Brand Activism

Activism

From Purpose to Action

CHRISTIAN SARKAR
& PHILIP KOTLER

Published by IDEA BITE PRESS
www.ideabitepress.com

"The **companies** that **perform best** over time build a **social purpose** into their operations that is as important as their **economic purpose.**"

— *Rosabeth Moss Kanter*

To the poor who can't sleep,
To the vanishing middle who are still distracted,
To the billionaires who are uneasy,
And to the beautiful planet that's losing patience with all of us....

Let us come together for the **Common Good**.

CONTENTS

The "Voices" interviewed in Chapter 10 include:

Hanneke Faber: The Future of Branding Is Activism
Scott Galloway: Algorithms, Democracy, And Capitalism
Martin Whittaker: Ranking America's Most Just Companies
John Elkington: Beyond the Triple Bottom Line
Stephen Hahn-Griffiths: From CSR To Corporate Reputation
Raj Sisodia: From Conscious Capitalism to Healing Organization
John Ehrenreich: Third Wave Capitalism
Nigel Sizer: Will the Amazon Fires Wake Up the World?
Christopher Davis: A Return to Activism
Stephen M.R. Covey: The Trust Crisis: What Do Leaders Do Now?
Anjana Das: Conscious Fashion
Hennie Botes: The Challenge of Affordable Housing
Elsie Maio: Does Your Business Have A Soul?
Stuart L. Hart: Capitalism at The Crossroads
David Hinds: Where There Is No Justice
Clark Fox: Enough Is Enough
Hazel Henderson: Some Prescriptions for Human & Planetary Health
Philip Kotler: The War for The Soul of Capitalism

ACKNOWLEDGMENTS

This book would not have happened without the help and support of so many people:

Special thanks to Nancy Kotler for her patience and understanding.

Thanks to Jenny and Aryssa for the endless enthusiasm and all that editing.

Thanks to Lena, Pranab, and Monica Sarkar – for your support and encouragement.

To Mikaela and Katrianna – keep going!

Thanks to Mark Blessington, Karl Hellman, and Frank Grillo. Without the work we did at *FIXCapitalism.com* and *The Marketing Journal,* none of this would be happening.

Thanks to Jonathan Ballantine – for your help and generosity. The "chance" meeting in Madrid will not soon be forgotten.

To the artists and musicians who see trouble first – you are the canaries in this coal mine.

To our many friends around the world who are truly making a difference, including the ones interviewed in this book – thank you!

Finally, to this, our **Common Home**, our beautiful planet – we hear your voice.

BRAND ACTIVISM TOOLKIT

© Christian Sarkar and Philip Kotler 2018

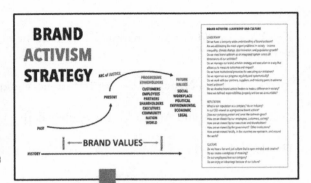

BRAND ACTIVISM STRATEGY

BRAND ACTIVISM MAPS

THE BRAND ACTIVISM CANVAS

BRAND ACTIVISM X MATRIX

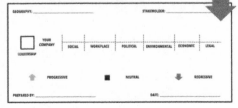

BRAND ACTIVISM SCORE

LETTER TO THE READER

Times have changed. In the past, a company could selectively choose the issues it wanted to engage in. No more.

In a highly polarized world, it's no longer *good enough to be neutral.* Furthermore, the issues are going to be chosen by the customer, your employees, and the public at large. Across the world, young people – your future customers – are using social media and taking to the streets to stand up against all forms of injustice.

Brands are expected to solve, not aggravate, the world's biggest problems.

You're now a **BRAND ACTIVIST**, whether you like it or not.

This book is a call to action for business leaders.

Time is running out.

We know that some of the views we present in this book will not be popular, but as Roethke said: "In a dark time, the eye begins to see" …

Will *you* get up, **stand up?**

Christian Sarkar
Philip Kotler

January 2020
www.activistbrands.com

PREFACE

Christian Sarkar and Phillip Kotler brilliantly illustrate in this important body of work, we have witnessed a changing expectation in society -- and we are now in a new era (like it or not) where the emergent expectation for "Brand Activism" is increasingly becoming the new reality. Beyond the realm of sycophantic politics and marketing hyperbole -- and in the midst of one of the largest pandemics (Covid-19) ever to hit human civilization – it is highly apparent in that how companies and brands are being judged is fundamentally changing. Rather than merely being assessed on the merits of the promise they fulfill, or the benefits they might deliver through consumption, corporate brands, and products and services brands alike, are being evaluated based on a new set of criteria such as their values, ethics, morality, commitment to sustainability – even judged on the social issues with which they align.

Given this societal shift in expectations and in the light of the declaration of the Business Roundtable in 2019, where 181 CEOs of multi-national companies universally pledged to deliver on purpose beyond just profits, there is a need for experts in brand, reputation, and even purpose, to completely rethink how they position the brands they represent With the elevated expectation among the general public for "doing and saying the right thing" and the imposition of other mandated guidelines such as the Sustainable Development Goals (SDGs) from the United Nations, there is a powerful and inspiring new agenda for marketers to follow based on the need for all companies to deliver on branding with a conscience.

Based on recent events I think it is fair to say that stakes for acting and behaving more responsibly as a company just got even higher. in this brave new world that's increasingly impacted by major cultural and societal life forces, such as the #MeToo movement, personal and data privacy concerns, fake news, and Black Lives Matter—business leaders at all companies (not just marketers) are increasingly expected to make responsible decisions in fulfilling the greater pursuit of living to and believable delivering on a company's stated purpose. That means not only being fiscally responsible and responsible for your employees in satisfying profit, sales, and employee motivations, but also delivering on the expectations of social and environmental responsibility.

Through-out my career, both as a practitioner and strategy leader in the heady-heights of the ad agency stratosphere, and more recently as a brand, reputation, and purpose-driven thought-leader in management consulting, I've seen these types of changes meaningfully evolve with the sands of time. But in recent times, the rate of evolutionary changes is gathering pace. As a keen observer of culture, society, business ecosystems, and the role that brands play as part of a world of influence, its really fascinating to see how these emergent super powers of brand activism have become part of the social fabric. In practicing brand activism and aligning with the communities they serve companies are not only helping themselves, but additionally helping to make the world a better place to live. In being able to measure the consequential impact of living to and fulfilling a higher purpose for brands in the work I have done at RepTrak -- as the world's preeminent leader in reputation (previously known as the Reputation Institute) -- the evidence for doing and saying the right thing is emphatic. Promoting brand activism, taking a stand on the issues that matter to the stakeholders you serve, through unleashing the power of a higher purpose, not only translates into good will but also leads to good business, in driving elevated sales, net promoter scores, enhanced employer brand status, and even higher levels of market capitalization. Indeed, as a point of example, based on a most recent study in 2020 among the general population across the G15 economies, RepTrak identified companies that were believably associated with a strong sense of purpose had the potential to establish a dominant market position -- and to drive purchase intent at levels above 57% of their total market potential.

So, what does this all mean for CEOs, strategic business leaders, brand evangelists, marketing experts, reputation advisors, and purveyors of insight?

It means they are expected to manage and advise the companies they work with more purposefully, and with a higher level of integrity than in the past. Beyond satisfying shareholders, meeting the needs of commercial business leaders, and pleasing their clients and bosses, Captains of Industry and Champions of Strategy will need to serve and fulfill a broader social agenda, while meeting the expectations of employees, consumers, customers, investors, regulators, and media stakeholders—to name a few. And so, with this need to be viewed as more purposeful comes the added requirement to radically change the priorities of how a company and its brands are managed. It means business leaders need to be as concerned about the company's impact on society, as they are about the bottom line -- or market share.

Consistent with this POV and alignment with the changing macro-economic market forces of the world, the concept of fulfilling a "higher purpose" has evolved as a term that is used to describe a company's reason for being—essentially capturing how a company contributes to society beyond profits to make the world a better place. That premise changes the emphasis of "why a company exists" from merely selling products and services, to justifying its license to operate, validating its very existence, and motivating employees to fulfill higher expectations. Interestingly, this was further reinforced by RepTrak's 2020 study of Global Trends which indicated that among marketing, corporate communications, and reputation leaders around the world, the fulfillment of a higher purpose is the single most important thing they are grappling with to make their company more successful.

With all this in mind, and the complexities of how you go to market taken into consideration, I am so privileged to have been able to contribute to this book, and to have learned so much from the deftly insightful and deeply profound minds of Kotler and Sarkar. As seasoned marketing experts, brand luminaries, and purposeful provocateurs who are highly attuned to the cultural realities and social changes of the twenty-first century, they provide us all with a cornucopia of perspective, observation, and frameworks that make sense of best to position your brand during a time of social and environmental activism. You'll find this book to be a refreshing guiding light on how companies and brands can best navigate complexity to make the world a better place to live. In that regard, it is a highly useful business intelligence tool, as well as a means by which to channel your inner Jiminy Cricket. Let your conscience be your guide to help you better unleash the power of purpose through brand activism -- and use this book to get smart on how to win with nobility versus the competition.

Stephen Hahn-Griffiths
EVP, RepTrack

INTRODUCTION

As humanity faces a growing number of existential challenges, we find that governments and institutions are not doing their jobs – they are failing us precisely at the moment we need them most. The apocalypse has many horsemen: social unrest, inequality, environmental collapse, species extinction, pandemics, trade wars, and yes, old-fashioned war. Even the tired wars of ideology have returned. We are facing an **ecosystem of wicked problems**:

What is to be done? And what does this have to do with business? Your business?

Corporate Social Responsibility (CSR) was not enough. The **Business Roundtable** has finally decided "maximizing shareholder value" is not such a great idea.[1]

The **World Economic Forum** has joined the conscious party as well. Its 2020 manifesto[2] describes an inclusive world of "stakeholder capitalism."

This too is not enough.

Why? Because the fundamental **narrative**[3] of capitalism is broken. What is needed now is a new narrative, a new form of commitment and integrity from business.

It is a commitment to a *fair and just future for all.* What we need now is **activism** – inspired by the great movements of the past – for the **Common Good**.

How can companies become activists? And what is the new role of business in this unsteady world? Time is running out, as we mentioned earlier. That is why we wrote this book. You'll discover what we mean when we say that brand activism can be regressive, and what it means to be a

---

[1] "Now that CEOs found purpose, what are they going to do with it?" Christian Sarkar and Philip Kotler, *FixCapitalism.com* http://fixcapitalism.com/now-that-ceos-found-purpose-what-are-they-going-to-do-with-it/

[2] "Davos Manifesto 2020: The Universal Purpose of a Company in the Fourth Industrial Revolution," *WEForum.org* https://www.weforum.org/agenda/2019/12/davos-manifesto-2020-the-universal-purpose-of-a-company-in-the-fourth-industrial-revolution/

[3] "Competing on Stories: Marketing and Cultural Narratives," Christian Sarkar and Philip Kotler, *The Marketing Journal* http://www.marketingjournal.org/competing-on-stories-marketing-and-cultural-narratives-christian-sarkar-and-philip-kotler/

progressive brand activist. You'll learn how brand activism is the future of marketing, and how your company can make a difference.

Afraid of politics? Stop right there. **It is corruption of our politics that has gotten us to this point, and it will be politics *or* war, that ends it.** We prefer politics – specifically democracy.

Join us. Together we must meet the challenge – the ecosystem of wicked problems.

THE ECOSYSTEM *of* WICKED PROBLEMS

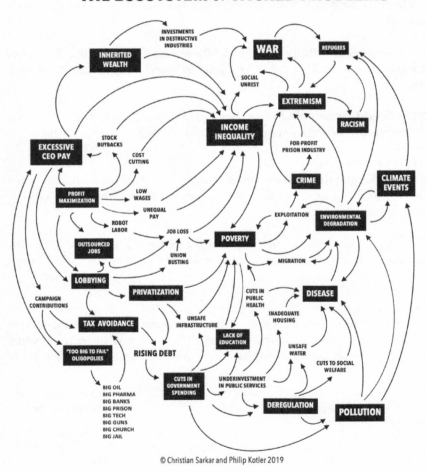

© Christian Sarkar and Philip Kotler 2019

1. PHILOSOPHICAL FRAGMENTS

We recall these wise words from Phil's friend, the late **Peter Drucker**. They set the stage for our thinking.

"…an institution, like an individual, is not an island unto itself. It has to solve the basic problem of balancing the need for concentration and for self-limitation with concern for its environment and compassion for its community."
— Peter Drucker, *The Concept of the Corporation*, 1946

"The corporation as a representative institution of American society must hold out the promise of adequately fulfilling the aspirations and beliefs of the American people."
— Peter Drucker, *The Concept of the Corporation*, 1946

"A free-enterprise society would become impossible if we had to live under total depression or total war."
— Peter Drucker, *The Concept of the Corporation*, 1946

"Few top executives can even imagine the hatred, contempt and fury that has been created—not primarily among blue-collar workers who never had an exalted opinion of the 'bosses'—but among their middle management and professional people."[1]
— Peter Drucker, *Forbes*, March 10, 1997

(the corporation) "…is in trouble because it is seen increasingly by more and more people as deeply at odds with basic needs and basic values of society and community."
— Peter Drucker, *The Concept of the Corporation*, 1946

"An industrial society based on the corporation can only function if the corporation contributes to social stability and to the achievement of the social aims independent of the good will or the social consciousness of individual corporation managements."
— Peter Drucker, *The Concept of the Corporation*, 1946

---

[1] "Seeing things as they really are" Robert Lenzner and Stephen S. Johnson, *Forbes.com*
https://www.forbes.com/forbes/1997/0310/5905122a.html#2d2f6af424b9

"That the President can be elected in this country without having given any proof of his ability as a leader of men or as a maker of political and administrative decisions is probably the most serious weakness of our political system."
— Peter Drucker, *The Concept of the Corporation*, 1946

"Few people – and probably no one outside the executive suite – sees much reason for these very large executive compensations. There is little correlation between them and company performance."
— Peter F. Drucker, *The Frontiers of Management*, 1986

"The Western Democracies have to realize that totalitarian fascism cannot be overcome by socialism, by capitalist democracy, or by a combination of both. It can only be overcome by a new noneconomic concept of a free and equal society…a noneconomic society striving for the freedom and the equality of the individual."
— Peter Drucker, *The End of Economic Man*, 1939

"It should therefore be asserted uncompromisingly that a monopolistic enterprise or a monopolistic industry always impairs social stability and economic efficiency. This effort of monopoly is inherent in its nature— simply because absolute power always means abuse of power."
— Peter Drucker, *The Concept of the Corporation*, 1946

"When Hitler and Mussolini set out to "re-establish authority" they intend to crush all freedom and all liberties and to prove that might is right. Yet 'authority' always meant the reign of right over might."
— Peter Drucker, *The End of Economic Man*, 1939

"If all the superrich disappeared, the world economy would not even notice. The superrich are irrelevant to the economy."[2]
— Peter Drucker, *Forbes*, March 10, 1997

"It is the responsibility of business to think through and work for the appropriate regulation before there is a scandal."
— Peter F. Drucker, *Management: Tasks, Responsibilities, Practices,* 1973

"I am not very happy with the unbalanced emphasis on stock price and market cap and short-term earnings…The most critical management job is to balance short term and long term. In the long term, today's one-sided

---

[2] "Seeing things as they really are" Robert Lenzner and Stephen S. Johnson, *Forbes.com*
https://www.forbes.com/forbes/1997/0310/5905122a.html#2d2f6af424b9

emphasis is deleterious and dangerous."[3]
— Peter Drucker, *New York Times*, November 17, 1999

"We can't learn anything by simplifying difficult issues. We've got to complexify them."[4]
— Peter Drucker, *Inc.*, March 10, 1997

[3] "MANAGEMENT: IDEAS INTO ACTION; The Sage of Value and Service" Fred Andrews *New York Times*
https://www.nytimes.com/1999/11/17/business/management-ideas-into-action-the-sage-of-value-and-service.html
[4] "Peter's Principles" Harriet Rubin, *Inc.com*
https://www.inc.com/magazine/19980301/887.html

2. THE TRUST CRISIS

One benchmark for trust is the **Edelman Trust Barometer**. In 2018, The Edelman Trust Barometer[1] revealed that trust in the U.S. had suffered the largest-ever-recorded drop in the survey's history among the general population. Trust among the **informed public** in the U.S. imploded, plunging 23 points to 45, making it now the lowest of the 28 markets surveyed, *below* Russia and South Africa.

You may also be surprised to hear that fewer than half of young Americans viewed capitalism positively.[2]

The disappointment with our elected officials is understandable. It's one reason why Trump was elected: *to drain the swamp.*

In 2019, there were still more changes. The 2019 Edelman Trust Barometer reveals that trust has changed profoundly in the past year with "my employer" emerging as the most trusted institution. Globally, "my employer" (75 percent) is significantly more trusted than NGOs (57 percent), business (56 percent), government (48 percent) and media (47 percent).

"The last decade has seen a loss of faith in traditional authority figures and institutions," said Richard Edelman, president and CEO of Edelman. "More recently, people have lost confidence in the social platforms that fostered peer-to-peer trust. These forces have led people to shift their trust to the relationships within their control, most notably their employers."

This shift to localized trust is unfolding against the backdrop of a return to the largest-ever trust gap (16 points) between the informed public (65 percent) and mass population (49 percent). The separation is driven by record-high spikes in trust among the informed public in developed markets, while mass population trust remains relatively flat. The trust gap is severe in developed nations (UK – 24 points; Canada – 20 points; France – 18 points; U.S. – 13 points) and has now moved into the developing world (India – 17 points; China – 12 points).

---

[1] *Edelman Trust Barometer* https://www.edelman.com/trust-barometer
[2] Democrats More Positive About Socialism Than Capitalism, *Gallup.com*
https://news.gallup.com/poll/240725/democrats-positive-socialism-capitalism.aspx

The trust disparity is also partly explained by gender. The gender trust gap is in the double digits in several developed markets, such as Germany (12 points) and the U.S. (11 points), mostly driven by *women's lower trust in business.*

There is also a growing feeling of pessimism about the future, with only one-in-three mass population respondents in the developed world believing his or her family will be better off in the next five years.

"Divergent levels of confidence between the mass population and informed public about the future signal a continued underlying rot in the structure of society," says Stephen Kehoe, global chair, Reputation. "While not everyone is taking to the streets, the data shows why protests like the Gilet Jaunes in France, the women's marches in India and walkouts by employees at some major tech companies could become more mainstream."

CEOs are expected to lead the fight for change. More than three-quarters (76 percent) say they want CEOs to take the lead on change instead of waiting for government to impose it. And 73 percent believe a company can take actions that both increase profits and improve economic and social conditions in the community where it operates.

Employees expect prospective employers to actively join them in advocating for social issues (67 percent). Companies that do are rewarded with greater commitment (83 percent), advocacy (78 percent) and loyalty (74 percent) from their employees.

We can also agree that many of our institutions are losing their credibility because they are not doing their jobs. The Edelman survey shows that trust in the four institutions – NGOs, Government, Business, and Media are all still depressingly low.

We're in a full-blown **trust crisis**.

THE TRUST CRISIS IS GLOBAL

Climate Crisis.

Income Inequality.

Trump.

Brexit.

#MeToo.

Charlottesville.

#BlackLivesMatter.

War without end.

Fascism 2.0.

The world as we know it is falling apart. Across the world, people are expressing their discontent with the *status quo*.

As we write these words, here's a snapshot of what's going on in the world:

In the **United States**, the Judiciary Committee has begun drafting articles of impeachment against president Trump. Meanwhile, the gap between the richest and the poorest U.S. households is now the largest it's been in the past 50 years. The number of hate groups in the U.S. has reached an all-time high.

In **Latin America**, people have taken to the streets to protest in Chile, a coup "happened" in Bolivia, and the Amazon is burning.

In **Europe**, even as support for the EU[3] has increased, we see the Brexit election in Britain, France struggling to cope with its *gilets jaunes* protests, Germany with an austerity problem, and across the continent we see NATO in crisis[4], migration problems[5], and recessionary fears[6] that are turning into reality. Only 19% of Italians trust their parliament[7] (but that's an improvement from 2018!).

---

[3] "Views of the European Union over time" *Pew Research Center*
https://www.pewresearch.org/global/2019/10/14/the-european-union/pg_10-15-19-europe-values-04-015/
[4] "NATO at 70: An alliance in crisis," *Harvard Kennedy School*,
https://www.hks.harvard.edu/faculty-research/policy-topics/international-relations-security/nato-70-alliance-crisis
[5] "Europe migrant crisis: Calls to redistribute migrants as arrivals rise," *BBC News*,
https://www.bbc.com/news/world-europe-49752380
[6] "Fall in EU firms' debt issuance fuels recession fears," *Reuters*
https://www.reuters.com/article/us-eu-markets-regulation/fall-in-eu-firms-debt-issuance-fuels-recession-fears-idUSKBN1WV0LV
[7] "REPORT FOR ITALIANS AND THE STATE – 2018," *DEMOS*
http://www.demos.it/a01557.php

In **Africa**, corruption continues even as extremism grows across West Africa in Mali, Burkina Faso, Niger, and Chad, with growing economic unrest in countries like South Africa. Pirates just boarded a super tanker off the coast of Nigeria.

In **Asia**, we have riots and protests in Hong Kong, Chinese social engineering in Xinjiang - with Uyghurs facing cultural genocide, problems in Indian Kashmir, continuing conflict with Israel and the Palestinians, and Turkish militias going after Kurd civilians.

The **Pacific** is not spared. Australia is also experiencing devastating wildfires which are turning New Zealand's glaciers pinkish-red. The Great Barrier Reef is as endangered as ever, and parts of the Solomon Islands have disappeared under the sea.

The **collapse of trust in the U.S. is driven by a staggering *lack of faith in government***, which fell 14 points to 33 percent among the general population, and 30 points to 33 percent among the informed public. The remaining institutions of **business, media** and **NGOs** also experienced declines of 10 to 20 points.

"The United States is enduring an unprecedented crisis of trust," says Richard Edelman, president and CEO of Edelman, speaking in 2018. "This is the first time that a massive drop in trust has not been linked to a pressing economic issue or catastrophe like the Fukushima nuclear disaster. In fact, it's the ultimate irony that it's happening at a time of prosperity, with the stock market and employment rates in the U.S. at record highs. The root cause of the is fall is the lack of objective facts and rational discourse.

For the first time, the **media** is the least trusted institution globally. In 22 of the 28 markets surveyed it is now distrusted.

The demise of confidence in the Fourth Estate is driven primarily by a significant drop in trust in platforms, notably search engines and social media. Sixty-three percent of respondents say they do not know how to tell good journalism from rumor or falsehoods or if a piece of news was produced by a respected media organization.

The lack of faith in media has also led to an **inability to identify the truth** (59 percent), **trust government leaders** (56 percent) and **trust business** (42 percent).

EXPECTATIONS FOR BUSINESS

Business is now expected to be an agent of change.

The Edelman Trust Barometer also tells us that the employer is the new safe house in global governance, with 72 percent of respondents saying that they trust their own company. And 64 percent believe **a company can take actions that both increase profits and improve economic and social conditions in the community where it operates.**

Another interesting insight from the survey was the fact that the past year saw **CEO credibility** rise sharply by seven points to 44 percent after a number of high-profile business leaders voiced their positions on the issues of the day.

Nearly two-thirds of respondents say they want CEOs to take the lead on policy change instead of waiting for government, which now ranks significantly below business in trust in 20 markets.

This show of faith comes with new expectations; **building trust (69 percent) is now the No. 1 job for CEOs**, surpassing producing high-quality products and services (68 percent).

Across the globe, we learn that trust in business has increased in 14 of 28 markets, with distrust at an all-time high for the USA, which experienced a 10-point decline from the previous year.

The USA, as a country, experienced a 5-point decline as a country brand. The survey points out that **"where trust loss is extreme, business is the retaining wall."**

Turning again to the expectations for CEOS, 84% of survey respondents expect CEOs to inform conversations and policy debates on the following issues:

- Jobs
- The economy
- Automation
- Regulations
- Globalization
- Corruption
- Global Warming

- Discrimination
- Infrastructure
- Cost of living
- Education
- Healthcare
- Immigration

52% agree that CEOs should regularly communicate directly to the public using social media.

THE REPUTATION ECONOMY

What are the companies with the best reputations doing right?

We turn to Stephen Hahn-Griffiths of the Reputation Institute for a deeper understanding. Here's what he stated[8] in an interview:

*If you look at the top 10 in 2017—we are talking about companies like Lego, Google, Sony, Rolex and Walt Disney—they all operate with honesty and integrity and **they stand for things that matter to people around the world**, such as diversity and inclusiveness, environmental sustainability and education. Their **companies have become associated with issues and causes which makes their reputation stronger because they are known to be doing the right thing.***

More and more we are seeing that reputation moves markets. There is a strong correlation between the market capital valuation of a business and its ability to create a good reputation. The past few years have shown the power of reputation to change the world; it had a hand to play in Brexit, in the election of Donald Trump, in the emergence of the #MeToo movement. The reputation of CEOs around the world is now being scrutinized because of cases of inappropriate sexual behavior.

*We are seeing the emergence of the dawn of the reputation economy—**reputation is now the currency on which everything else will depend**. On a company level it drives whether people say good things about you. On a personal level it defines your job, your career, and your next move in life. Reputation is all around us and it is driving human behavior.*

---

[8] "How Do Companies Earn Top Marks for Reputation?" *Biz Blog*
https://www.lexisnexis.com/communities/lexisnexis_biz/b/bizblog/archive/2018/03/16/how-do-companies-earn-top-marks-for-reputation.aspx

MORAL MYOPIA

And what do we see with the worst-ranked companies? The dubious honor of the worst rating of the 100 most visible companies goes to Takata, responsible for "the largest and most complex safety recall[9] in U.S. history." The Weinstein Company[10] is next. Equifax is the third[11]. The Trump Organization[12] ranks *5th-from the bottom* out of the 100 companies.

But rankings only **take** us so far. Let's look at the policies beneath the rankings.

How do companies pursue profit over people?

A notable example is the Epipen[13], where **Mylan Pharmaceuticals** chose to hike prices to $600 up from roughly $100 when they acquired the life-saving product.

Another example of *the disconnect between profit-seeking and values* come to us from **Goldman Sachs**, where an analyst actually asked: "Is curing patients a sustainable business model?"[14] The investor's dilemma is described in simple but chilling terms:

"The potential to deliver "one shot cures" is one of the most attractive aspects of gene therapy, genetically engineered cell therapy, and gene editing. However, such treatments offer a very different outlook with regard to recurring revenue versus chronic therapies… While this proposition carries tremendous value for patients and society, it could represent a challenge for genome medicine developers looking for sustained cash flow."

---

9 "Takata Airbag Recall: Everything You Need to Know," *Consumer Reports*, https://www.consumerreports.org/car-recalls-defects/takata-airbag-recall-everything-you-need-to-know/
10 "Weinstein Company Files for Bankruptcy and Revokes Nondisclosure Agreements," *New York Times*, https://www.nytimes.com/2018/03/19/business/weinstein-company-bankruptcy.html
11 "Equifax data breach: What you need to know," *CNN*, https://money.cnn.com/2017/09/08/technology/equifax-hack-qa/index.html
12 "The Trump brand's shrinking power," *CBS News*, https://www.cbsnews.com/news/the-trump-brands-shrinking-premium/
13 "The EpiPen uproar, explained," *The Week*, https://theweek.com/articles/646256/epipen-uproar-explained
14 "Is curing patients a sustainable business model?" Goldman Sachs analysts ask *TECHNICA* https://arstechnica.com/tech-policy/2018/04/curing-disease-not-a-sustainable-business-model-goldman-sachs-analysts-say/

These are examples of **moral myopia**, where the pursuit of profit crosses the line of civilized behavior and ventures into "evil" territory.

This tone-deaf mindset is not, unfortunately, an exception. For many businesses, it is part of the engine of profit-making.

WHAT IS DOING THE RIGHT THING?

Many public relations experts talk about "active reputation management[15]" to help salvage broken reputations. This is the old world, where expensive campaigns and staged press conferences are used to mitigate reputation damage, while the underlying causes remain unaddressed. In a sense this was ***#fakevirtue*** – where the appearance of virtue is more important than virtue itself. In the past, our understanding of what is damaging has been restricted to surveys and polls of the public. Here are the **most damaging scenarios for corporate reputations** via the Harris Poll[16]:

- Lying or misrepresenting the facts about a product or service
- Intentional wrongdoing or illegal actions by company leaders (corporate malfeasance)
- A security or data breach that exposes personal information
- Product recall due to contamination that may cause illness
- Unfair work conditions and culture
- Workplace discrimination
- Leadership conduct that reflects poorly on the company
- An environmental mishap or accident
- Product recall due to a safety concern that may cause injury
- Negative financial news about a company
- Product recalls due to technical or equipment failure
- Employee conduct that reflects poorly on the company
- An employee strike or work stoppage

The idea that companies must ***do the right thing*** has been around since the very beginning, but what does this really mean?

---

[15] "Brand Reputation Management: Your Seven-Point Game Plan" Lorna Walkden, *MarketingProfs* http://www.marketingprofs.com/articles/2013/11004/brand-reputation-management-your-seven-point-game-plan
[16] "The most damaging scenarios for corporate reputations" *Marketing Charts* https://www.marketingcharts.com/industries/government-and-politics-65871/attachment/theharrispoll-most-damaging-scenarios-corporate-reputations-feb2016

ASK: *What is my brand, my organization, doing to build trust in the market, in society?*

3. WHAT IS BRAND ACTIVISM?

What happens when businesses and their customers don't share the same values?

Or, for that matter, when employees of a company don't share the same values as their executives?

Companies no longer have a choice. If the gap between a business and its values and its customers or society and his other stakeholders is too large, business will inevitably suffer.

So, what can be done?

How do brands align their values with the values of their customers, their employees, and society at large?

A common way to understand what issues matter to customers is to survey them, and continuously try to understand what issues matter most. Experts tell us that companies must select issues that align most closely with the brand. This is a myopic way to look at issues because it sees the world and reality from the inside out. What is needed, now more than ever, is a mindset that views reality from the *outside in.*

It is no small irony that in the Western world, where we claim to cherish freedom and democracy, our companies function like totalitarian states, complete with authoritarian rulers and dysfunctional bureaucracies.

And when business leaders lose touch with society, their employees, customers, and the everyday struggles of the local population, they start to make bad decisions. By bad, we are referring to decisions that are shortsighted, don't include the common good for their employees or society, and end up being detrimental to the future of the brand. This is an all too common recipe for value-destruction.

Is your industry, the industry your business belongs to, regressive or progressive? If so, there's still hope — as long as your company is viewed as the most progressive in a regressive field. Even better? Transform your industry by disrupting it.

From a marketing perspective, historically, most brands have been marketed on their performance characteristics. "Our toothpaste is better than yours." We're better at "whitening teeth," "preventing cavities," or giving you "fresh breath."

Positioning was the name of the game in brand marketing.

But *positioning is no longer enough*.

Just consider marketing to millennials, one of today's largest demographic groups. Millennials have high expectations for brands. Millennials live in a world filled with constant problems – air pollution, bad drinking water, crime and violence. Many would like brands to show concern not just for profits but for the communities they serve, and the world we live in. In fact, more and more, we see a yearning for jobs that have a higher meaning than profit-making[1].

Generation Z is even more "political" than the Millennials. In the aftermath of the Parkland shootings, they took on one of the most powerful lobbies in the world – the NRA, and succeeded in igniting a national dialogue where even President Barack Obama failed.

The World Economic Forum's Global Risks Report 2018[2] states:

Despite unprecedented levels of peace and global prosperity, in many countries a mood of economic malaise has contributed to anti-establishment, populist politics and a backlash against globalization. The weakness of the economic recovery following the global financial crisis is part of this story, but boosting growth alone would not remedy the deeper fractures in our political economy. More fundamental reforms to market capitalism may be needed to tackle, in particular, an apparent lack of solidarity between those at the top of national income and wealth distributions and those further down.

For organizations today, it's not enough to have a higher purpose. Purpose-driven means nothing if your behavior doesn't match your vision. What matters now is **action**: how your brand lives and behaves in the real world. Your actions, or lack of action are signals to your customers and society at large.

---

[1] "Why Making Money Is Not Enough" Ratan Tata, Stuart L. Hart, Aarti Sharma and Christian Sarkar, *MIT Sloan Management Review*
https://sloanreview.mit.edu/article/why-making-money-is-not-enough/
[2] "The Global Risks Report 2018" *Zurich Forum*
https://www.zurich.com/knowledge/topics/global-risks/the-global-risks-report-2018

The **Body Shop** was one of the first companies to fight for its ethical values and beliefs. Its founder and CEO, **Anita Roddick**, not only wanted to make really fine skincare products but also fight for animal rights, civil rights, fair trade, and environmental protection. Body Shop clients said they were interested in her products but also approved of her activism and often gathered to march together for the causes they shared. She was a true business revolutionary, and her pioneering voice still reverberates throughout the halls of businesses that are awakening to the new reality.

Companies must learn to keep up with their customers. How do you keep up with your customers' values and hopes and dreams?

ASK: What is my brand, my organization, doing to solve the problems of the world – the problems my future customers and employees care about?

In his book *The Concept of the Corporation* (1946), Peter Ducker warned us:

(the corporation) "…is in trouble because it is seen increasingly by more and more people as deeply at odds with basic needs and basic values of society and community."

and

"An industrial society based on the corporation can only function if the corporation contributes to social stability and to the achievement of the social aims independent of the good will or the social consciousness of individual corporation managements."

Now, customers, especially progressive customers like Millennials and Generation X, are demanding that companies make a difference in the world by trying to solve the most urgent wicked problems facing society – like income inequality, corruption, and climate change.

It is no longer enough to simply make profits and worship at the altar of shareholder value. Issue after issue, companies must take the side of society.

What does this mean for the future?

Enter **brand activism**.

BRAND ACTIVISM: A WORKING DEFINITION

To begin, let's examine activism at the individual level. *Wikipedia* tells us:

"Activism consists of efforts to promote, impede, or direct social, political, economic, and/or environmental reform or stasis with the desire to make improvements in society. Forms of activism range from writing letters to newspapers or to politicians, political campaigning, economic activism such as boycotts or preferentially patronizing businesses, rallies, street marches, strikes, sit-ins, and hunger strikes."

Using this definition as a starting point, we developed a **brand activism framework** that allows organizations to execute an **activist strategy**. This is what we present in this book – a way to see and understand **what is required of business** if it intends to continue to thrive in society. A warning: we should be clear in saying that activism doesn't have to be **progressive**; it can be **regressive** as well.

The poster-child for **regressive activism** is Big Tobacco – the tobacco companies that for so many years denied the harm their products did to consumers, even when their own research revealed otherwise. They promoted the "virtues" of smoking in a way that actually hurt consumers. Companies that lobby our politicians for regressive policies are brand activists.

On the **progressive activism** side, we see more and more companies seeking to have an impact on the biggest societal problems. These companies have a larger purpose than simple profit-seeking, and are increasingly seen as leaders in their industries.

With this in mind, here is our working definition for brand activism:

Brand Activism consists of business efforts to promote, impede, or direct social, political, economic, and/or environmental reform or stasis with the desire to promote or impede improvements in society.

This brand activism is a natural evolution beyond the values-driven Corporate Social Responsibility (CSR) and Environmental, Social and Governance (ESG) programs that are too slowly transforming companies across the world.

In *Corporate Social Responsibility: Doing the Most Good for Your Company and Your Cause* (2005), Nancy Lee and Philip Kotler identified six major areas for corporate social-responsibility activities. They were marketing-driven or corporate-driven – based on what it means to be a good corporate citizen.

Brand activism is different because it is driven by a fundamental concern for the *biggest* and most *urgent problems facing society*.

It gives life to what it means to be a "values-driven" company. You can't be a values-driven company and disregard society – your employees, your customers, the communities you work in, *and* the world. The proof is in what **you do, not what you say.**

MARKETING-DRIVEN

CAUSE PROMOTION
CAUSE-RELATED MARKETING
CORPORATE SOCIAL MARKETING

CORPORATE-DRIVEN

CORPORATE PHILANTHROPY
WORKFORCE VOLUNTEERING
SOCIALLY RESPONSIBLE BUSINESS PRACTICES

SOCIETY-DRIVEN

BRAND ACTIVISM

ASK: What are the urgent, wicked problems of the world?

Let's dig deeper:

- What is the current state of our world?
- What are the most urgent issues facing society?
- How did we get here? What are the root causes?
- What must be done now?
- How can we find common ground?
- What is the job of the leader?
- What does the future demand from business?

The top 5 trends are listed in the World Economic Forum's *Global Risks Report 2018* are:

- Rising income and wealth disparity
- Changing climate
- Increasing polarization of societies
- Rising cyber dependency
- Aging population

According to World Economic Forum Founder and Executive Chairman **Klaus Schwab**, "The threat of a less cooperative, more inward-looking world also creates the opportunity to address global risks and the trends that drive them. This will require responsive and *responsible leadership* with a deeper commitment to inclusive development and equitable growth, both nationally and globally. It will also require **collaboration** across multiple interconnected systems, countries, areas of expertise, and stakeholder groups with the aim of having a greater societal impact."

Schwab has unveiled the **Davos Manifesto 2020** which embraces "stakeholder capitalism." He explains[3]:

"Stakeholder capitalism," a model I first proposed a half-century ago, positions private corporations as trustees of society, and is clearly the best response to today's social and environmental challenges.

---

[3] "Why we need the 'Davos Manifesto' for a better kind of capitalism" *World Economic Forum* https://www.weforum.org/agenda/2019/12/why-we-need-the-davos-manifesto-for-better-kind-of-capitalism/

For Schwab, this is the "best response." But is it? If private companies are the trustees of society, where does that leave government and democracy? What if government was capable of serving the needs of society? One must ask why this isn't so.

To his credit, Schwab outlines what is needed: (1) a new measure of "shared value creation" to include "environmental, social, and governance"

(ESG) goals as a complement to standard financial metrics, (2) executive remuneration, which should be tied to long-term shared value creation, and (3) the understanding that business is a major stakeholder in our common future, and should work with other stakeholders to improve the state of the world.

We'll also return to the Davos Manifesto 2020 when we look at potential frameworks for Brand Activism – in Chapter 7.

ASK: Who will provide "responsible leadership"?

Brand activism has emerged as a values-driven agenda for companies that care about the future of society and the planet's health. The underlying force for *progress* is a drive or movement towards justice and fairness for all.

What domains or categories come under the umbrella of brand activism? While the issues may shift over time, we've identified six areas that will be familiar to all; broad categories that capture some of the largest problems facing society:

© 2018 Christian Sarkar and Philip Kotler

Social activism includes areas such as equality – gender, LGBT, race, age, etc. It also includes societal and community issues such as Education, Healthcare, Social Security, Privacy, Consumer Protection, etc.

Workplace activism is about governance – corporate organization, CEO pay, worker compensation, labor and union relations, supply chain management, governance, etc.

Political activism covers lobbying, privatization, voting, voting rights, and policy (gerrymandering, campaign finance, etc.)

Environmental activism deals with conservation, ecocide, land-use, air and water pollution, emission control, environmental laws and policies.

Economic activism includes wage and tax policies that impact income inequality and redistribution of wealth.

Legal activism deals with the laws and policies that impact companies, such as tax, citizenship, and employment laws.

Intuitively, we all recognize these categories – but what is puzzling is why our leaders continue to "kick the can down the road" – by not facing the realities and challenges until they become crises, and often, not even then.

In his book *Building Strong Brands*, Phil's friend **David Aaker** introduced us to four brand identity perspectives:

- Brand as product
- Brand as organization
- Brand as person
- Brand as symbol

Now, it's time to add to add a fifth dimension to brand identity – **Brand as activist**.

REGRESSIVE VS PROGRESSIVE ACTIVISM

How do we know if a brand's behavior is "regressive" or "progressive"?

One way is to take a **survey of public opinion**, a straightforward approach that is and has been used since the dawn of public polling. For example, a recent online survey [4] asked respondent to vote on their choice for the three **"most shameful"** corporations, and proceeds to list out the contenders for the **Corporate Hall of Shame 2018.**

The choices?

Bayer – for **further monopolizing the seed and chemical industry** by merging with Monsanto, threatening to force even more small and family farms out of business globally.

Beretta – for **profiting richly from manufacturing weapons**—and using those profits to fund the NRA and its obstruction of popular, commonsense gun safety measures that would save countless lives.

ExxonMobil – for **deceiving the public** about climate change for more than 30 years, then attempting to intimidate the cities and states working to hold it accountable.

The GEO Group, Inc. – for **profiting from the mass incarceration of people of color and immigrants** at its private prisons, while spending millions on lobbying and elections to protect its profiteering.

---

[4] "Corporate Hall of Shame 2018 Official Ballot" *signforgood*
https://surveys.signforgood.com/CorporateHallOfShame-2018/

Goldman Sachs – for **continuing to exploit people in Puerto Rico**— despite the devastation caused by Hurricane Maria—through predatory loans that squeeze maximum corporate profits from the island's government and its people.

Koch Industries, Inc. – for **working to dismantle the EPA** in the name of fossil fuel profits, while the Koch Brothers' network aims to pour a record-breaking $400 million into influencing the 2018 U.S. midterm elections.

Nestle – for **extracting Michigan's groundwater for mere pennies** just down the highway from Flint, where residents pay some of the highest rates in the country for poisoned water.

Phillip Morris International – for **launching a massive foundation to health wash its image** and undermine implementation of the global tobacco treaty.

Shell – for its **role in violent suppression** of opposition to its oil projects in Nigeria and beyond, and continuing to **block lifesaving climate policy** globally.

Veolia – for **its role in the lead crises** in Pittsburgh and Flint, which have endangered tens of thousands of people, particularly people of color and low-income communities.

The survey also leaves open a final option for you to "Write in your own shameful corporation."

This **brandshaming**[5] project was underwritten by the following organizations: Americans for Tax Fairness, Climate Hawks Vote, Common Cause, Corporate Accountability, Corrections Accountability Project, Daily Kos, Democracy Initiative, Dream Defenders, Enlace, Friends of the Earth Action, Green America, HEAL Food Alliance, Million Hoodies Movement for Justice, Peace is Loud, Pesticide Action Network, People for the American Way, Plastic Pollution Coalition.

In effect, it is a political marketing campaign designed to highlight the shameful actions of **regressive brands**.

---

5 "Brandshaming: The Kids vs. The NRA" Philip Kotler and Christian Sarkar, *THE MARKETING JOURNAL*
http://www.marketingjournal.org/brandshaming-philip-kotler-and-christian-sarkar/

What's happening here is that the brand's perspective is at odds with what Drucker called the **"basic needs and basic values of society and community."**

The "values gap" can be measured through surveys, issue by issue, at regular intervals.

The diagram below illustrates this values gap. Note that this gap could also be played in reverse — that is, the brand view could be *ahead* of its stakeholders.

That's called *leadership* – or **progressive brand activism**.

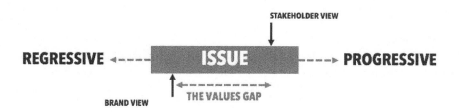

The brand "conscience" cannot be indifferent to injustice, and so, because of its position of power, must act for justice. To look the other way is to turn your back on the future, and invite the wrath of your future customer.

When governments and other institutions fail to act, business must step up to take up the slack.

Progressive brand activism is becoming a new point of differentiation for businesses across the world. Let's look at a few examples of companies that are taking brand activism to new heights.

Here are a few examples of **progressive brand activism**:

Patagonia
"The Activist Company[6]" launched *The President Stole Your Land*[7] campaign is the latest and perhaps the most progressive act we've seen from

6 The Activist Company, *patagonia*
https://www.patagonia.com/the-activist-company.html
7 The President Stole Your Land, *patagonia*
https://www.patagonia.com/protect-public-lands.html

Patagonia in their fight to protect public lands for almost 30 years. While other outdoor retailers also protested the Trump administration's plan, Patagonia was the only one to act by filing a lawsuit. Their commitment to social and environmental justice goes a lot further[8].

Unilever
In addition to its leading sustainability[9] efforts, Unilever does not invest in digital platforms which create division in society, and promote anger or hate. It promotes transparency[10] in influencer marketing to combat fake news. Former CEO **Paul Polman** has set the standard for a vision and strategy[11] to fully decouple its growth from its overall environmental footprint and increase its positive social impact through the Unilever Sustainable Living Plan. Also of note, Unilever co-developed a Circular Business Model[12] that aims to link up all material flows in an infinite process circle in order to use resources most efficiently.

Levi Strauss
Its recent support for gun violence prevention[13] has catapulted the company and CEO **Chip Bergh** into the limelight. "Americans shouldn't have to live in fear of gun violence," says Bergh.

EY
Demonstrated a commitment to Inclusive Capitalism[14], by developing a proof-of-concept framework that will be tested and further developed by some of the world's largest asset owners, asset managers, and asset creators (corporations). The proposed framework is a tool for asset owners and asset managers and other stakeholders to understand, measure and compare the investments made by asset creators in their purpose, brand, intellectual

[8] "Finally, Brand Activism!" – Philip Kotler and Christian Sarkar, *THE MARKETING JOURNAL* http://www.marketingjournal.org/finally-brand-activism-philip-kotler-and-christian-sarkar/
[9] Unilever named industry leader in Dow Jones Sustainability Index, *Unilever* https://www.unilever.com/news/press-releases/2018/unilever-named-as-an-industry-leader-in-djsi.html
[10] Unilever calls on industry to increase trust, transparency and measurement in influencer marketing, *Unilever* https://www.unilever.com/news/press-releases/2018/unilever-calls-on-industry-to-increase-trust-transparency-and-measurement-in-influencer-marketing.html
[11] Sustainable Living, *Unilever* https://www.unileverusa.com/sustainable-living/
[12] https://www.unilever.com/news/press-releases/2018/unilever-calls-on-industry-to-increase-trust-transparency-and-measurement-in-influencer-marketing.html
[13] "Why Business Leaders Need to Take a Stand on Gun Violence, *FORTUNE* https://fortune.com/2018/09/04/levi-strauss-gun-violence-parkland/
[14] "Embankment Project for Inclusive Capitalism" *EY* https://www.ey.com/Publication/vwLUAssets/ey-at-embankment-project-inclusive-capitalism/$FILE/EY-the-embankment-project-for-inclusive-capitalism-report.pdf

property, products, employees, environment and communities.

Ben & Jerry's

Quite possibly the most activist company in the world, specific issues[15] include: Democracy[16], Climate Justice[17], GMO Labeling[18], LGBT Equality[19], Fairtrade[20], opposing rGBH[21], overturning *Citizen's United* [22], and Peace Building[23]. In 2016, Ben & Jerry's publicly announced their support for Black Lives Matter[24] and opposition to systemic racism[25]. In many ways Ben & Jerry's is a **justice-brand** – taking a stand for social issues most businesses avoid by design. It's also a B-Corporation[26].

Nike

When **Nike** decided[27] to make **Colin Kaepernick** the face of the 30th anniversary commemoration of their *Just Do It* campaign, they were instantly commended (and reviled) as a leader in brand activism.

Seventh Generation

Another Unilever subsidiary, also B-Corp and a mission-driven[28] company. The mission – **to inspire a consumer revolution that nurtures the health of the next seven generations**– is based on the Great Law of the Iroquois[29]

15 Issues We Care About, *Ben & Jerry's*
https://www.benjerry.com/values/issues-we-care-about
[16] We believe Democracy only works when it works for Everyone, *Ben & Jerry's* https://www.benjerry.com/values/issues-we-care-about/democracy
17 Time is Running Out, *Ben & Jerry's*
https://www.benjerry.com/values/issues-we-care-about/climate-justice
18 Our Non-GMO Standard, *Ben & Jerry's* https://www.benjerry.com/values/issues-we-care-about/support-gmo-labeling/our-non-gmo-standards
[19] LGBT Equality, *Ben & Jerry's*
https://www.benjerry.com/values/issues-we-care-about/marriage-equality
20 Fairtrade, *Ben & Jerry's* https://www.benjerry.com/values/issues-we-care-about/fairtrade
21 rBGH, Ben & Jerry's https://www.benjerry.com/values/issues-we-care-about/rbgh
[22] Get the Dough Out of Politics! *Ben & Jerry's*
https://www.benjerry.com/values/issues-we-care-about/get-the-dough-out-of-politics
[23] Peace-Building, *Ben & Jerry's*
https://www.benjerry.com/values/issues-we-care-about/peace-building
[24] Black Lives Matter, *Ben & Jerry's*
https://www.benjerry.com/whats-new/2016/why-black-lives-matter
[25] 7 Ways We Know Systemic Racism Is Real, *Ben & Jerry's*
https://www.benjerry.com/whats-new/2016/systemic-racism-is-real
[26] Certified B Corporation, *Ben & Jerry's* https://bcorporation.net/directory/ben-and-jerrys
[27] BEHIND NIKE'S DECISION TO STAND BY COLIN KAEPERNICK Jelani Cobb, *The New Yorker* https://www.newyorker.com/news/daily-comment/behind-nikes-decision-to-stand-by-colin-kaepernick
[28] We're on a mission to transform the world, *Seventh Generation* https://www.seventhgeneration.com/insideSVG/mission
[29] Great Law of the Iroquois Confederacy, *Fast Company* https://www.fastcompany.com/665006/great-law-iroquois-confederacy

– which holds it appropriate to think seven generations[30] ahead (about 140 years into the future) and decide whether the decisions they make today would benefit their children seven generations into the future.

The Body Shop

When the late **Anita Roddick** started the Body Shop, here's how she expressed her vision: "the business of business should not be about money, it should be about responsibility. It should be about public good, not private greed." Today, the Body Shop is returning to its founding principles. Their commitment to future-fitness[31] is an integrated systematic approach which includes a commitment to citizenship, paying taxes, employee wages and health, eco-product development, green stewardship, and renewable energy. By pursuing future-fitness, companies protect infrastructure they rely upon while managing business disruption and enhancing societal acceptance.

Marks and Spencer

Over ten years ago, M&S launched Plan A by making 100 commitments to tackle five big issues – climate change, waste, resources, fair partnerships, and health. Now Plan A 2025[32] adds a sense of urgency and 100 new targets.

Starbucks

Starbucks promised to hire 10,000 refugees[33] by 2022 in response to President Trump's "Muslim-ban" executive order.

What is striking about these initiatives is that they are fast becoming an expectation of business behavior.

Businesses that miss this point will miss the future.

ASK: In our industry, do we lead or do we follow – on our responsibilities to society? Are we viewed as progressive or regressive brand on the issues that matter most to our key stakeholders?

---

30 The Role of Chief, *Seven Generations*
http://www.pbs.org/warrior/content/timeline/opendoor/roleOfChief.html
31 *future-fitness* https://futurefitbusiness.org/

32 "Plan A 2025 Commitments" *Marks & Spencer*
https://corporate.marksandspencer.com/documents/plan-a/plan-a-2025-commitments.pdf
33 "Starbucks Makes Global Commitment to Hire 10,000 Refugees by 2022" *Starbucks*
https://www.starbucks.com/responsibility/community/refugee-hiring

THE COMMON GOOD: JUSTICE AS STRATEGY

One of the problems with constantly measuring the "values gap" between your company's conscience and the conscience of the various stakeholders is the difficulty of "staying the course" based on public opinion.

We decided to try another method, a more consistent way to measure brand activism, that we think will make sense for all.

It's based on the concept of the **Common Good**[34].

Wikipedia defines the common good as follows:

What is shared and beneficial for all or most members of a given community, or alternatively, what is achieved by citizenship, collective action, and active participation in the realm of politics and public service.

The question then arises, what is the community? **For the multi-national business, community is local, regional and global.**

It matters how you treat your employees all over the world.

Polluting one side of the world to profit on the other side is not a viable strategy, in fact, it is a crime.

With this in mind we can define **regressive brand activism as company actions that go against the common good.**

Progressive brand activism promotes the common good.

---

34 *Wikipedia* https://en.wikipedia.org/wiki/Common_good

We can think of the earth as our "common home," and the climate as "common good." Companies that damage the environment are thus hurting the common good, and can be classified as regressive.

Where does your industry stand? Where do your customers stand? Your employees? The rest of the stakeholders?

When your target customer is progressive, *you* had better be a progressive company.

Different industries have different norms, but even within industries such as oil and gas, for example, there will be leaders and laggards in each domain.

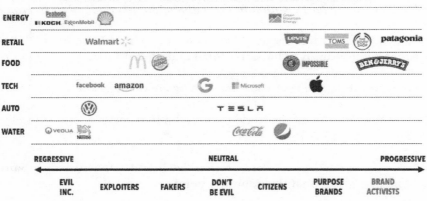

SOURCE: *DLM survey of 17-20-year-old students (2018)*

It would be an interesting and meaningful exercise to measure and rank all businesses by industry with clear indicators of where they stand.

It might be even more interesting to measure their long-term success in the market as well.

PROGRESSIVE

PROGRESSIVE
CUSTOMERS

**REGRESSIVE
COMPANY**

PROGRESSIVE
CUSTOMERS

PROGRESSIVE
COMPANY

**REGRESSIVE
CUSTOMERS**

**REGRESSIVE
COMPANY**

**REGRESSIVE
CUSTOMERS**

PROGRESSIVE
COMPANY

CUSTOMERS

REGRESSIVE   PROGRESSIVE
COMPANY

The strategy is justice. In an age of instant transparency, companies that do the right thing will increasingly command a premium. **Progressive brand activism becomes brand equity.**

ASK: Where are our progressive stakeholders headed? What are the values of the future?

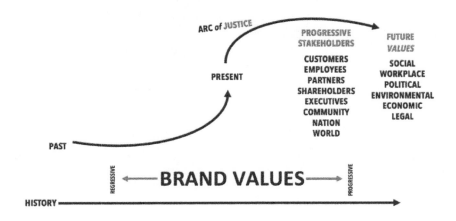

37

THE WICKED SEVEN

The inevitable question, one that we get asked all the time, is: "OK great, so what problem should my company work on?"

Our answer is what does your **future customer** care about?

And, if your company is a global multinational, we ask – what is it that is the most urgent issue of your local customers – country by country, region by region? Inevitably we find a common set of wicked problems that come up time and time again.

We have identified seven wicked problems that companies interested in pursuing brand activism may want to consider. We call them the "Wicked 7" because they are key components of the "ecosystem of wicked problems"[35] – intertwined and not easily solved – and yet, these are the very problems your future customer expects you to work on.

THE WICKED 7

---

35 "The Ecosystem of Wicked Problems" Christian Sarkar, *Global Peter Drucker Forum Blog* https://www.druckerforum.org/blog/?p=2365

Here is the list of the **Wicked7**:

Climate Collapse: the interlinked global crisis of weather-related events from heat waves, forest fires, flooding, hurricanes, ecosystem degradation, and species extinction.

Inequality: economic inequality is a way to measure social and gender inequality. The growing gap between the 1% and the rest of the population creates an unequal and unjust society.

Hate: the growing intolerance, polarization, and extremism fueled by identity-based and ideological groups which create social unrest, conflict, and commit acts of violence and terror.

War: includes militarism, the culture of war, armies, arms, industries, policies, plans, propaganda, prejudices, and rationalizations that lead to lethal group conflict.

Health and Livelihood: the worldwide challenge of public wellbeing – economic and physical health. Includes the economy, the future of work, employment, education, and the new skills and capabilities required to "make a living."

Corruption: the dishonest conduct by those in positions of power or those seeking to influence them using fraud and bribery. Corruption creates a system that governs not for the many, but for the few.

Population: the domestic and global population growth leads to increased conflicts over water, energy, food, open space, transportation, and schooling. Carrying capacity, the number of people, other living organisms, or crops that a region can support without environmental degradation – becomes a key metric for local and national wellbeing. growing problem of refugees and asylum seekers, mainly from the "global south" – the euphemism for poor countries.

How do you choose between the Wicked 7? We've started an online project at www.wicked7.org. Learn more and join our discussion.

BRANDSHAMING

On Valentine's Day 2018, Marjory Stoneman Douglas High School in Parkland, Florida lost 17 students to a mass shooting. The students stood up[36] in revolt against our politicians – asking them to **do something** instead of offering "thoughts and prayers."[37]

In the past, the NRA has exerted pressure on lawmakers, critics, and even gun manufacturers[38] through political lobbying[39]. But now, Generation Z[40] and their parents[41] have touched a nerve. The NRA put out a video ad ridiculing anyone who wasn't supportive of their agenda.

Parkland student **Sarah Chadwick**[42] responded with a blow-for-blow parody. The result? The **brandshaming** of the NRA[43] and its partners.

As the NRA is increasingly viewed as a **dangerous brand**, businesses are taking **measures that defy the NRA and are stricter on gun sales than federal or state laws.** Increasing pressure from consumers has caused companies to cut their ties with the NRA. Companies eliminating their NRA-member discount programs include:

- Airlines: Delta Air Lines, United Airlines
- Car Rentals: Enterprise, Alamo, National, Hertz, Avis, Budget
- Tech: Symantec, Starkey Hearing Technologies
- Miscellaneous: TrueCar, MetLife, SimpliSafe, First National Bank of Omaha, Dick's Sports

The Parkland students have shown us that **Generation Z** may be even *more conscious than the Millennials.*

---

[36] "Florida school shooting survivors take movement nationwide" *YouTube*
https://www.youtube.com/watch?time_continue=148&v=Ejze6-2lLAc
[37] "How 'thoughts and prayers' went from common condolence to cynical meme" *CNN*
https://www.cnn.com/2018/02/20/us/thoughts-and-prayers-florida-school-shooting-trnd/index.html
[38] "Smith and Wesson was once a leader in gun safety. Then the NRA stepped in" *Quartz*
https://qz.com/1215914/parkland-florida-school-shooting-smith-and-wesson-was-a-leader-in-gun-safety-until-the-nra-stepped-in/
[39] "This is how the NRA swings elections" *YouTube*
https://www.youtube.com/watch?v=kVJbA7KQIo0
[40] "American history suggests Centennials could turn the tide on the NRA" *Micheline Maynard, ABC.* https://www.abc.net.au/news/2018-02-19/generation-z-nra-gun-control-florida-high-school-massacre/9460720
[41] "Grieving father to Trump: I'm pissed" *YouTube*
https://www.youtube.com/watch?v=WvD7IYQv8B8
[42] Sarah Chadwick https://twitter.com/brutamerica/status/971828370282565633
[43] "Brandshaming: The Kids vs. The NRA" – Philip Kotler and Christian Sarkar, *THE MARKETING JOURNAL*
http://www.marketingjournal.org/brandshaming-philip-kotler-and-christian-sarkar/

Brandshaming is a revolt against regressive behavior. Think of it as the exact opposite of the Net Promoter Score.[44]

The NRA is the new face of **regressive brand activism**, replacing Big Tobacco, the previous champions.

When did the NRA lose sight of its public responsibilities?

Historically, up until 1977 the NRA often supported gun-control[45] legislation. But today, the NRA is fighting our kids – whose very lives the NRA has placed in danger. The kids[46], meanwhile, are taking to the streets. At last count, **Emma Gonzalez** had more Twitter followers than the NRA.

How have brands reacted to the NRA brandshaming?

When Dick's Sporting Goods CEO **Ed Stack** decided eliminate selling assault-style weapons and large-capacity magazines from more than 700

---

[44] *Wikipedia* https://en.wikipedia.org/wiki/Net_Promoter
[45] "The NRA once supported gun control" *Salon*
https://www.salon.com/2013/01/14/the_nra_once_supported_gun_control/
[46] Parkland survivor: Trump 'owned' by NRA just like other politicians by *JACQUELINE THOMSEN, THE HILL* https://thehill.com/homenews/administration/377878-parkland-survivor-trump-is-still-owned-by-the-nra

stores nationwide, the backlash was inevitable. In his book[47], *It's How We Play the Game: Build a Business. Take a Stand. Make a Difference*, we learn about how Stack's "toughest business decision" came in the wake of the Marjory Stoneman Douglas High School in Parkland, Florida.

Dick's became the first major retailer to pull all semi-automatic weapons from its shelves and raise the age of gun purchase to 21. Despite being a gun owner himself who'd grown up around firearms, Ed's strategy included destroying the five million dollars of assault-style-type rifles then in Dick's inventory.

If Congress wasn't going to take a stand on sensible gun laws in the wake of those tragedies, then someone else had to step in, Stack explains. If had to be Dick's, so be it. "AR-15s and other military-style rifles are like catnip to the deranged... The military variant of the AR-15 has just one purpose: to kill people."

Stack explains that firearms are a low-margin business, and that when the guns were removed, the floor space was dedicated to higher-margin merchandise.

The result? While gun advocates boycotted the store, Dick's ended up expanding its customer base, driving more traffic to the store, and recently achieved its best quarterly results[48] in six years!

ASK: What is my brand doing to embarrass itself and destroy its reputation with the customers of the future?

IS BRAND ACTIVISM GOOD FOR BUSINESS?

How does Brand Activism boost the bottom line?

Unilever CEO **Alan Jope** explains[49]: "We believe the evidence is clear and compelling that brands with purpose grow. Purpose creates relevance for a brand, it drives talkability, builds penetration and reduces price elasticity. In

---

[47] "It's How We Play the Game: Build a Business. Take a Stand. Make a Difference" by Ed Stack https://www.amazon.com/Its-How-Play-Game-Difference/dp/B07P886RCV
[48] "Dick's Sporting Goods posts best sales quarter in six years" by Jeff Platsky, *USA Today* https://www.usatoday.com/story/money/2019/11/26/dicks-sporting-goods-posts-best-sales/4308285002/
[49] "The ROI of Brand Activism: Unilever's Latest Findings" by Christian Sarkar & Philip Kotler, *activistbrands.com*
http://www.activistbrands.com/the-roi-of-brand-activism-unilevers-latest-findings/

fact, we believe this so strongly that we are prepared to commit that in the future, every Unilever brand will be a brand with purpose."

He tells us:

- In 2018, Unilever's Sustainable Living Brands grew 69% faster than the rest of the business, compared to 46% in 2017;
- Unilever now has 28 Sustainable Living Brands – the four new entrants are Close Up (toothpaste), Wheel (laundry), Calve and Bango (dressings);
- Seven of Unilever's top ten brands – Dove, Knorr, Omo/Persil, Rexona/Sure, Lipton, Hellmann's and Wall's ice cream – are all Sustainable Living Brands.

Unilever's Sustainable Living Brands are those that communicate a strong environmental or social purpose, with products that contribute to achieving the company's ambition of halving its environmental footprint and increasing its positive social impact. According to Jope, while all of Unilever's brands are on a journey towards sustainability, Sustainable Living Brands are those that are furthest ahead.

What about **Nike**? As we mentioned earlier, when Nike decided to make **Colin Kaepernick** the face of the 30th anniversary commemoration of their *Just Do It* campaign, they became an overnight poster child for brand activism.

By taking a public stand against President Trump and, to some extent, the NFL, Nike has rekindled the national debate over rights, patriotism, and the politicization of sports. The initial reaction was shrill and predictable. President Trump engaged his followers in bashing Nike, and once again created a moment of polarization and divisiveness:

A few "patriots" burned their Nike shoes or cut the Nike logo off their merchandise. Analysts like Professor **Scott Galloway**, for example, had a different take[50].

Within less than 24 hours since Kaepernick first revealed the spot on Twitter, *Bloomberg* reports[51] that Nike received more than $43 million worth

---

[50] "The Gangster Marketing Move of 2018" *YouTube*
https://www.youtube.com/watch?v=qLXzPDteFks
[51] Kaepernick Campaign Created $43 Million in Buzz for Nike
by Eben Novy-Williams, *Bloomberg* https://www.bloomberg.com/news/articles/2018-09-04/kaepernick-campaign-created-43-million-in-buzz-for-nike-so-far

of media exposure. Most tellingly, Nike's **online sales jumped 31%** in the four-day period following Kaepernick's announcement. Nike's stock price dipped but then came back, despite some threatening to boycott the company. The stock price went on to an all-time high.

Why is brand activism the next logical step for purpose-driven or values-based companies?

Because actions speak louder than words (or ads). Also, it can be profitable. In some cases, taking a stand is a strategic move that improves profits.

Here are the numbers, via Scott Galloway[52], who says:

Nike registers $35B in revenues — $15B domestically and $20B abroad. Two-thirds of Nike consumers are under the age of 35. A younger consumer who can afford $150 Flyknit racers likely has substantial disposable income and lives in a city. The term for this cohort? Progressive. Of the $20B international customer base, how many believe the US is currently a "beacon on a hill" and is handling race issues well? I'll speculate, none. Nike has risked $1-3B in business to strengthen their relationship with consumers who account for $32-34B of their franchise. The math? Nike just did it.

FUN UPDATE: Nike's stock has risen over 18 percent in 14 months after the announcement of the Kaepernick deal, adding a whopping $26.2 billion to the company's bottom line and valuing it at nearly $146 billion.

What this means is that companies must understand the trajectory of their future customer's beliefs, and race to meet them. The leaders will, in all probability, profit over the laggards.

What's next, Nike?

As Nike starts down this road of brand activism, they are going to have to be more progressive in order to combat the image of exploitative sweatshop labor[53] and gender inequality[54] in the workplace.

---

[52] "Stand for Something: Brand Activism at Nike" by Christian Sarkar and Philip Kotler, *THE MARKETING JOURNAL* http://www.marketingjournal.org/stand-for-something-brand-activism-at-nike-christian-sarkar-and-philip-kotler/
[53] "How Nike Solved Its Sweatshop Problem" by Max Nisen, *BUSINESS INSIDER* https://www.businessinsider.com/how-nike-solved-its-sweatshop-problem-2013-5
[54] "Fairness in its corporate corridors? Nike should just do it" by Jennifer Wells, *THE STA* https://www.thestar.com/business/opinion/2018/09/06/fairness-in-its-corporate-corridors-nike-should-just-do-it.html

Nike's progressive customers would not have it any other way.

ASK: What is the cost of our silence in the face of injustice?

Similar to NIKE, the sports brand PUMA has its own brand activist project launched by none other than Tommie Smith.

50 years ago, when US sprinter Tommie Smith took the gold in the 200 meters in a world-record-setting time at the 1968 Olympic Games in Mexico City, he used his moment on the podium to enter the history books. His countryman John Carlos, who won bronze in the same race, also took a stand.

Together, they raised their fists in protest.

The **ACLU**[55] describes the scene, and places it in perspective with our current climate:

Smith and Carlos won the gold and bronze medals respectively in the 200-meter event. What came next shocked the world. As Smith and Carlos walked to the podium, they took off their shoes to protest poverty. They wore beads and a scarf to protest lynchings — the last lynching of the 20th century had not yet occurred in 1968. Carlos unzipped his Olympic jacket, in defiance of Olympic etiquette, but in support of "all the working-class people — black and white — in Harlem who had to struggle and work with their hands all day."

Carlos also deliberately covered up the "USA" on his uniform with a black t-shirt to "reflect the shame I felt that my country was traveling at a snail's pace toward something that should be obvious to all people of good will." And when the national anthem was played, Smith and Carlos lowered their heads and raised their fists. They only had one pair of gloves so Smith put a black glove on his raised right fist; Carlos covered his left fist. The world was watching.

Smith and Carlos were protesting Black poverty that existed in a sea of prosperity. They were protesting police violence against Blacks and other people of color who spoke up about America's shortcomings. Yet just as we fail to see the connection between King and young Black activists today[56], we are blind to the parallels between Smith and Carlos on

---

[55] "The Spirit of 1968 Lives on Today in Athletes like Colin Kaepernick" by Jeffery Robinson, *ACLU* https://www.aclu.org/blog/racial-justice/race-and-economic-justice/spirit-1968-lives-today-athletes-colin-kaepernick
[56] "Back in the day: What critics said about King's speech in 1963" by *Morgan Whitaker*, *MSNBC* http://www.msnbc.com/msnbc/back-the-day-what-critics-said-about-king

the one hand and Colin Kaepernick and other modern day protesting athletes on the other. The protests are mirror images of each other and, sadly, the issues are the same.

The protest cost Smith dearly – he was suspended from the U.S. Olympics team, received death threats, and also faced repercussions from family and friends.

Now, inspired by Tommie Smith, the sports brand PUMA has launched #REFORM, a new platform that will give activists from the worlds of sports, music and entertainment support in championing causes and encouraging conversations around issues such as **universal equality** and **criminal justice reform**.

Joining Smith is rapper **Meek Mill** (who will focus on *criminal justice reform*), and WNBA All-Star **Skylar Diggins-Smith** (*gender equality*).

All proceeds from PUMA's Power Through Peace[57] collection will go towards charity partners fighting for universal equality, including the **American Civil Liberties Union** (ACLU).

Will this campaign help PUMA financially? As a brand ambassador for Africa – a majority of the continent's soccer teams are sponsored by PUMA – it probably already has.

ASK: *Do we celebrate those who stand for social justice?*

---

[57] "Puma Celebrates Tommie Smith and the Olympic Games with "PWR THRU PEACE" Capsule" *SneakerNews* https://sneakernews.com/2018/10/12/puma-power-through-peace-collection-release-date-photos/

4. THE EMPLOYEE AS BRAND ACTIVIST

What happens when employees decide their company should not pursue a customer or a project?[1]

Do they have the right to be **conscientious objectors**?

This letter to Google CEO **Sundar Pichai** was submitted with over 3000 signatures:

Dear Sundar,

We believe that Google should not be in the business of war. Therefore, we ask that Project Maven be cancelled, and that Google draft, publicize and enforce a clear policy stating that neither Google nor its contractors will ever build warfare technology.

Google is implementing Project Maven, a customized AI surveillance engine that uses "Wide Area Motion Imagery" data captured by US Government drones to detect vehicles and other objects, track their motions, and provide results to the Department of Defense.

Recently, Googlers voiced concerns about Maven internally. Diane Greene responded, assuring them that the technology will not "operate or fly drones" and "will not be used to launch weapons." While this eliminates a narrow set of direct applications, the technology is being built for the military, and once it's delivered it could easily be used to assist in these tasks.

This plan will irreparably damage Google's brand and its ability to compete for talent. *Amid growing fears of biased and weaponized AI, Google is already struggling to keep the public's trust. By entering into this contract, Google will join the ranks of companies like Palantir, Raytheon, and General Dynamics. The argument that other firms, like Microsoft and Amazon, are also participating doesn't make this any less risky for Google. Google's unique history, its motto Don't Be Evil, and its direct reach into the lives of billions of users set it apart.*

We cannot ***outsource the moral responsibility of our technologies to third parties.*** *Google's stated values make this clear: Every one of our users is trusting us. Never jeopardize that. Ever. This contract puts Google's reputation at risk and stands in direct opposition to our core values.* ***Building this technology to assist the US***

---

[1] "Don't Be Evil: When Employees Stand Up to Save the Brand" by Philip Kotler and Christian Sarkar http://www.marketingjournal.org/dont-be-evil-when-employees-stand-up-to-save-the-brand-philip-kotler-and-christian-sarkar/

Government in military surveillance – and potentially lethal outcomes – is not acceptable.

Recognizing Google's moral and ethical responsibility, and the threat to Google's reputation, we request that you:

1. Cancel this project immediately
2. Draft, publicize, and enforce a clear policy stating that neither Google nor its contractors will ever build warfare technology

The Googlers are objecting to Google's involvement in Project Maven, a Department of Defense project that focuses on computer vision—an aspect of machine learning and deep learning—that autonomously extracts objects of interest from moving or still imagery.

What's more, after Google chose to continue working on the project, reports indicate that nearly a **dozen employees actually resigned in protest**. They don't want to be a party to developing the "kill chain" for autonomous robotic warfare.

If some of the world's best and brightest are walking away from their jobs, shouldn't Google management get the hint? Employee pushback has worked in the past. In 2015, employees and users successfully challenged Google's ban on sexually explicit content posted to Blogger.

ASK: Do we understand the impact of our work on our brand? On our employees? Do we listen to employee concerns about our brand?

DON'T BE EVIL

The Google brand used to be famous for its code of conduct "Don't be evil" coined by an employee in 2000. While the code has been altered since, the last line still reads (at the time of this printing) as follows:

"And remember… don't be evil, and if you see something that you think isn't right – speak up!"

The objection is not restricted to Google. The backlash against Pentagon contracts is spreading throughout the tech industry[2]. The Tech Workers Coalition issued its own petition for the entire industry.

---

[2] "Tech should not be in the business of war" *coworker.org*
https://www.coworker.org/petitions/tech-should-not-be-in-the-business-of-war

From our vantage point, standing outside Google and Alphabet, the decision to pursue this war project seems to go against the Google brand promise. Have the senior executives considered what it means to join the military-industrial complex?

The employees are right to question their leadership. What does it do for consumer-trust in the long run? Do Google customers want to support a company that aided and abetted autonomous killing?

The reckless pursuit of profit can blind the best of leaders. Decisions like this can turn out to be a costly brand-destruction exercise for tech companies that are driving for growth at all cost.

Here's a thought[3] from the International Committee for Robot Arms Control:

"We are at a critical moment. The Cambridge Analytica scandal demonstrates growing public concern over allowing the tech industries to wield so much power. This has shone only one spotlight on the increasingly high stakes of information technology infrastructures, and the inadequacy of current national and international governance frameworks to safeguard public trust. Nowhere is this more true than in the case of systems engaged in adjudicating who lives and who dies."

We have not heard the last of AI and war. There is too much profit in the military-industrial war machine.

Unfortunately, the executives in charge may just be too close to the action to think and act rationally. **While executives may have failed to think strategically, Google's employees did not.**

ASK: Do our leaders listen to the voice of employees who risk their jobs to stand up?

---

[3] "Open Letter in Support of Google Employees and Tech Workers" *ICRAC*
https://www.icrac.net/open-letter-in-support-of-google-employees-and-tech-workers/

WHEN TALENT REBELS

At the consulting giant McKinsey, we saw an **employee backlash** on its decision to work with the Trump administration on "detention savings opportunities"[4] at ICE, the Immigration and Customs Enforcement agency.

ProPublica's Ian MacDougall explains that the money-saving recommendations the consultants came up with even made some career ICE staff "uncomfortable." MacDougall writes:

> *They proposed cuts in spending on food for migrants, as well as on medical care and supervision of detainees, according to interviews with people who worked on the project for both ICE and McKinsey and 1,500 pages of documents obtained from the agency after ProPublica filed a lawsuit under the Freedom of Information Act.*

> *McKinsey's team also looked for ways to accelerate the deportation process, provoking worries among some ICE staff members that the recommendations risked short-circuiting due process protections for migrants fighting removal from the United States. The consultants, three people who worked on the project said, seemed focused solely on cutting costs and speeding up deportations — activities whose success could be measured in numbers — with little acknowledgment that these policies affected thousands of human beings.*

Other reputational problems for McKinsey:

- Helping to turbo-charge the sale of opioids[5] for **Purdue Pharma**
- Dealings with corrupt[6] officials in **South Africa**
- In **Ukraine**, McKinsey and President Trump's convicted campaign chairman Paul Manafort were "paid by the same oligarch to help burnish the image of a disgraced presidential candidate, Viktor F. Yanukovych, recasting him as a reformer."
- producing a report[7] that tracked critics who were promoting negative views of Saudi Arabia on Twitter

---

[4] "How McKinsey Helped the Trump Administration Detain and Deport Immigrants" by Ian MacDougall, *ProPublica* https://www.propublica.org/article/how-mckinsey-helped-the-trump-administration-implement-its-immigration-policies
[5] "McKinsey Advised Purdue Pharma How to 'Turbocharge' Opioid Sales, Lawsuit Says" *The New York Times* https://www.nytimes.com/2019/02/01/business/purdue-pharma-mckinsey-oxycontin-opiods.html
[6] "McKinsey overhauls South Africa office after graft scandal" by Joe Brock, *Reuters* https://www.reuters.com/article/us-mckinsey-safrica/mckinsey-overhauls-south-africa-office-after-graft-scandal-idUSKBN1JY0ZM
[7] "Statement in response to today's New York Times article" https://nyti.ms/2yPncs7, *McKinsey & Company* https://twitter.com/mckinsey/status/1053838356826808320?lang=en

- Working closely with the Chinese government and state-owned Chinese companies despite the alleged human rights abuse of ethnic Uighurs in

All of this has led **Michael Posner**, professor of ethics and finance at NYU Stern School of Business and director of the Center for Business and Human Rights, to argue[8] that the firm "needs to develop more rigorous protocols for its government engagements that would address three fundamental issues: when should it decline to engage with a government, how should it respond when a government client asks for advice on a matter that violates fundamental rights, and when should it extricate itself from existing but inappropriate government contracts."

Working with authoritarian regimes[9] in the pursuit of profits is not the best way to win the hearts and minds of your employees. The reputational risk to McKinsey is considerable.

ASK: Are we risking our reputation by working with certain customers?

GUIDELINES FOR EMPLOYEE ACTIVISM

A survey[10] commissioned by global communications and marketing solutions firm **Weber Shandwick** in partnership with **KRC Research** and **United Minds**, reveals that 71% of employees feel they can make a difference in society, with 62% believing they can make a greater impact than business leaders can. Millennials are significantly more likely than older generations to feel empowered.

The study also finds that most U.S. employees believe employees are right to speak up about their employers, whether they are in support of them (84%) or against (75%). The belief that employees have a right to speak up in support of their employers is consistent across generations. Millennials are the only generation that think employees are just as right to speak out against their employers as they are to support (82% vs. 85%, respectively).

---

[8] "How McKinsey & Co. Fails As A Global Leader" Michael Posner, *Forbes* https://www.forbes.com/sites/michaelposner/2018/12/18/how-mckinsey-co-fails-as-a-global-leader/#11bc0c86376d
[9] "How McKinsey Has Helped Raise the Stature of Authoritarian Governments" *The New York Times* https://www.nytimes.com/2018/12/15/world/asia/mckinsey-china-russia.html
[10] "Employee Activism in the Age of Purpose: Employees (UP)Rising" *Weber Shandwick in partnership with KRC Research and United Minds.* https://www.webershandwick.com/wp-content/uploads/2019/06/Employee-Activism-in-the-Age-of-Purpose-FINAL.pdf

The report offers seven **guidelines** for navigating the new wave of employee activism:

1. Embrace employee activism as a positive force to propel your reputation and your business.

2. Ensure your corporate purpose and culture are known from the point of applicant interview and onboarding through employee tenure.

3. Be mindful of what is on employees' minds.

4. Cultivate a culture of openness and transparency.

5. Establish a response protocol.

6. Clearly articulate and communicate your company's values.

7. Make your company's values part of the solution.

ASK: Have we established a policy and guidelines for engaging with our employees in activism for the Common Good?

During the course of writing this book, we encountered several employees who left Facebook because they were shamed by the **Cambridge Analytica**[11] story.

Their point of view?

"I don't want to work for a company that I cannot believe in."
Mark Zuckerberg, the Facebook chief executive has been dubbed "the most dangerous person in the world"[12] by New York University Stern School of Business professor **Scott Galloway**.

One has to ask how we have reached this point. Is no one minding the store? Is there no adult supervision?

---

[11] "The Cambridge Analytica scandal changed the world – but it didn't change Facebook" *The Guardian* https://www.theguardian.com/technology/2019/mar/17/the-cambridge-analytica-scandal-changed-the-world-but-it-didnt-change-facebook
[12] "Why 'Mark Zuckerberg is the most dangerous person in the world,' according to this NYU business professor," *CNBC* https://www.cnbc.com/2019/08/09/scott-galloway-why-mark-zuckerberg-is-dangerous.html

5. THE CEO AS BRAND ACTIVIST

The U.S. has one of the lowest voter participation rates in the developed world, recently as low as 36 percent, and one of the most common reasons that people give for not voting is that they are too busy, or have work and life demands that prevent them from voting. To change this paradigm, a diverse coalition of companies including Kaiser Permanente, Levi Strauss & Co., Patagonia, PayPal, Tyson Foods and Walmart are coming together, starting with the 2018 November elections, to increase voter turnout[1].

While Patagonia plans to again give all its roughly 1,500 U.S. employees a paid day off on Election Day, other participating corporations are doing things differently. Lyft, for instance, plans to provide discounted rides to polling stations and free rides to people in underrepresented communities. So, rather than give its one million plus drivers the day off, it's instead making sure they have the information they need to file absentee ballots.

The campaign's big success is that it's managed to enlist CEOs from **both sides of the political spectrum**. In addition to Walmart's 1.5 million American employees, companies like Tyson Foods (which employs 122,000 people), Kaiser Permanent (216,199), and VF Corporation (70,000) have signed on.

In our view, the **Make Time to Vote** project is good citizenship and definitely in the realm of political brand activism, especially when certain political parties have worked hard at voter suppression[2] tactics.

The following statements are from the **CEOs** of some of the 150 participating companies:

"Our democracy needs strong participation to stay vibrant and healthy," said **Eric Dayton**, CEO of **Askov Finlayson**. "At a time when fewer people are voting than ever, businesses have a vital role to play by empowering our employees to exercise their fundamental right to vote in the upcoming election."

"Beautycounter is proud to give our teams the day off to participate in democracy and head to the polls," said **Gregg Renfrew**, Founder & CEO,

---

[1] *MAKE TIME TO VOTE* https://www.maketimetovote.org/
[2] "Voter Suppression Is Warping Democracy" by Vann R. Newkirk II, *The Atlantic* https://www.theatlantic.com/politics/archive/2018/07/poll-prri-voter-suppression/565355/

Beautycounter. "Business leaders can play an important role in making it easy for American workers to vote for elected officials that best represent their values. The time is now for us to engage in the democratic process in a meaningful way. As a company dedicated to non-partisan advocacy, we couldn't find a better way to support our mission than to join the Time to Vote initiative."

"At Deckers, we believe in doing business in a way that keeps us engaged and makes a positive impact on the world around us," said **Dave Powers**, CEO of **Deckers Brands**. "But that isn't just a business philosophy – it's something that extends to each and every employee. We encourage everyone at Deckers to make their voices heard and positively impact our community and environment."

"DICK'S Sporting Goods is proud to join the Time to Vote campaign," said **Ed Stack**, Chairman & CEO, **DICK'S Sporting Goods**. "We are happy to provide flexibility for our teammates to make voting easier and more convenient. We encourage everyone at DICK'S to take the time to register and visit the polls."

"I believe that each of us can be a catalyst for change," said **Eileen Fisher**, Founder and President of **EILEEN FISHER, Inc.** "When we exercise our right to vote, we can have a profound impact. As the founder of a values-based company, I want to encourage every employee - across our entire organization – to exercise their right to create change. Any opportunity that allows us to make a difference in our communities is of vital importance."

"We have long believed that employers should make it possible for their employees to vote," said **Charlie and Carolyn Kimbell**, Owners of **Elevation Clothing**. "It is a civic duty of the voter and a corporate responsibility of the employer."

"Too many prospective voters face legitimate hurdles in exercising the most necessary and fundamental right of voting," said **Ian Golden**, CEO of **Finger Lakes Running**. "Paired with an apathy, or cynicism as to the impact that one vote can have, we have one of the lowest voter turnout rates among comparable and developed nations. We're long overdue for a greater number of voters to exercise their right to make their voices heard, for politicians to empower and not disenfranchise prospective voters, and for we as employers to do our parts in making that happen. I'm thankful to be a part of this necessary endeavor."

"I know from firsthand jousting with so many of my colleagues that our people are truly passionate about politics – on both sides of the aisle," said **John Saunders**, president and CEO **FleishmanHillard**. "However, during a full-out, typically hectic PR consultancy day it can be too easy to neglect to vote. So we are saying: Stop. Time out. Go vote - it's too important not to."

"Voting is crucial to participating in the future of our country and helping to enact change, whether it's to protect our planet or our own healthy lifestyles," says **Kara Goldin**, Founder and CEO of **hint, Inc.** "This November, it's important to have your voice heard, please vote wherever you are, it matters."

"To create healthier communities, we must build more engaged communities — and this includes encouraging as many Americans as possible to exercise their right to vote," said **Kaiser Permanente** Chairman and CEO **Bernard J. Tyson**. "Voting is a privilege of living in America, and we are proud to join other major employers to ensure our position on exercising your right to vote is encouraged and supported."

"As a proud immigrant and son of a Holocaust survivor, I deeply value our vibrant democracy, which cannot be taken for granted and requires our active participation," said **Daniel Lubetzky**, Founder & CEO of **KIND Healthy Snacks**. "KIND is proud to join other businesses in the Time to Vote campaign, as exercising our right to vote is one important way to build stronger communities."

"The purest expression of any person's freedom occurs in the voting booth - it is our collective moral duty as CEOs to accommodate every citizen in pursuing that privilege," said **Todd Carmichael**, CEO of **La Colombe**.

"Lyft takes our civic responsibility seriously, which is why we are providing free and discounted rides to the polls on election day," said **John Zimmer**, Co-Founder and President of **Lyft**. "Last election, it is estimated that 15 million registered citizens did not vote because of transportation issues. We're thrilled to be a part of the Time to Vote movement, to help community members exercise their rights through initiatives like in-office voter registration, and voter education on early voting and vote by mail."

"People have fought and died for the right to vote in America and as business leaders we have a role to play in helping our employees participate in the democratic process," said **Levi Strauss & Co.** President and CEO **Chip Bergh**. "This campaign isn't about any particular party or candidate or issue – it's about encouraging more people to vote without having to make the hard choice between going to work and going to the polls."

"Every election is an important one, and democracy dies without engagement," said **New Belgium Brewing** CEO, **Steve Fechheimer**. "As business leaders, we aspire to foster engagement within our workplaces, and we have the power to enable engagement in our democracy as well. We raise our glasses to the organizations that have joined the campaign and to all those considering taking action."

"Our democracy simply works better when people go vote," said **Patagonia** CEO **Rose Marcario**.   "Demonstrating your company's commitment to voting reinforces the idea that American businesses can protect our democracy. I have been heartened to see business leaders from every corner of the country and across a range of industries prioritizing the health of our democracy and I look forward to seeing this movement grow."

"It is not fair, it is lazy, it is undemocratic and cowardly to sit on the sidelines and complain and whine about the sorry state of affairs our politics are in and the attacks on our environment and our deficits and our wars and dysfunctional politicians and NOT VOTE!" said **Vinny McClelland**, CEO of **The Mountaineer.**

"It's powerful to see companies coming together in support of voter participation," said **Arne Arens**, **The North Face Brand** president. "We feel responsible for creating opportunities for our people to vote, and we encourage them to actively engage in civic life. We're proud to be a part of Time to Vote, and continue to advocate for all Americans to make their voice heard."

"No matter your core beliefs, voting this midterm will have major implications in our communities, with our environment, and to the landscape of outdoor recreation areas," said **Bryan Wolf**, owner of **Roads Rivers and Trails**. "So for those of you on the fence about voting, we want to be the positive voice that tells you, your vote matters!"

"At sweetgreen, we know that when we act together, we can make a change and it takes only one small change influence the world," said **sweetgreen** Co-Founder and CEO **Jonathan Neman**. "That's why we're proud to be a part of the Time to Vote campaign and encourage each and every person at sweetgreen, and across the country, to make their voice heard and to vote."

"The opportunity to vote is one of our most powerful forms of expression, and a necessary part of a thriving democracy," said **Patrick Spence**, CEO **Sonos**. "As employers, it is our duty to society to empower those who work for us to use their voices at the polls. Sonos is proud to be part of this important initiative."

What is truly amazing, if we stop to think about it, is that our Election Day in the USA is ***not*** a national holiday.

How can we hold our democracy together if we can't even find the commitment to make it a priority for all our citizens? Should we move Election Day to coincide with Martin Luther King's birthday or George Washington's? Sen. Bernie Sanders has proposed a bill to designate "Democracy Day" as a national election holiday to make it easier for Americans to vote.

ASK: *Does our CEO support Democracy?*

THE ROLE OF THE CEO

Larry Fink's now infamous letter to CEOs is titled "A Sense of Purpose"[3], and in it he makes the case for the CEO leadership for societal good. As the CEO of Blackrock, the largest asset manager in the world, Fink manages more than $6 trillion in investments through 401(k) plans, exchange-traded funds and mutual funds.

In the past, Fink's BlackRock has been viewed[4] as a passive investor.

People like Bill Ackman, Carl Icahn, and Paul Singer, on the other hand, are considered "activist" investors, because they claim to look out for shareholders by pushing companies to innovate and change. Their maneuvers often deal with share buybacks and breakups – profit maximization, often in the short-term, to the detriment of the brands they purport to be saving. Profits without prosperity[5], is what this "activist" approach has been termed in the past.

Fink's sense of responsibility is to be commended.

---

3 "A Fundamental Reshaping of Finance" by Larry Fink *BlackRock*
https://www.blackrock.com/corporate/investor-relations/larry-fink-ceo-letter
4 The world's largest investment firm wants corporations to "serve a social purpose", *Vox*
https://www.vox.com/policy-and-politics/2018/1/17/16898496/blackrock-larry-fink
5 Profits without prosperity, *Harvard Business Review*
https://hbr.org/resources/pdfs/comm/fmglobal/profits_without_prosperity.pdf

Sceptics may ask, "Why now?" and to them, Fink answers:

We also see many governments failing to prepare for the future, on issues ranging from retirement and infrastructure to automation and worker retraining. As a result, society increasingly is turning to the private sector and asking that companies respond to broader societal challenges. Indeed, the public expectations of your company have never been greater.

The failure of government to do its job has caused companies to take up the slack. This is not uncommon in developing nations, where we've seen companies in India, the Tata Group[6] for example, cast a wide social[7] net.

Again, in his letter, Fink makes an important shift from **shareholder** to **stakeholder**:

*Society is demanding that companies, both public and private, serve a social purpose. To prosper over time, every company must not only deliver financial performance, but also show how it makes a positive contribution to society. Companies must **benefit all of their stakeholders**, including shareholders, employees, customers, and the communities in which they operate.*

Without a sense of purpose, no company, either public or private, can achieve its full potential. It will ultimately lose the license to operate from key stakeholders.

For reference[8], Blackrock's ESG (Environmental, Social, Governance) commitment spans a range of issues, including measures of company carbon emissions, labor and human rights policies, and corporate governance structures.

Fink is not alone in his views. The **World Economic Forum** has called this the **New Age of CEO activism**[9]. The World Economic Forum is stimulating CEOs and their companies to take more interest in addressing social problems found around the world.

---

[6] *Tata* http://www.tata.com/sustainability/articlesinside/corporate-social-responsibility
[7] "Transformational Sustainability at the Tata Group" – Stuart Hart, Aarti Sharma and Christian Sarkar, Green Leap Review
http://www.greenleapreview.com/transformational-sustainability-at-the-tata-group-stuart-hart-aarti-sharma-and-christian-sarkar/
[8] EXPLORING ESG: A Practitioner's Perspective, *BLACKROCK*
https://www.blackrock.com/corporate/literature/whitepaper/viewpoint-exploring-esg-a-practitioners-perspective-june-2016.pdf
[9] "The new age of CEO activism" *World Economic Forum*
https://www.weforum.org/agenda/2018/01/new-age-of-ceo-activism/

Additionally, the *Harvard Business Review* published *The New CEO Activists*[10], by Aaron K. Chatterji and Michael W. Toffel, in which they make an important point: **the more CEOs speak up on social and political issues, the more they will be expected to do so.**

And increasingly, CEO activism has strategic implications: **In the Twitter age, silence is more conspicuous.**

Weber Shandwick, in partnership with KRC Research, released *CEO Activism in 2017: High Noon in the C-Suite*.[11] The survey measures attitudes toward the trend of chief executive officers (CEOs) speaking out on hot-button societal topics, revealing stark generational differences when it comes to perspectives on CEO activism.

The opinion about CEO activism varies in different age groups. Millennials (ages 18-36) like the idea, as illustrated in the following percentages:

- 47% believe CEOs have a responsibility to speak up about issues that are important to society
- 56% agree CEOs and other business leaders have greater responsibility today for speaking out on hotly debated current issues than they used to
- 48% have heard or read about CEOs taking public positions on hotly debated current issues
- 74% of those who have heard or read about CEO activism have taken an action based on a CEO's stance on a hotly debated current issue, most commonly talking about the stance with friends and family (26%), as well as with coworkers (23%)
- 51% would be more likely to buy from a company led by a CEO who speaks out on an issue they agree with
- 42% are more favorable of CEOs who take public positions on issues. 20% are less favorable
- 37% would be more favorable of a CEO who took a public position on an issue even if that issue is not directly related to the company's business. 26% would be less favorable

---

10 "The New CEO Activists" by Aaron K. Chatterji Michael W. Toffel, *Harvard Business Review* https://hbr.org/2018/01/the-new-ceo-activists
11 https://www.webershandwick.com/uploads/news/files/ceo-activism-in-2017-high-noon-in-the-c-suite.pdf

- 44% of those who are employed full-time would be more loyal to their organization if the CEO took a public position on an issue. 19% would be less loyal
- 36% think CEOs take public positions on hotly debated current issues to get attention in the media (their top perceived reason)
- 21% say CEOs speak out to build the company's reputation (their #2 perceived reason)

The evolution of brand activism in business is an opportunity for differentiation and **purpose-driven engagement**. This sentiment is explained in *Why Making Money is Not Enough[12]:*

The problem with industrial capitalism today is not the profit motive; the problem is how the profit motive is usually framed. There is a persistent myth in the contemporary business world that the ultimate purpose of a business is to maximize profit for the company's investors. However, the maximization of profit is not a purpose; instead, it is an outcome. We argue that the best way to maximize profits over the long term is to not make them the primary goal.

Traditionalists strongly believe that companies should "stick close to their knitting" and work hard to create profits to satisfy the expectations of the company's owners and investors. Professor Milton Friedman of the University of Chicago passionately believed that CEOs and companies have the fiduciary responsibility of maximizing the returns to the company's owners and investors. Why would investors want to receive less than the maximum return? Why let CEOs decide on which social problems the company should invest its hard-earned profits? Let investors make the social decisions that they want.

Not anymore.

What are the key considerations for the CEO?

- the CEO helps **create** and **nurture** the brand
- the CEO is the **guardian** of the brand, protecting it from short term actions which may result in longer-term value destruction
- the CEO safeguards the **continuity** of the brand, ensuring consistency across time

---

[12] "Why Making Money Is Not Enough" by Stuart Hart, Aarti Sharma, and Christian Sarkar, *MIT Sloan Management Review*
https://sloanreview.mit.edu/article/why-making-money-is-not-enough/

- the CEO is the **architect of the future** of the brand

What makes a leader trustworthy? Untrustworthy?

The **CEO** is the **Brand Guardian**[13]. The culture of a company is the direct reflection of the tone set by the chief executive.

Studies show that employees rate their leaders on trust through their actions. In their article *Why People Believe in Their Leaders — or Not*[14], Daniel Han Ming Chng, Tae-Yeol Kim, Brad Gilbreath, and Lynne Andersson cite two critical elements lie at the heart of credibility: perceived competence and trustworthiness. The difference between trustworthy and untrustworthy leaders is stark:

Trustworthy Leaders:

- Communicate and act in a consistent manner
- Protect the organization and employees
- Embody the organization's vision and values
- Consult with and listen to key stakeholders
- Communicate openly with others
- Value employees
- Offer support to employees and key stakeholders

Untrustworthy leaders:

- Promote an unethical climate in the organization
- Communicate dishonestly
- Act in a self-serving manner
- Behave in an inconsistent manner
- Communicate in a guarded or inconsistent manner
- Ignore the input of employees and key stakeholders
- Treat employees as expendable

Trustworthy leaders *listen* to their employees and key stakeholders.

---

13 "The CEO as Brand Guardian" by Christian Sarkar and W. Rodgers, *edgemi*
http://edgemi.org/ceobrand.shtml
14 Why People Believe in Their Leaders by Daniel Han Ming Chng, Tae-Yeol Kim, Brad Gilbreath, and Lynne Andersson, MIT Sloan https://sloanreview.mit.edu/article/why-people-believe-in-their-leaders-or-not/

Apple CEO **Tim Cook** has said that as government fails to deliver, business and other areas of society need "to step up." All businesses benefit from a well-working economy with good infrastructure and well-trained and motivated workers.

ASK: Do our employees trust our CEO to do the right thing?

Let's dig deeper. **What tone should the CEO be setting?** For that we looked at the behavior of **Howard Schultz, Starbucks'** former Chairman and CEO, who sent the following message to all partners (employees) on January 29, 2017:

Dear partners,

I write to you today with deep concern, a heavy heart and a resolute promise. Let me begin with the news that is immediately in front of us: we have all been witness to the confusion, surprise and opposition to the Executive Order that President Trump issued on Friday, effectively banning people from several predominantly Muslim countries from entering the United States, including refugees fleeing wars. I can assure you that our Partner Resources team has been in direct contact with the partners who are impacted by this immigration ban, and we are doing everything possible to support and help them to navigate through this confusing period.

We are living in an unprecedented time, one in which we are witness to the conscience of our country, and the promise of the American Dream, being called into question. These uncertain times call for different measures and communication tools than we have used in the past. Kevin and I are going to accelerate our commitment to communicating with you more frequently, including leveraging new technology platforms moving forward. I am hearing the alarm you all are sounding that the civility and human rights we have all taken for granted for so long are under attack, and want to use a faster, more immediate form of communication to engage with you on matters that concern us all as partners.

I also want to take this opportunity to announce specific actions we are taking to reinforce our belief in our partners around the world and to ensure you are clear that we will neither stand by, nor stand silent, as the uncertainty around the new Administration's actions grows with each passing day:

***Support for DACA:** As I wrote to Senators Graham and Durbin[15] this week, we are enthusiastically behind their work to support "Dreamers" across our country —*

---

[15] Letter from Howard Schultz to U.S. Senators Lindsey Graham and Richard Durbin, *STARBUCKS STORIES* https://stories.starbucks.com/stories/2017/letter-from-howard-schultz-to-senators-lindsey-graham-and-richard-durbin

including those young men and women who are part of the Deferred Action for Childhood Arrivals (DACA) program. There are nearly three quarters of a million hardworking people contributing to our communities and our economy because of this program. At Starbucks, we are proud to call them partners and to help them realize their own American Dream. We want them to feel welcome and included in our success, which is why we reimburse them for the biennial fee they must pay to stay in the program and why we have offered DACA-related services at our Opportunity Youth hiring fairs.

Hiring Refugees: *We have a long history of hiring young people looking for opportunities and a pathway to a new life around the world. This is why we are doubling down on this commitment by working with our equity market employees as well as joint venture and licensed market partners in a concerted effort to welcome and seek opportunities for those fleeing war, violence, persecution and discrimination. There are more than 65 million citizens of the world recognized as refugees by the United Nations, and we are developing plans to hire 10,000 of them over five years in the 75 countries around the world where Starbucks does business. And we will start this effort here in the U.S. by making the initial focus of our hiring efforts on those individuals who have served with U.S. troops as interpreters and support personnel in the various countries where our military has asked for such support.*

Building Bridges, Not Walls, With Mexico: *We have been open for business in Mexico since 2002, and have since opened almost 600 stores in 60 cities across the country, which together employ over 7,000 Mexican partners who proudly wear the green apron. We have sourced coffee from Mexico's producers and their families for three decades and last fall, we also announced the creation of a farmer support center in Chiapas to help accelerate our collective ability to grow and export some of the world's finest coffees from this important growing region, while donating more than $2 million to support the livelihood, food security and water quality of coffee producing communities in Oaxaca. With the support of thousands of Starbucks partners and millions of customers, we have also donated over a million coffee trees to support 70,000 families, and we will be expanding the initiative this year to generate another 4 million tree donations. Coffee is what unites our common heritage, and as I told Alberto Torrado, the leader of our partnership with Alsea in Mexico, we stand ready to help and support our Mexican customers, partners and their families as they navigate what impact proposed trade sanctions, immigration restrictions and taxes might have on their business and their trust of Americans. But we will continue to invest in this critically important market all the same.*

Our Healthcare Commitment to You: *Finally, let me restate what we have recently communicated with you about the Affordable Care Act – our commitment remains that if you are benefits eligible, you will always have access to health insurance through Starbucks. Many of you have expressed concerns that recent government actions may jeopardize your ability to participate in the Affordable Care Act. If the recent Executive Order related to health care remains in place and the Affordable Care Act is repealed* *causing you to lose your healthcare coverage, you will always have the ability to return and can do so within 30 days of losing that coverage rather than having to wait for an open enrollment period. If you have any questions or concerns, please contact the Benefits Center at 877-728-9236.*

In the face of recent events around the world, let me assure you that we will stay true to our values and do everything we can possibly do to support and invest in every partner's well-being while taking the actions that are squarely within our ability to control. This is our focus: providing a Third Place of respite for those around the world who seek it, daily.

Starbucks has and will always stand for opportunity — opportunity for our young people who are working to land their first job in the 75 countries where we do business, opportunity for our farmers who care so deeply for the highest of quality coffee we offer to customers all around the globe, and yes, opportunity for those who come to America in search of their own fresh start — whether that is with Starbucks directly, or through our suppliers or our partner companies.

If there is any lesson to be learned over the last year, it's that your voice and your vote matter more than ever. We are all obligated to ensure our elected officials hear from us individually and collectively. Starbucks is doing its part; we need you to use the collective power of your voices to do the same while respecting the diverse viewpoints of the 90 million customers who visit our stores in more than 25,000 locations around the world.

So, while we seek to understand what the new Administration's policies mean for us and our business both domestically and around the world, I can assure you that we will do whatever it takes to support you, our partners, to realize your own dreams and achieve your own opportunities. We are in business to inspire and nurture the human spirit, one person, one cup and one neighborhood at a time — whether that neighborhood is in a Red State or a Blue State; a Christian country or a Muslim country; a divided nation or a united nation. That will not change. You have my word on that.

Onward,

Howard

This sort of message is inevitably seen as political, because it is. **When polarization is a political strategy, then business leaders have a responsibility to lead us *back* to civility.** That inclusivity is what Schultz is promoting.

Another outstanding example[16] of Schultz's brand leadership comes to us via **Frederick Allen**, the leadership editor at *Forbes*:

At an annual meeting, a shareholder complained the company had lost customers because of its support for gay marriage.

"In the first full quarter after this boycott was announced, our sales and our earnings, shall we say politely, were a bit disappointing," said the shareholder, Tom Strobhar, whom the Huffington Post identifies[17] at the founder of the anti-gay marriage Corporate Morality Action Center.

Schultz's response?

"Not every decision is an economic decision. Despite the fact that you recite statistics that are narrow in time, we did provide a 38% shareholder return over the last year. I don't know how many things you invest in, but I would suspect not many things, companies, products, investments have returned 38% over the last 12 months. Having said that, it is not an economic decision to me. **The lens in which we are making that decision is through the lens of our people.** We employ over 200,000 people in this company, and we want to embrace diversity. Of all kinds…If you feel, respectfully, that you can get a higher return than the 38% you got last year, it's a free country. You can sell your shares in Starbucks and buy shares in another company. Thank you very much."

The audience cheered.

The final consideration is whether the brand delivers *brand beneficence*[18]. We believe that most companies would benefit from making their brands more activist. And the job of the CEO is to lead the charge.

ASK: Is our CEO viewed as "force for good"?

---

[16] "Howard Schultz to Anti-Gay-Marriage Starbucks Shareholder: 'You Can Sell Your Shares'" *Forbes* https://www.forbes.com/sites/frederickallen/2013/03/22/howard-schultz-to-anti-gay-marriage-starbucks-shareholder-you-can-sell-your-shares/#45fa4a3143fa
[17] "Starbucks Gay Marriage Stance: CEO Puts Smackdown On Anti-Marriage Equality Shareholder" by Hunter Stuart, *Huffington Post*
https://www.huffpost.com/entry/starbucks-gay-marriage-howard-schultz_n_2931734
[18] "Branding: From Purpose to Beneficence" by Philip Kotler, *THE MARKETING JOURNAL* http://www.marketingjournal.org/brand-purpose-to-beneficence-philip-kotler/

THE TEAM OF TEAMS: THE B TEAM

What happens when activist CEOs team up for good?

The **B Team** is a not-for-profit initiative formed by a global group of business leaders to catalyze a better way of doing business, for the wellbeing of people and the planet.

Here's how they describe themselves:

Founded in the belief that the private sector can, and must, redefine both its responsibilities and its own terms of success, we are developing a 'Plan B'[19] – for concerted, positive action that will ensure business becomes a driving force for social, environmental and economic benefit. Plan A – where business has been motivated primarily by profit – is no longer an option. We are focused on driving action to meet a set of Challenges that underpin Plan B – by starting 'at home' in our own companies, taking collective action to scale systemic solutions and using our voice where we can make a difference.

The team includes the who's who of progressive business leaders from across the planet: Oliver Bäte, Sir Richard Branson, Marc Benioff, Sharan Burrow, Kathy Calvin, Bob Collymore, David Crane, Christiana Figueres, Mats Granryd, Arianna Huffington, Dr. Gro Harlem Brundtland, Dr. Mo Ibrahim, Yolanda Kakabadse, Guilherme Leal, Andrew Liveris, Strive Masiyiwa, Dr. Ngozi Okonjo-Iweala, Arif Naqvi, François-Henri Pinault, Paul Polman, Mary Robinson, Ratan Tata, Zhang Yue, Professor Muhammad Yunus, Jochen Zeitz.

This sort of collaborative requires an **ego-free mindset** so desperately required in this, our crisis-ridden world. What's important is how their good intentions are realized in action. The B-Team's **Vision of The Future** is a world in which **the purpose of business is to become a driving force for social, environmental and economic benefit.**

Plan B takes on 10 issues that cause companies to remain trapped in "business as usual":

1. **Drive full transparency**
    Be open, transparent and free from corruption, with good governance and accountability at all levels of our organizations.

---

[19] THE B MOVEMENT https://bteam.org/our-movement/overview

2. **Foster collaboration**
   Work with other businesses, governments, trade unions, and civil society to foster open dialogue and forge new partnerships that accelerate positive change.

3. **Restore nature**
   Ensure our companies significantly reduce their environmental impacts and invest in new business models that help regenerate the environment.

4. **Scale true accounting**
   Measure and communicate social and environmental impacts, as well as our plans for improvement.

5. **Create thriving communities**
   Help create environments inside and outside our companies that enable employees and our communities to thrive.

6. **Reinvent market incentives**
   Encourage government policies, corporate structures and tax systems that deliver the best outcomes for people and the planet, helping capital flow towards delivering true returns.

7. **Ensure dignity and fairness**
   Ensure that people throughout our supply chains are treated with dignity and respect, working in a safe, equitable and empowering environment, where they receive a fair share of the value they create and their rights are fully supported.

8. **Redefine reward systems**
   Support fair rewards in our companies, integrating social and environmental performance targets into our compensation systems, and champion efforts to close the pay gap throughout the business world.

9. **Value diversity**
   Cultivate and celebrate diversity, including gender, at all levels of business while ensuring equality of opportunity for all employees.

10. **Lead for the long run**
    Adopt longer reporting cycles and nurture inclusive, collaborative leadership focused on delivering long-term value to all stakeholders.

The hope is that the prestige, power, and example of these global titans will inspire others to join them – peer-pressure for the CEO crowd. This is a positive sentiment, and, perhaps, a last best hope. We are going to have to institutionalize the spirit of Plan B across not just businesses, but governments, nations, and other institutions.

Where do we sign up?

A fun question: where are Bill Gates and Warren Buffet? Obama? Bono? Klaus Schwab? Did they miss the bus?

But seriously, this is *the* real challenge: **How do progressive CEOs mitigate the impact of regressive CEOs?** How does Plan B – Branson and friends take on the Koch brothers and the Mercers? We will come back to this question later.

ASK: What is our Plan B?

INCLUSIVE DECISION-MAKING

Are your business decision-making processes that look beyond "shareholder-value maximization"? Are there lessons from progressive brands that we can learn from?

In this article[20], we find an alternative **screen for decision-making** used by the **Tata Group.**

Founder **Sir J.N. Tata** believed that the "acquisition of wealth was only a secondary object of life"; he considered Tata Sons' mission was to **"serve and help" the communities in which it operated.**

---

[20] "Transformational Sustainability at the Tata Group" – Stuart Hart, Aarti Sharma and Christian Sarkar, *Green Leap Review* http://www.greenleapreview.com/transformational-sustainability-at-the-tata-group-stuart-hart-aarti-sharma-and-christian-sarkar/

Even today, despite the growing wealth of the Tata Group, company leaders are *not* featured in the listings of the richest people in India or the world. This is because two-thirds of the shares of Tata Sons, the holding company of the group, belong to the Tata Trusts, including the Sir Ratan Tata Trust, the Sir Dorabji Tata Trust, and the JRD and Thelma J Tata Trust.

As one of the largest and oldest Indian philanthropic foundations, the Tata Trusts have long supported causes and institutions aimed at the greater good of India and mankind, including the Indian Institute of Science, the Tata Institute of Social Sciences, and the Tata Memorial Hospital.

The employees of the Tata group are also connected to its tradition of giving back to society through active encouragement of volunteering as a way of life – Tata Engage, the group-level volunteering program, is listed as one among the top 10 corporate volunteering programs in the world having achieved a million volunteering hours annually.

The **Tata Group** has developed a set of straightforward guidelines[21] (next page) to ensure that its core beliefs about sustainability are not lost in the pursuit of growth and profits.

ASK: What will make my company more inclusive? What will it take for outside voices – the customer, society, the planet, to be heard?

What sort of screen does your company need to ensure it does not end up in the **Corporate Hall of Shame**?

21 "Transformational Sustainability at the Tata Group" – Stuart Hart, Aarti Sharma and Christian Sarkar, *Green Leap Review* http://www.greenleapreview.com/transformational-sustainability-at-the-tata-group-stuart-hart-aarti-sharma-and-christian-sarkar/

1. MOTIVATE WITH PURPOSE

Frame business motives around solving economic, environmental and/or social problems

Offer business products and services that build and support communities

Improve stakeholders' quality of life

2. CHANGE THE RULES OF THE GAME

Question the industry status quo

Challenge existing business practices

Demonstrate transformational sustainability through economically empowering, socially inclusive and environmentally conscious business practices

3. INCUBATE LOCAL, DISTRIBUTED, SOLUTIONS

Solve social, economic and environmental problems through decentralized solutions

Adapt clean technologies to socio-economic and environmental conditions of local communities

Provide small scale and distributed clean technological solutions to meet local needs

4. EMBED BUSINESS BACK INTO SOCIETY

Address socio-economic and environmental inadequacies of communities to expand current business or create new businesses

Identify business supply chain inadequacies to create local business opportunities for stakeholders

Strengthen supply chain capabilities through stakeholder training

5. SHATTER TRADE-OFFS AMONG STAKEHOLDERS

Develop business strategies that curb social injustice

Address socio-economic and environmental needs of marginalized stakeholders

Create sustainable communities around industrial facilities through win-win strategies

6. THE CUSTOMER AS BRAND ACTIVIST

A brand activist company has three choices if it wants to engage its customers: it can follow them, it can lead them, or it can work with them to co-create a future worth having.

It starts by asking two questions: 1) what do customers want? and 2) what do we think must be done? If the two questions give you the same answer, then it's time to do it. If not, then there is a need for education – either the customer will educate you, or you have a responsibility to educate the customer. Or, and this is a third option, you can learn together.

In this section we'll introduce two ideas for engaging with your customers and beyond:

1) **The Internet of Purpose** – in which your **product** becomes a catalyst and instrument of activism
2) **The Purpose Platform** – in which your brand builds a movement around the Common Good; this goes well beyond your customers to include society

But first, let's look at what the people want.

WHAT DO CUSTOMERS WANT?

What does the data say? A survey[1] by **Sprout Social** reveals these key findings:

People want brands to take stands on important issues, and social media is the place for it. Two-thirds of consumers (66%) say it's important for brands to take public stands on social and political issues, and more than half (58%) are open to this happening on social media – the top channel for consumer receptivity.

Brands can't change minds, but they can effect change. Sixty-six percent of respondents say posts from brands rarely or never influence their opinions on social issues. Rather, respondents believe brands are more effective on social media when they announce donations to specific causes (39%) and encourage followers to take specific steps to support causes (37%),

---

[1] *#BrandsGetReal: Championing Change in the Age of Social Media*
https://sproutsocial.com/insights/data/championing-change-in-the-age-of-social-media/

such as participating in events or making their own donations.

Liberals are galvanized by brands that take stands, while conservatives are indifferent. Seventy-eight percent of respondents who self-identify as liberal want brands to take a stand, while just about half (52%) of respondents who self-identify as conservative feel the same. Likewise, 82% of liberals feel brands are credible when taking stands, compared to just 46% of conservatives.

Relevance is key to reception. Consumers say brands are most credible when an issue directly impacts their customers (47%), employees (40%) and business operations (31%).

Brands face more reward than risk. Consumers' most common emotional reactions to brands taking a stand on social were positive, with intrigued, impressed and engaged emerging as the top three consumer reactions. Likewise, when consumers' personal beliefs align with what brands are saying, 28% will publicly praise a company. When individuals disagree with the brand's stance, 20% will publicly criticize a company.

What's more the survey also discovers that respondents want brands to take stands depending on the issue:

WHEN CONSUMERS WANT BRANDS TO TAKE STANDS - BY ISSUE

	YES	only if related to products/ service	NO
EDUCATION	45%	34	21
ENVIRONMENT	45	36	20
GENDER EQUALITY	48	27	26
HEALTHCARE	42	39	20
HUMAN RIGHTS	58	25	17
IMMIGRATION	33	37	31
LABOR LAWS	55	29	16
LGBTQ RIGHTS	34	30	35
POVERTY	48	31	21
RACE RELATIONS	43	28	30

source: sprout social

72

Yet another survey[2] by **BRANDfog** and **McPherson Strategies** tells us that **93%** of respondents believe CEOs make a difference:

"When CEOs issue statements about the key social issues of our time and I agree with the sentiment, I am more likely to make a purchase from that company."

86% of people think that **CEOs who publicly defend the rights of others** on social media **are seen as great leaders.**

PRODUCT ACTIVISM: THE INTERNET OF PURPOSE

We've all heard about the **Internet of Things**, but what if a company used its products to build an **Internet of Purpose (IoP)**?

Does anyone remember the days when bad news was printed on milk cartons[3]? The product (milk-cartons) would raise public awareness of missing children through the message on the cartons. Now imagine an intelligent product which allows the customer to engage with a cause they care about. As the product is used, the customer is awarded points which can be redeemed in ways that make a difference towards the cause they support. Social recognition and social rewards are powerful tools for encouraging good behavior. *The **Internet of Purpose** (IoP) is the product/device ecosystem that engages the customer with relevant and meaningful opportunities to do good.*

THE INTERNET *of* PURPOSE
"embedding purpose in your connected-product"

---

[2] CEOS SPEAKING OUT ON SOCIAL MEDIA SURVEY, *brandfog*,
 http://brandfog.com/survey/2018_ceo_survey.pdf
[3] When Bad News Was Printed on Milk Cartons, *The Atlantic*
https://www.theatlantic.com/technology/archive/2017/02/when-bad-news-was-printed-on-milk-cartons/516675/

To design a brand-activism program that employs the Internet of Things as an Internet of Purpose, a company will have to understand the psychology and cultural narrative[4] that resonates best with its customer.

Here's the step-by-step process:

1. Pick the **issue** or **cause** that resonates most with your target customer
2. Identify how you will **support the cause**
3. Design a product architecture that **connects the cause to the consumer**
4. Create advertising that builds a **narrative for change**
5. Ensure the **packaging** is consistent with the narrative
6. Build the **"activism-in-use"** component embedded in the product
7. Design the elements of the brand activism campaign that will nurture the consumer as activist: **education**, **calls to action**, and **alerts**
8. Implement a **social rewards program** that enables activist customers to support the cause
9. Measure and **communicate the impact**, the collective campaign results, with the customer

How could Nike develop an *Internet of Purpose* to have an exponential impact with its Kaepernick "Just Do It" campaign?

The key would be to **connect the shoe to the cause.** Every step you take must help the cause. How? Imagine: Nike pledges to donate $1 million dollar each month to *one* of Colin Kaepernick's favorite causes – anti-police brutality, youth initiatives, community reform, minority empowerment, health reform, and nourishment. The winning cause is determined by points donated by shoe owners who accumulate a point for *every step they take.*

---

[4] "Competing on Stories: Marketing and Cultural Narratives" by Christian Sarkar and Philip Kotler, *THE MARKETING JOURNAL* http://www.marketingjournal.org/competing-on-stories-marketing-and-cultural-narratives-christian-sarkar-and-philip-kotler/

Points are awarded via a "K7" app, and can be tagged by shoe owners towards the cause they select. At the end of the month, the winning cause is awarded the $1 million. *Repeat each month.* Note: Causes may change, as selected by Kaepernick, over the course of the brand-activism campaign.

A similar approach can be employed by almost any company – even if your products aren't smart. So a cereal maker could connect its product packaging to a website with a call to action. It could even connect the consumer to a *purpose platform, and invite them to help solve a problem!*

ASK: *Can we use our product ecosystem to engage our customers and create a movement for the Common Good?*

THE PURPOSE PLATFORM

What happens when a company's **brand-activism** leads it to engage with actors well *beyond* the closed walls of the business? What happens when you approach a problem with radical humility?

Simone Cicero, the leading expert on platform design[5], says: "platforms are about scaling interactions so that solutions can emerge organically from all the interactions in the system. This is what happens when brands don't have all the answers, especially in a complex age, with wicked problems arising." Cicero is a proponent of platforms as a vehicle for self-organization and connection.

What's the difference between building products versus a platform? Cicero explains: "platforms are channels that connect people and services so that everyone can fully leverage their potential. This is different than just providing everybody with a consumable solution. Building products is similar to building houses, which are a specific answer to a need for shelter. Building platforms is like building a city where you just need an infrastructure: you make the zoning laws, but then the participants build the houses."

The Brand Activist asks: ***What is my brand, my organization, doing to solve the pressing problems of the world – the problems my future customers and employees care about?***

What is a **purpose platform**[6]?

We define it as **a platform to mobilize people across society – experts and community members – to create lasting and sustainable solutions to society's most pressing challenges,** i.e. the **Common Good**[7].

Purpose platforms mobilize people to act. They may even build a social movement. History tells us that movements (Civil Rights, Woman's Suffrage, etc.) were all platforms for societal change. In a digital world, we see platforms for change sprout up all the time – from Move to Amend[8] to Black Lives Matter[9]. While we *don't* see many companies building platforms of purpose, more and more are participating and supporting platforms outside

---

[5] Platform Design Toolkit https://platformdesigntoolkit.com/

[6] How Companies can Build a Purpose Platform for the Common Good" by Christian Sarkar and Philip Kotler, *ACTIVISTBRANDS.COM* http://www.activistbrands.com/how-companies-can-build-a-purpose-platform-for-the-common-good/

[7] *Advancing the Common Good: Strategies for Businesses, Governments, and Nonprofits* by Philip Kotler, *PRAEGER* https://www.amazon.com/Advancing-Common-Good-Strategies-Governments/dp/1440872449/

[8] We Move to Amend. https://movetoamend.org/

[9] Black Lives Matter https://blacklivesmatter.com/

their companies – see **jovoto**[10], the **BoP Global Network**[11], or **OpenIdeo**[12], for example of these types of purpose platforms.

We even see the emergence of new standalone platforms like **Needslist**[13] - a real-time needs registry for disaster relief and humanitarian aid. The Needslist platform aggregates needs from vetted nonprofits, matching them with corporate resources to increase the speed, efficiency, and transparency of crisis response.

Another platform, the **Accountability Framework initiative**[14] brings together collaborators like the Rainforest Alliance, Greenpeace, WWF, Imaflora, The Nature Conservancy, the World Resources Institute, etc. to help multi-national companies seeking to eliminate deforestation from their supply chains.

The Accountability Framework was developed from 2017 through May 2019 through an open consultative process involving diverse stakeholder groups. This process included three public consultation periods (October-December 2017 on the 1st draft Core Principles; July-November 2018 on the 2nd draft Core Principles and 1st batch Operational Guidance; and December 2018-March 2019 on the full draft Framework). These consultations included multi-stakeholder workshops in several tropical commodity-producing countries as well as in-depth conversations with companies, industry groups, government representatives, and peer initiatives working on issues of commodities, deforestation, and human rights.

The Accountability Framework provides a practical roadmap, offering principles and guidance at each stage of a company's ethical supply chain journey.

There is a sense of urgency that is being communicated:

In recent years, hundreds of companies have pledged to eliminate deforestation from product supply chains by 2020 and to respect the rights of indigenous peoples, local communities, and workers. But with only months left until the deadline, these commitments have yielded disappointing results. Farms and plantations continue to replace forests, grasslands, and wetlands, and human rights abuses remain widespread. While some companies have made progress, most are far from achieving their targets, and many have

---

[10] jovoto https://www.jovoto.com/
[11] BoP Global Network https://www.bopglobalnetwork.org/
[12] OpenIDEO https://www.openideo.com/
[13] Needslist https://needslist.co/
[14] Accountability Framework https://accountability-framework.org/

barely begun the journey.

Yet another purpose platform is **Base of the Pyramid** BoP - Global Network founded by **Stuart L. Hart** in 2000. The original Base of the Pyramid (BoP) Learning Lab was established by Hart at the University of North Carolina. Since then, Hart has played an integral role in helping to catalyze and launch *eighteen* new BoP Labs around the world.

The goal? The platform was established to bring together global leaders to share knowledge and disseminate information regarding the theory and practice of sustainable business at the base of the economic pyramid. Rather than using traditional aid methodologies to help the poor and improve their quality of life, the BoP Learning Labs promote research and development of entrepreneurial business methods. The goal is to stimulate new enterprises that are economically competitive, environmentally sustainable, and culturally appropriate. This innovative idea has caught the attention of numerous academic institutions and other organizations around the world.

Today, the BoP Global Network has become a vibrant community of academics and practitioners in over 18 countries, engaged in knowledge creation and dissemination about the theory and practice of creating sustainable businesses at the base of the economic pyramid.

What about social business?

Enspiral is a network of groups and people, a DIY collective of social enterprises, ventures, and individuals working collaboratively across the world while fulfilling their purpose.

In many ways, Enspiral is a post-capitalist company. It's an active network of 150+ contributors and friends from New Zealand and around the world, who participate together to support and amplify individual purpose, and steward the collective to its highest potential impact.

Their concept of "microsolidarity"[15] is an explanation[16] of how ecosystems of purpose will disrupt the world of business:

---

[15] "Microsolidarity Part 2: A Theory of Groups and Groups of Groups" by Richard D. Bartlett, *Enspiral Tales* https://medium.com/enspiral-tales/microsolidarity-part-2-a-theory-of-groups-and-groups-of-groups-7c6e7ce63eda
[16] Microsolidarity Part 4. An Unorthodox Recipe For Social Change by Richard D. Bartlett, *Enspiral Tales* https://medium.com/enspiral-tales/microsolidarity-part-4-an-unorthodox-recipe-for-social-change-a947d881f4b8

*If you want to be agile and adaptive in a complex and rapidly changing environment, you **must** move as much decision-making power as possible into groups that are small enough to be governed by spoken dialogue, not written policy.*

Who can build a purpose platform? Anyone: a business; an institution: a school or college; a non-profit.

One can argue, as **Greta Thunberg** does so effectively, that *No One Is Too Small to Make a Difference*[17]. Her individual efforts have sparked a global movement based on the power and conviction of her message: "I want you to act as if your house was on fire."

Typically, we find a core team of passionate individuals at the heart of such platforms. They are the ones Margaret Mead might have been talking about: *"Never doubt that a small group of thoughtful, committed citizens can change the world; indeed, it's the only thing that ever has."*

But what the world needs now is a "coalition of the willing" – businesses, institutions, and individuals who come together to act.

Why build a purpose platform?

Organizations must choose their *why* carefully. It must inspire and mobilize participants.

We feel that human beings are inspired by **action projects** driven by the **Common Good**, by **purpose**, more than they are by profit or greed. The key is to *act* – to make a difference in the outcomes that are important to society.

Participants in such a platform must ask: what and how do we measure the outcomes? What **public value** do we create? Are we solving the root cause of our challenge?

How do we define **public value**?

Let's understand **Timo Meynhardt**'s disarmingly simple definition:

Public value is value for the public. Watch Professor Meynhardt's videos[18] on how organizations can contribute towards the Common Good.

---

[17] *No One Is Too Small to Make a Difference* by Greta Thunberg, *Penguin Books*
https://www.amazon.com/One-Too-Small-Make-Difference/dp/014313356X/
[18] "Public Value – Common Good and the Society" *HSG animated film series "Little Green Bags"* https://www.youtube.com/watch?v=tLGAQ4q_Sb0&feature=youtu.be

ASK: *What action(s) can we take to maximize our contribution to public value?*

A purpose platform brings together the sponsors of public value creation, stakeholders, local and global partners, all with a single purpose:
to **act** to **solve problems** for the **Common Good**.

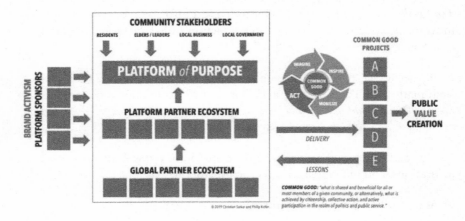

Platform Sponsors: the companies, institutions, even government agencies that get behind the mission of the platform and fund its work.

Community Stakeholders: the people and organizations affected by the problem being addressed.

Local Partner Ecosystem: the actors that will deliver and maintain the solution in the community being served.

Global Partner Ecosystem: the institutions that can help find and create solutions by tapping into their knowledge networks and supply chains.

A Purpose Platform: the technical and social ecosystem that allows participants to find each other and work on projects.

Common Good Projects: co-developed to make a positive impact for local communities.

Outcomes: the public value created by these projects.

Participants could work on a single or multiple projects to create public value, while constantly improving their knowledge and understanding of the various issues. For a business or businesses that decide to sponsor a platform of purpose, the process begins with **"purpose alignment"** – making sure the goals and objectives are inspirational enough and concrete enough to launch a **movement**. By definition, a movement is about societal change.

EXTENDING IMPACT
with a **PURPOSE PLATFORM**

© 2019. Christian Sarkar & Philip Kotler

A purpose platform is an engine to design urgent, meaningful, engagement leading to external impact. That's **brand activism *strategy*.**

7. BRAND ACTIVISM STRATEGY

What is required to architect a meaningful brand activism strategy? We start with traditional strategy to ask 5 questions.

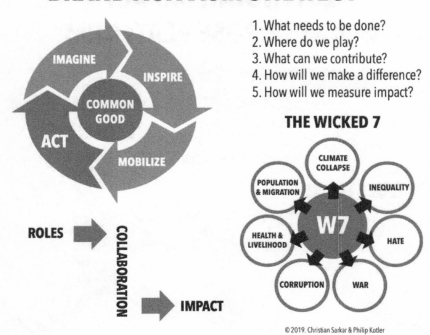

BRAND ACTIVISM STRATEGY

1. What needs to be done?
2. Where do we play?
3. What can we contribute?
4. How will we make a difference?
5. How will we measure impact?

© 2019. Christian Sarkar & Philip Kotler

THE 5 QUESTIONS

Brand Activism is not a static process – like any strategic process it is dynamic and fluid. Unlike more traditional strategic approaches, it is distinct because it begins and ends with meeting societal needs that lie outside the business.

1. What needs to be done? Do we understand the most urgent "unmet needs" for society today? Can we create a mission to serve the Common Good?

2. Where do we play? What is the scope of our involvement? Local, national, international?

3. What can we contribute? Do we have specialized expertise and resources we can contribute to solve problems, or do we support the organizations and people that do?

4. How will we make a difference? What specific strengths can we bring to help the situation? How can we help those already doing a good job?

5. How will we measure impact? What does success mean, and how will we communicate it in a way that creates even more engagement?

Answering these 5 questions is a continuous task – the answers are always in development. Nevertheless, metrics must be developed - and measured - and improved.

Companies that embrace brand activism must do it in a spirit of inquiry and learning. Internal commitments are even more critical than external ones.

A company that wants to understand the future and shape it, must assess its internal culture and understanding before it can begin the journey.

We've included a set of questions that cover: 1) Mindset, 2) Leadership, 3) Reputation, and 4) Culture.

MINDSET

- Do we have a common understanding and vocabulary of what we mean by Brand Activism?

- Do we have a framework or system that we think we can use effectively?

- What kinds and how many stakeholders are likely to care about our company's level and type of activism?

- Who are our *future* stakeholders – the employees and customers of the future?

- Will consumers believe that our company authentically and passionately believes in the cause(s) we support?

- Will the cost of implementation require us to raise our prices?

- Will our consumers be willing to pay a little more?

- Does the governance structure and executive leadership understand how and why brand activism makes a difference?

- How blind are we to our own shortcomings?

- Are we able to see the world as it is, or do we reduce it to our own internal mindset and ideology?

- How do we learn? Are we continuously curious about what and how the world is changing? What role does technology play?

- How does our activism make us a *workplace of meaning* to engage and inspire our employees?

- How do we function in a 100% transparent world?

- How do we protect *ourselves* and society from tyranny? Do we care about inclusivity or are we promoting apartheid?

- What kinds and how many stakeholders are likely to care about our company's level and type of activism?

- Who are our *future* stakeholders – the employees and customers of the future?

- Will consumers believe that our company authentically and passionately believes in the cause(s) we support?

- Will the cost of implementation require us to raise our prices?

- Will our consumers be willing to pay a little more?

- Does the governance structure and executive leadership understand how and why brand activism makes a difference?

- How blind are we to our own shortcomings? Are we able to see the world as it is, or do we reduce it to our own internal mindset and ideology?

- How do we learn? Are we continuously curious about what and how the world is changing?

- What role does technology play?

- How does our activism make us a *workplace of meaning* to engage and inspire our employees?

- How do we function in a 100% transparent world?

- How do we protect ourselves and society from tyranny? Do we care about inclusivity or are we promoting apartheid?

LEADERSHIP

- Do we have a company-wide (and industry-wide) understanding of brand activism?

- Are we addressing the most urgent problems in society – income inequality, climate change, discrimination, and population growth?

- Do we view brand activism as an integrated system across all dimensions of our activities?

- Do we manage our brand activism strategy and execution in a way that allows us to measure outcomes and impact?

- Do we have institutional processes for executing our initiatives?

- Do we report on our progress regularly and systematically?

- Do we work with our partners, suppliers, and industry peers to advance brand activism?

- Do we develop brand activist leaders to make a difference in society?

- Have we defined responsibilities properly and are we accountable?

REPUTATION

- What is our reputation as a company? As an industry?

- Is our CEO viewed as a progressive brand activist?

- Does our company protect and serve the common good?

- How are we viewed by our employees, customers, society?

- How are we viewed by our executives and shareholders?

- How are we viewed by the government? Other institutions?

- How are we viewed locally, in the countries we operate in, and around the world? By our future stakeholders?

CULTURE

- Do we have a fair and just culture that is open-minded and creative?

- Do we create a workplace of "meaning"?

- Do our employees love our company?

- Do we enjoy an advantage because of our culture?

- Are we ready to be radically transparent?

These are the basic considerations that brand activists must take into account *before* they start designing their purpose platforms.

THE 6 Ps of BRAND ACTIVISM

At Ben and Jerry's **Jay Curley**, Global Head of Integrated Marketing, says that activism "turns your marketing organization into a campaigning organization, and marketers into activists. It means you sell not just more stuff, but big ideas." He describes[1] the approach they take:

"At Ben & Jerry's, we do not invent campaigns, issues, or causes. And we don't parachute into a community with money. We take our lead from the activists and leaders of frontline and impacted communities. We ensure our work supports the strategies of leading progressive organizations driving these movements forward. We build our campaigns based on their goals and in support of their strategy. *They* are the experts in knowing what their communities need."

Curley's critical advice? You need to deploy the 6P's of brand activism:

PURPOSE—Your Core Values
Business Activism is not driven by the values of your customers or the issues they care about. It is driven by the values of your brand and the things that you and your company care about. Why does your company exist, and what are your core values? Be clear about your values—make sure they are rooted in something real and that they can stand the test of time.

POLICY—Tangible Change
Stand for real policy changes that address the root cause of issues. Don't pursue empty actions that don't support and align with larger movements. Be transparent and be direct in this ask with your customers to bring them along.

PEOPLE—Of the Movement
Your employees must truly believe in and be connected to the issues and the movements you aim to support. They must be passionate about creating change. This work cannot be wholly outsourced to agencies.

POWER—Resources
Businesses have immense power and influence over policymakers, the media, and consumers. This includes expertise in consumer research, performance marketing, world-class creative development, and big budgets. Let's leverage all of that to better the world, not just sell more stuff.

PUBLISHING—Storytelling
Use your voice and your consumer touch-points for ongoing storytelling and creative content that brings your consumers into these movements. Offer an easy onramp to participation, such as signing a petition or joining a

---

[1] "The 6P's of Brand Activism" by Jay Curley, https://www.linkedin.com/pulse/6ps-brand-activism-jay-curley/

march.

POP CULTURE—Relevancy

Use your brand positioning and tone to cut through the cluttered media landscape. Your connection with your consumers can help you drive them to movements, and your support of movements can make your brand relevant and top of mind.

BUILDING A MOVEMENT

The easy part is designing the brand activism strategy. Execution is, as all strategists know, the key to success. What transforms a campaign into a **movement**? The ability to transfer a common vision to engage and get others to join in collaborative action.

Have you ever arrived somewhere and wondered how you got there? Scientists at the University of Leeds[2] believe they may have found the answer, with research that shows that humans flock like sheep and birds, subconsciously following a minority of individuals. Apparently, it just takes a small minority of committed participants to sway the larger population. This is what politicians play to – and unfortunately, exploit – to manipulate the public.

BUILDING A MOVEMENT

IMAGINE · INSPIRE · COMMON GOOD · ACT · MOBILIZE

© 2019 Christian Sarkar and Philip Kotler

Our research tells us that building a movement has 5 clear components:

[2] "Sheep In Human Clothing: Scientists Reveal Our Flock Mentality"
https://www.sciencedaily.com/releases/2008/02/080214114517.htm

1) Begin by creating a noble mission that is based on the **Common Good**
2) **Imagine** what the movement must achieve and how
3) How will we **inspire** people to engage and participate?
4) **Mobilize** committed participants
5) **Act** – coordinate joint action to make a difference

To clarify what we mean by movement, we'll examine the "Greta Thunberg Effect."

No matter your opinion on **Greta Thunberg**, we can all agree that she has brought a new sense of **awareness** and **urgency** to the **climate crisis**.

Skolstrejk för Klimatet - Greta Thunberg
(photo: Anders Hellberg)

In traditional debates, we have been taught that a message is convincing because of the three elements of persuasion: **ethos, pathos**, and **logos**[3] (we'll dismiss *kairos*).

But now, in a post-truth age, in a time of "fake news" and "alternative facts," we add one more critical element: the spirit of the messenger themselves – *thumos*, the messenger's enthusiasm and passion for the message.

In the past we knew that all good salesmen believe in the product they sell, but now, this has become a far more critical component.

How does this translate to a brand?

Brands must become more authentic, more human, more believable. You can't fake enthusiasm. Employees at Costco, Southwest Airlines, Starbucks and Zappo's are excellent examples of this **culture of enthusiasm**. In fact, if we investigate their hiring practices, all four of these companies "hire for cultural fit."

What is the impact on the receiver of your message? In our theory of the structure of cultural narratives, we propose four dimensions that influence the receiver's worldview: **myth, ideology, history**, and **identity**. Of these, **identity** is the most important because it is the most personal.

Hence, Greta Thunberg's message resonates with those whose identity is tied to the future: the young.

The "Greta effect"[4] has begun affecting the political landscape as well. Even as increasing numbers of school children heed her call to action, radical lobbyist groups[5] have begun attacking her message in a concerted campaign to discredit her.

Thunberg's activism is a model for building movements for the Common Good.

How do companies build a movement? They must engage with the dominant cultural narratives in society.

---

[3] "Modes of persuasion" *Wikipedia* https://en.wikipedia.org/wiki/Modes_of_persuasion
[4] "The 'Greta Effect' On Student Activism and Climate Change," *neaToday*
http://neatoday.org/2019/09/19/the-greta-effect-student-activism-climate-change/
[5] Attacks on Greta Thunberg Are About More Than Anti-Environmentalism, *DESMOGUK*
https://www.desmog.co.uk/2019/09/15/attacks-greta-thunberg-right-wing-free-market-network

As old cultural narratives are replaced by new ones, companies must tune themselves to the future. A cultural narrative creates meaning for our place in the world, and provides a map for the journey.

The vision or message is a promise (brand-promise) to take the participant (customer, member, or citizen) from the present to a desired future place or state.

The heart of all activism is action, and there is no movement without action. For leaders, understanding the cultural traditions of the organization vis-a-vis the cultural narratives of society can help guide strategic decisions. Why? **Because decisions that go against the dominant culture are more likely *to fail*.**

Sometimes the cultural shifts required to compete can be daunting, even fatal. For this reason, despite the best intentions of managers and executives, change agendas fail even before they begin.

Taking your activism to market requires a clear message that resonates with the audience. Your message is meaningful or meaningless: either your message aligns with the dominant cultural narrative and is accepted relatively easy, or your message must alter the cultural narrative before it gains widespread acceptance.

- What makes a message convincing?
- What is the right narrative?
- What makes it dominant?
- How does a message gain cultural acceptance?
- How does one shift or disrupt a cultural narrative?

BRAND ACTIVISM STRATEGY EXECUTION

	IMAGINE	INSPIRE	MOBILIZE	ACT
ORGANIZATION				
EMPLOYEE				
PARTNER				
CUSTOMER				
SOCIETY				

© 2019. Christian Sarkar & Philip Kotler

Brand Activism can also be a strategy of **resonance**. The values your company stands for must align with the values of your future customer. If they don't, you have lost the market of the future. Brand activist movements are designed to influence behavior, with the Common Good as the vehicle for alignment.

It may be that your brand cannot afford to start a movement. That is not in itself a bad thing. What if you joined a movement already in the works?

ASK: *Should we start our own movement to make the world a better place, or should we join one that already exists?*

EXISTING FRAMEWORKS

There are several useful frameworks in use today to help your business on its Brand Activism journey:

- The UN Global Compact
- Plan B
- Future Fit Business Benchmark
- The Reputation Institute
- JUST Capital
- The Business Roundtable
- The Davos Manifesto 2020

While these frameworks are not designed as Brand Activism frameworks, we feel that they serve a useful purpose, and encourage businesses to explore and understand each one. What we do want to warn you about is the purpose-consulting practices of the more traditional consulting companies. Many of the destructive narratives of the past were developed and promoted by these organizations, and many of them remain wedded to outmoded business thinking. The same applies to some of the more famous business schools. Our hope is that your company is a critical thinker, and questions the assumptions we were taught in B-School. Remember, if they already had the answers, we would not be where we are now.

The UN Global Compact

The primary purpose of the **UN Global Compact**[6] is to align business with Ten Principles on human rights, labor, environment and anti-corruption.

---

[6] *United Nations Global Compact* https://www.unglobalcompact.org/

The Ten Principles[7] are listed below under four categories:

Human Rights

Principle 1: Businesses should support and respect the protection of internationally proclaimed human rights; and
Principle 2: make sure that they are not complicit in human rights abuses.

Labor

Principle 3: Businesses should uphold the freedom of association and the effective recognition of the right to collective bargaining;
Principle 4: the elimination of all forms of forced and compulsory labor;
Principle 5: the effective abolition of child labor; and
Principle 6: the elimination of discrimination in respect of employment and occupation.

Environment

Principle 7: Businesses should support a precautionary approach to environmental challenges;
Principle 8: undertake initiatives to promote greater environmental responsibility; and
Principle 9: encourage the development and diffusion of environmentally friendly technologies.

Anti-Corruption

Principle 10: Businesses should work against corruption in all its forms, including extortion and bribery.

In addition to the UN Global Compact, we are fans of the **Global Goals for Sustainable Development**[8]. In 2015, world leaders agreed to 17 goals for a better world by 2030. These goals have the power to end poverty, fight inequality and address the urgency of climate change. Guided by the goals, it is now up to all of us, governments, businesses, civil society and the general public to work together to build a better future for everyone.

---

[7] The Ten Principles of the UN Global Compact, *United Nations Global Compact*
https://www.unglobalcompact.org/what-is-gc/mission/principles/principle-1

[8] THE GLOBAL GOALS FOR SUSTAINABLE DEVELOPMENT
https://watch.globalgoals.org/

Learn more >> www.unglobalcompact.org

Plan B

Plan B – the CEO collective, as we like to call it – focuses on 10 issues:

Drive full transparency
Be open, transparent and free from corruption, with good governance and accountability at all levels of our organizations.

Foster collaboration
Work with other businesses, governments, trade unions, and civil society to foster open dialogue and forge new partnerships that accelerate positive change.

Restore nature
Ensure our companies significantly reduce their environmental impacts and invest in new business models that help regenerate the environment.

Scale true accounting
Measure and communicate social and environmental impacts, as well as our plans for improvement.

Create thriving communities
Help create environments inside and outside our companies that enable employees and our communities to thrive.

Reinvent market incentives
Encourage government policies, corporate structures and tax systems that deliver the best outcomes for people and the planet, helping capital flow towards delivering true returns.

Ensure dignity and fairness
Ensure that people throughout our supply chains are treated with dignity and respect, working in a safe, equitable and empowering environment, where they receive a fair share of the value they create and their rights are fully supported.

Redefine reward systems
Support fair rewards in our companies, integrating social and environmental performance targets into our compensation systems, and champion efforts to close the pay gap throughout the business world.

Value diversity
Cultivate and celebrate diversity, including gender, at all levels of business while ensuring equality of opportunity for all employees.

Lead for the long run
Adopt longer reporting cycles and nurture inclusive, collaborative leadership focused on delivering long-term value to all stakeholders.

Learn more >> www.bteam.org

Future Fit Benchmark

The Future-Fit Business Benchmark highlights extra-financial criteria that all businesses must meet if they are going to thrive in an increasingly volatile and resource-constrained world. The Benchmark identifies the extra-financial break-even point for business, expressed as a unified set of social and environmental goals. Each goal is complemented by indicators designed to support effective monitoring of progress.

The benchmark includes the following categories:

Business Inputs

- Energy is from renewable sources
- Water use is environmentally responsible and socially equitable
- Natural resources are managed to respect the welfare of ecosystems, people and animals

Business Activities

- Procurement safeguards the pursuit of future-fitness

- Operational emissions do not harm people or the environment
- Operations emit no greenhouse gases
- Operational waste is eliminated
- Operations do not encroach on ecosystems or communities
- Community health is safeguarded

Employees

- Employee health is safeguarded
- Employees are paid at least a living wage
- Employees are subject to fair employment terms
- Employees are not subject to discrimination
- Employee concerns are actively solicited, impartially judged and transparently addressed

Products

- Product communications are honest, ethical, and promote responsible use
- Product concerns are actively solicited, impartially judged and transparently addressed
- Products do not harm people or the environment
- Products emit no greenhouse gases
- Products can be repurposed

Citizenship

- Business is conducted ethically
- The right tax is paid in the right place at the right time
- Lobbying and corporate influence safeguard the pursuit of future-fitness
- Financial assets safeguard the pursuit of future-fitness
- Positive Pursuits

Learn more >> www.futurefitbusiness.org

The Reputation Institute

To earn and maintain a *strong* to *excellent* reputation, organizations must go beyond CSR, and deliver in the areas of social, fiscal, environmental, and employer responsibility. In the new "Reputation Economy," brands are ranked on the emotional bond established by perceptions of Esteem, Admiration, Trust, and overall Feeling.

Their proprietary Reputation Intelligence System yields insights along seven dimensions:

- *Products/Services*
  Do you deliver on a world-class experience? High-quality Products and Services can profoundly shape reputation.
- *Innovation*
  Is your company static or dynamic? Forward-thinking and creatively-inspired companies have a reputational advantage.
- *Workplace*
  Corporate culture directly impacts recruitment, retention, and talent acquisition. Positive perceptions of a workplace can help you achieve employer of choice status.
- *Governance*
  Can your company be trusted to do the right things when no one is looking? Practicing good governance is key in earning trust in times of crisis.
- *Citizenship*
  How does your company align with social values? Being a good corporate citizen has a positive impact that helps to make the world a little better.
- *Leadership*
  Companies with executives who align brand purpose with daily business activities outperform those focused solely on financials.
- *Performance*
  Financials matter, but it is important to link your financial success with positive social impact to maintain a license to operate.

Learn more >> www.reputationinstitute.com

JUST Capital

JUST Capital is the only independent nonprofit that tracks, analyzes, and engages with large corporations and their investors on how they perform on the public's priorities. The public identified 29 Issues essential to just business, which are classified according to the stakeholders they most impact. The organization is committed to stakeholder capitalism, with a stated goal to "restore faith in business during this era of declining trust and mobilize the private sector in support of the country's most pressing societal challenges."

The stakeholders include: workers, customers, communities, environment, and shareholders.

Priorities closely mirror those in the framework recently adopted by the Business Roundtable, including how a company:

- Invests in its Workers. (35% weight)
- Treats its Customers. (24% weight)
- Supports Communities, including its international supply chain. (18% weight)
- Impacts the Environment. (11% weight)
- Serves its Shareholders through good governance. (11% weight)

Learn more >> www.justcapital.com

The Business Roundtable

The Business Roundtable's decision to move from "shareholder" to "stakeholder" capitalism is not Brand Activism. Yet, it is an admission that change is nigh. The main points of their Statement on the Purpose of the Corporation commit to:

- Delivering value to our customers. We will further the tradition of American companies leading the way in meeting or exceeding customer expectations.
- Investing in our employees. This starts with compensating them fairly and providing important benefits. It also includes supporting them through training and education that help develop new skills for a rapidly changing world. We foster diversity and inclusion, dignity and respect.
- Dealing fairly and ethically with our suppliers. We are dedicated to serving as good partners to the other companies, large and small, that help us meet our missions.
- Supporting the communities in which we work. We respect the people in our communities and protect the environment by embracing sustainable practices across our businesses.
- Generating long-term value for shareholders, who provide the capital that allows companies to invest, grow and innovate. We are

committed to transparency and effective engagement with shareholders.

Is this a framework that is practical and measurable? Not yet.

Learn more >> www.businessroundtable.org

Davos Manifesto 2020

As a supporter of stakeholder capitalism, The **World Economic Forum**'s new "Davos Manifesto"[9] states that companies should pay their fair share of **taxes**, show **zero tolerance for corruption**, uphold **human rights** throughout their global supply chains, and advocate for a competitive **level playing field** – particularly in the "platform economy."

Here's the manifesto in full:

A. The purpose of a company is to engage all its stakeholders in shared and sustained value creation. In creating such value, a company serves not only its shareholders, but all its stakeholders – employees, customers, suppliers, local communities and society at large. The best way to understand and harmonize the divergent interests of all stakeholders is through a shared commitment to policies and decisions that strengthen the long-term prosperity of a company.

    i. A company serves its customers by providing a value proposition that best meets their needs. It accepts and supports fair competition and a level playing field. It has zero tolerance for corruption. It keeps the digital ecosystem in which it operates reliable and trustworthy. It makes customers fully aware of the functionality of its products and services, including adverse implications or negative externalities.

    ii. A company treats its people with dignity and respect. It honors diversity and strives for continuous improvements in working conditions and employee well-being. In a world of rapid change, a company fosters continued employability through ongoing upskilling and reskilling.

    iii. A company considers its suppliers as true partners in value creation. It provides a fair chance to new market entrants. It integrates respect for human rights into the entire supply chain.

---

[9] *World Economic Forum* https://www.weforum.org/the-davos-manifesto

iv. A company serves society at large through its activities, supports the communities in which it works, and pays its fair share of taxes. It ensures the safe, ethical and efficient use of data. It acts as a steward of the environmental and material universe for future generations. It consciously protects our biosphere and champions a circular, shared and regenerative economy. It continuously expands the frontiers of knowledge, innovation and technology to improve people's well-being.

v. A company provides its shareholders with a return on investment that takes into account the incurred entrepreneurial risks and the need for continuous innovation and sustained investments. It responsibly manages near-term, medium-term and long-term value creation in pursuit of sustainable shareholder returns that do not sacrifice the future for the present.

B. A company is more than an economic unit generating wealth. It fulfils human and societal aspirations as part of the broader social system. Performance must be measured not only on the return to shareholders, but also on how it achieves its environmental, social and good governance objectives. Executive remuneration should reflect stakeholder responsibility.

C. A company that has a multinational scope of activities not only serves all those stakeholders who are directly engaged, but acts itself as a stakeholder – together with governments and civil society – of our global future. Corporate global citizenship requires a company to harness its core competencies, its entrepreneurship, skills and relevant resources in collaborative efforts with other companies and stakeholders to improve the state of the world.

What is interesting about the World Economic Forum is its wider scope of understanding. It states[10] that "Corruption has the potential to undermine the successful implementation of all 17 goals. Without meaningful action against corruption, progress towards the other goals is likely to be extremely limited, hampering economic growth, increasing inequality and inhibiting prosperity." This is an important point that we touch on in detail at the end of this book.

---

[10] "Serious about sustainability? Get serious about corruption" *World Economic Forum* https://www.weforum.org/agenda/2019/09/serious-about-sustainability-get-serious-about-corruption/

Learn more >> https://www.weforum.org/the-davos-manifesto

ASK: *What can we learn from the various frameworks for better business?*

THE SARKAR-KOTLER BRAND ACTIVISM FRAMEWORK

The **Sarkar-Kotler Brand Activism Framework** is an outcome-based process we've developed to help companies develop and execute a strategy that deals with the challenges of the future. We present it as a guideline, as a starting point for building your own strategy.

Taken together, these the toolkit consists of the following:

Brand Activism Strategy
Questions to help your organization understand the scope and impact of brand activism

Brand Activism Maps
Mapping the six dimensions of brand activism – a guide to the issues that matter most

The Brand Activism Canvas
A tool to evaluate the values gaps between your stakeholders and your business strategy

The Brand Activism X Matrix
A Brand Activism "Hoshin Kanri" execution dashboard to manage your initiatives

The Brand Activism Scorecard
How to develop a simple status dashboard to communicate progress to employees and interested stakeholders.

BRAND ACTIVISM STRATEGY

The first section of this chapter describes the approach we've developed for businesses to begin the work of devising an appropriate brand activism strategy. Note the **5 Questions**, and the specific question sets on 1) Mindset, 2) Leadership, 3) Reputation, and 4) Culture.

BRAND ACTIVISM MAPS

The urgency that your stakeholders – especially future customers – feel is sometimes not perceived inside the walls of the business. That is why we must formulate questions that view the business world from the **outside in**. The following maps – six in all, address some of the most pressing issues as viewed by external stakeholders. The issues and questions we raise are based on a list of current and emerging and issues (www.activistbrands.com/the-issues).

Some may not be hot topics on your radar at present, but we expect them to become increasingly important. We hope you find these maps useful.

COMMON GOOD SCORING: for each issue try to understand expectations from your employees and customers.

On a scale of 1-10:
1-4 = strongly disagree (REGRESSIVE BRAND ACTIVISM)
5-6 = neutral (DON'T BE EVIL)
7-10 = strongly agree (PROGRESSIVE BRAND ACTIVISM)

To get an accurate reading, it's best that each issue is tracked for each stakeholder, and in three locations: local, national, and worldwide.

SOCIAL ACTIVISM

- Are we committed to equality – race, gender, sexual orientation, religion, etc.?
- Do we respect and support Human Rights?
- Do we protect the privacy rights of all?
- Are we working to improve access and quality to public goods and services like healthcare, education, safety, food security, for all members of society?
- Do we support immigration reform and amnesty?
- Do we prohibit forced labor - in the form of prison labor, indentured labor, bonded labor, human trafficking, around the world?
- Do we work to create a better social climate for the communities we work with? Society at large?
- Do we work to improve the standard of living?
- Do we support propped public health policies for all?
- Do we stand for just immigration policies?
- Do we stand against polarization and divisive agendas?
- Do we support consumer protection agencies and watchdog groups?
- Does senior management demonstrate high standards of personal propriety?

WORKPLACE ACTIVISM

- Do we provide our employees with a living wage?
- Do we provide our employees the opportunity to form unions?
- Do we put our employees' workers' voices at the heart of our business model?
- What is the ratio of CEO Pay to our frontline employees?
- Do we avoid exploiting our labor or the labor of our suppliers?
- Do we promote equal pay for equal work?
- Do our employees have a voice? Representation on the board?
- Do we provide training and safety for all employees and part-time workers?
- Do we practice work safety? Are employee concerns dealt with transparently?
- Do we encourage a democratic workplace?

- Do we respect workers' rights?
- Are integrity concerns openly and freely discussed in the workplace and is it safe to report suspected violations of integrity?

POLITICAL ACTIVISM

- Do we support Democracy?
- Do we promote a transparent and open government that allows for the meaningful participation of all stakeholders in the development and implementation of public policies?
- Do we support voter rights?
- Do we encourage our employees to vote, by giving them the time to do so?
- Do we oppose gerrymandering?
- Are we paying our fair share of taxes?
- Do we support campaign finance reform?
- Are we transparent with our lobbying activities?
- Do our lobbying efforts align with stakeholder values?
- Do we support fair trade?
- Do we support competition in our industry?
- Are we supporting long term policies in technology?
- Do we welcome just regulations? Do we support privacy and data security?
- Are we supporting a healthy and transparent foreign policy?
- Do we oppose public policies that give us an unfair advantage?
- Do we seek a level playing field without special consideration?
- Do we avoid corruption and seek to remove it from all levels of society and government?

ENVIRONMENTAL ACTIVISM

- Do we stand against ecocide – the destruction of entire ecosystems?
- Do we embed sustainability into all our activities and future plans?
- Do we support the Rights of Nature?
- Do we advocate and promote conservation and protection of our public lands?
- Have we redesigned our supply chain around a circular economy?
- Are we aware of the impact of biotech and its ramifications on the environment?
- Do we take environmental impact studies seriously?

- Do we have an action plan to eliminate water and air pollution?
- Do we get our energy from clean, renewable sources?
- Are we leading our industry in environmental stewardship?
- Do we take a stand against unnecessary development and exploitation of natural resources?
- Do we encourage public awareness and education?

ECONOMIC ACTIVISM

- Do we support policies that fight income inequality?
- Do we support just trade policies?
- Do we partner and encourage local small businesses and entrepreneurs?
- Do we support public interests like affordable transportation and housing?
- Do we support public investments in infrastructure and education?
- Do we pay our fair share of taxes to local, national, and global authorities?
- Do we avoid tax shelters and financial manipulation to escape our tax responsibilities?
- Do our employees (including part-timers) get paid enough to afford a living?
- Do we support the development and protection of local community interests?
- Do we balance our economic interests and the economic health of the public?

LEGAL ACTIVISM

- Do we support the rule of law?
- Do we respect employment and labor laws?
- Do we seek just business practices that avoid corruption and improper influence?
- Do we seek and encourage laws to promote workplace safety?
- Do we seek and stand for reasonable financial regulations that protect the rights of consumers?
- Do we work for just laws for all members of the community?
- Do we respect property laws and encourage public engagement and transparency?
- Do we respect and promote Human Rights?

- Do we have an agenda for promoting integrity?
- Does senior management participate in the development of the necessary legal and institutional frameworks for a just society?

Answering these questions and using them to begin a conversation about **living the values your brand aspires to** is the first step in beginning the progressive brand activism journey.

Where most companies falter is, they pick a few issues to work on whilst completely neglecting others. This was possible in times past, but will increasingly open the door for **brandshaming**.

In our opinion, brand activism is the "price of entry" for success in the future. Which brings us back to the **Wicked 7** – our shortcut. Pick these seven, and see where your business can make a difference *(see www.wicked7.org)*.

THE BRAND ACTIVISM CANVAS

How does a company identify and track the gaps between values and issues as seen from an internal perspective and the outside world?

The **Brand Activism Canvas** is a tool we created to help companies and leaders take stock of where they stand vis-à-vis the reality outside the company gates.

For each issue, we track the views of various stakeholders internal and external at three levels: in the local community, at the national level, and in the world – globally. We help you design a plan of action based on desired **outcomes** – with an emphasis on positive impact. We also want you to consider the "**return on trust**." What lessons have you learned? What does a **common good analysis** tell you?

VISIT www.activistbrands.com to download further instructions and tools for your use.

Content

THE BRAND ACTIVISM CANVAS

DESIGNED FOR _____   DESIGNED BY _____

VALUES
- Social
- Workplace
- Political
- Environmental
- Economic
- Legal

ISSUES
- Do our practices align with our values?
- Do our values align with our stakeholders' values?
- Are we participating to find solutions that work for all?
- Are we helping or hindering communities achieve what is best for society?
- Are we lobbying politicians in ways that seek unfair advantages?
- Are we creating an inclusive world or are we aiding in its polarization?
- Are we respectful of the common good, or are we seeking to exploit it for profit?

RIGHTS
- Human Rights
- Rights of Nature

STAKEHOLDERS

LOCAL
- Board
- C-Level
- Executives
- Managers
- Supervisors
- Unions

NATIONAL
- Customers
- Employees
- Partners
- Shareholders
- Community

WORLD
- Customers
- Employees
- Partners
- Shareholders
- Community

RIGHTS (STAKEHOLDERS)
- Customers
- Employees
- Partners
- Shareholders
- Community

GAP ANALYSIS
- Summary Findings
- Local Values Gap
- National Values Gap
- Global Values Gap

ACTION PLAN
- Jobs to be Done
- Promise
- Proof Points
- Operational Changes
- Cultural Changes
- Incentives
- Training
- Delivery
- Accountability
- Outcomes
- Schedule
- Responsibilities

RESULTS
- internal
- external

COST/BUDGET

COMMON GOOD ANALYSIS
- Outside In

RETURN ON TRUST

LESSONS LEARNED

www.activistbrands.com

DATE _____

THE BRAND ACTIVISM X MATRIX

The **Brand Activism X Matrix** is an adaption of the Japanese "Hoshin Kanri" methodology for planning and execution, with the goal of aligning short-term and long-term brand activism objectives. Hoshin Kanri is a convenient method of strategic planning and deployment to prioritize and communicate execution objectives, responsibilities, and metrics.

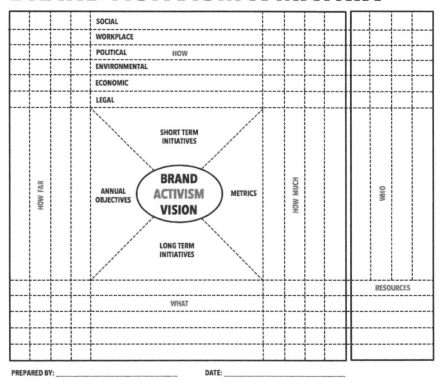

For businesses that don't have experience using this methodology we recommend a review of online resources at www.activistbrands.com.

THE BRAND ACTIVISM SCORECARD

Finally, it's a good idea to create a company-wide **Brand Activism Scorecard** to communicate the status of all your brand activism activities at a glance. The best scoring systems are developed by cross-company teams, involving your very own employee activists, tailored to the specific brand activism objectives of the division, region, or country. External frameworks and benchmarks can be useful to help stay in touch with industry leaders and get ahead of them.

HOW WOKE IS MY COMPANY?

ZOMBIE ➡ WOKE

BRAND ACTIVISM EMBEDDED IN YOUR COMPANY
COMPANY ACTIVITIES

BRAND IMPACT	STRATEGY	SOURCING	OPERATIONS	PRODUCT	DISTRIBUTION	USAGE	DISPOSAL	ADVERTISING	POLICIES
WORKPLACE	☐	☐	☐	☐	☐	☐	☐	☐	☐
SOCIAL	☐	☐	☐	☐	☐	☐	☐	☐	☐
ENVIRONMENTAL	☐	☐	☐	☐	☐	☐	☐	☐	☐
POLITICAL	☐	☐	☐	☐	☐	☐	☐	☐	☐
LEGAL	☐	☐	☐	☐	☐	☐	☐	☐	☐
ECONOMIC	☐	☐	☐	☐	☐	☐	☐	☐	☐

*How do we **eliminate** our **negative impact**?*
*How do we **maximize** our **positive impact**?*

© 2020 Christian Sarkar and Philip Kotler.

GEOGRAPHY: _____		STAKEHOLDER: _____

YOUR COMPANY LEADERSHIP	SOCIAL	WORKPLACE	POLITICAL	ENVIRONMENTAL	ECONOMIC	LEGAL

⬆ PROGRESSIVE ■ NEUTRAL ⬇ REGRESSIVE

PREPARED BY: _____ DATE: _____

We leave it to your *imagination* as to what a dashboard for Exxon-Mobil might look like. Jokes aside, it is critical that a brand activism scorecard is prepared at three levels – locally, nationally, and globally.

8. THE GREAT CORRUPTION

The question we must ask here is **how do brands lose their way?** How do businesses decide that making profits takes precedence over all else (people and planet be damned)?

Is it because they don't see the impact they cause?

Is it because the unfettered pursuit of "shareholder value[1]" makes them blind to reality?

Or is it because the government agencies that are responsible for regulating industry are failing to do their jobs? Why is government seemingly incapable of governing in the public interest?

And in the US especially, our educational system has not been honest. It does not highlight the inequality we are creating.

Who makes the rules?

THE VECTORS OF POWER

Who runs the world? We created this "vectors of power" to help us visualize the interests that influence our public policies and laws.

[1] Making Sense Of Shareholder Value: 'The World's Dumbest Idea' by Steve Denning, *Forbes* https://www.forbes.com/sites/stevedenning/2017/07/17/making-sense-of-shareholder-value-the-worlds-dumbest-idea/#60021e4e2a7e

Here's a quick refresher on concepts we ought to have paid attention to in our high school civics or government class. The problem, in each case, is the abuse of power by those that have it – regardless of type or form of government.

- **Theocracy:** laws made by and according to religious ideology (Iran, the Taliban in Afghanistan, the Christian Right in the US).

- **Military dictatorship:** when the military seizes power or controls the political domain (Pakistan, Iraq, Latin American dictatorships).

- **Corpocracy:** when political power and decision-making is increasingly concentrated in the hands of business interests (USA).

- **Oligarchy:** a form of power structure in which power rests with a small number of people. These people may be distinguished by nobility, wealth (Plutocracy), family ties, education or corporate, religious or political, military control. Such states are often controlled by families who typically pass their influence from one generation to the next, but inheritance is not a necessary condition for the application of this term (Saudi Arabia, Russia, the USA).

- **Democracy:** direct or representative – the power is in the hands of the majority of the people, and decisions are made in the public interest.

- **Social Democracy:** a political, social and economic ideology that supports economic and social interventions to promote social justice within the framework of a liberal democratic polity and capitalist economy (Nordic countries).

- **Communism:** When the politicians themselves become the ruling class in the name of the people (China, the old Soviet Union).

- **Monarchy:** When power is held by the individual King and related families (Saudi Arabia, the British Monarchy) of the aristocracy.

As we see almost daily, "freedom of speech, thought, and expression" and "academic freedom" is often at odds with totalitarian or authoritarian governments.

What is important is how and in whose interest is government working? Is it working for a few elite members of the ruling class, or does it work for the people?

What about the U.S.? Does our public policy reflect the preferences of the people? This question was explored by political scientists Martin Gilens of Princeton and Benjamin I. Page of Northwestern in a paper[2] titled *Testing Theories of American Politics: Elites, Interest Groups, and Average Citizens.* Here's what they said:

What do our findings say about democracy in America? They certainly constitute troubling news for advocates of "populistic" democracy, who want governments to respond primarily or exclusively to the policy preferences of their citizens. In the United States, our findings indicate, the majority does not rule—at least not in the causal sense of actually determining policy outcomes. When a majority of citizens disagrees with economic elites or with organized interests, they generally lose. Moreover, because of the strong status quo bias built into the U.S. political system, even when fairly large majorities of Americans favor policy change, they generally do not get it.

Former President **Jimmy Carter** says[3] that the US is "an oligarchy with unlimited political bribery."

Is he right? We looked at **Stanley F. Stasch**'s *The Creation and Destruction of the Great American Middle Class (1930-2010)*[4] to explain how the following events gave corporate and business interests too much power and influence in the United States:

During the 1970s:

- A program of government-guaranteed student loans rewarded bankers at the expense of students.

---

[2] "Testing Theories of American Politics: Elites, Interest Groups, and Average Citizens" *Cambridge Core* https://www.cambridge.org/core/journals/perspectives-on-politics/article/testing-theories-of-american-politics-elites-interest-groups-and-average-citizens/62327F513959D0A304D4893B382B992B/core-reader

[3] "Jimmy Carter: U.S. Is an 'Oligarchy With Unlimited Political Bribery'" *RollingStones* https://www.rollingstone.com/politics/politics-news/jimmy-carter-u-s-is-an-oligarchy-with-unlimited-political-bribery-63262/

[4] "The Creation and Destruction of the Great American Middle Class" (1930-2010), *Loyola eCommons* https://ecommons.luc.edu/cgi/viewcontent.cgi?referer=http://fixcapitalism.com/free-online-class-the-creation-and-destruction-of-the-great-american-middle-class-1930-2010-with-professor-stanley-stasch/&httpsredir=1&article=1004&context=business_facpubs

- Congress created a new bankruptcy law that favored the wealthy over the middle and lower classes.
- The Health Maintenance Organization Act of 1973 signed into law by President Nixon allowed medical insurance agencies, hospitals, clinics and even doctors, to function as for-profit business entities instead of the service organizations they were intended to be,
- The Supreme Court made a decision that allowed banks to charge very high interest rates on credit card balances.

During the 1980s:

- The Reagan presidency allowed corporations to replace pension plans with 401(k) plans, thus greatly reducing the retirement incomes of millions of middle-and-lower class workers.
- The government eliminated three important banking regulations, and their absence contributed to increasing income inequality and the housing crisis that culminated in the financial crash of 2007-2008.

During the 1990s:

- The government allowed the growing use of stock options to dramatically increase CEO compensation.
- Congress excluded waitresses and waiters when it increased the federal minimum wage, thus relegating them to poverty or near-poverty incomes.
- In 1995 the Republican-controlled Congress passed, over President Clinton's veto, the Private Securities Litigation Reform Act to severely limit the ability of shareholders and similarly-interested parties to take legal action against corporations and investment bankers.
- The government allowed "forced arbitration" clauses to exist in cable, cell phone, and other consumer contracts, which prevented consumers from participating in class action lawsuits when they felt that companies were unjustly taking small amounts of money each month from them and millions of other consumers.

During the 2000s:

- The business community helped President George W. Bush pass his tax cuts for the rich.
- The government bailed out "banks too big to fail" during the financial crisis of 2007-2008, but prevented distressed homeowners from declaring bankruptcy.
- Congress' new treaty greatly facilitated outsourcing U.S. manufacturing jobs to China and increasing imports from China.

- Congress allowed employers to steal billions of dollars from employees through legalized wage theft; low-level working supervisors and others were reclassified as managers and executives. By changing the law, Republicans essentially legalized wage theft. Because of that reclassification, millions of workers were forced to work more than forty hours a week without being paid overtime.
- The new bankruptcy law of 2005 favored the rich over the middle class.
- Congress and the president allowed U.S. companies to transform themselves into global corporations and move high tech jobs to foreign countries.
- Congress allowed the business community to block attempts to "cap" excessive CEO compensation.
- Congress failed in its attempt to reform banks and financial institutions after the financial crisis of 2007-2008.
- The Supreme Court under Chief Justice Roberts reached out in the Citizens United case, ruling that corporations and other business-like organizations were no longer restrained in contributing to a politician's campaign fund. They were now free to spend as much money as they wished to support or defeat any candidate for any office. This opened the floodgates for the Koch Brothers, the Mercers, and other donors in the billionaire class to influence elections at an unprecedented level.

And now, with the Trump administration, the pattern continues (via the Brookings[5] deregulatory tracker):

- The FCC, headed by Chairman Ajit Pai, a Trump appointee, voted 3-2 to repeal Net Neutrality.
- The Trump Interior Department proposed[6] to repeal most of the requirements of the Obama-era Methane Rule which regulated the gas released into the atmosphere during oil and natural gas production through venting, flaring, and equipment leaks.
- Nullification of a rule allowing class action lawsuits against banks and credit card companies to resolve financial disputes.

Effective nullification of a rule requiring communities to analyze racial residential segregation and submit plans to reverse it as a condition of receiving federal housing aid.

[5] "Tracking deregulation in the Trump era" *BROOKINGS*
https://www.brookings.edu/interactives/tracking-deregulation-in-the-trump-era/
[6] A Proposed Rule by the Land Management Bureau *NATIONAL ARCHIVES*
https://www.federalregister.gov/documents/2018/02/22/2018-03144/waste-prevention-production-subject-to-royalties-and-resource-conservation-rescission-or-revision-of

- Withdrawal of the Organic Livestock and Poultry Practices Rule requiring the humane treatment of "certified organic" animals.
- Rescission of Oil and Gas Fracking rule by the Department of the Interior on the grounds that it imposes burdensome reporting requirements and other unjustified costs on the oil and gas industry.
- Nullification of a rule requiring resource extraction issuers to disclose information about payments made to the U.S. government or foreign governments for the purposes of commercial development of oil, natural gas, or minerals. Advocates of the rule claimed that it prevented companies from bribing foreign governments and engaging in other forms of corruption. Detractors argued that the rule placed an excessive burden on U.S. companies.

The result of these actions has been a steady and systemic corruption of *all* our government institutions.

The problem is global.

Nick Dearden, director of Global Justice Now, says[7]:

The vast wealth and power of corporations is at the heart of so many of the world's problems – like inequality and climate change. The drive for short-term profits today seems to trump basic human rights for millions of people on the planet. Yet there are very few ways that citizens can hold these corporations to account for their behavior. Rather, through trade and investment deals, it is corporations which are able to demand that governments do their bidding.

Figures compiled by Global Justice Now show that top corporations continue to accrue revenues far in excess of most governments. Comparing 2017 revenues, 69 of the top 100 economic entities are corporations rather than governments. The top 10 corporations – a list which includes Walmart, Toyota and Shell as well as several Chinese corporations – raked in over $3 trillion last year.

Walmart, Apple and Shell all accrued more wealth than even fairly rich countries like Russia, Belgium, Sweden.

---

[7] "69 of the Richest 100 Entities on the Planet are Corporations, Not Governments, Figures Show" *Global Justice Now* https://www.commondreams.org/newswire/2018/10/17/69-richest-100-entities-planet-are-corporations-not-governments-figures-show

The non-profit **Friends of the Earth** explains[8] what unaccountable corporate power is doing to the world:

From a coal mine in Bangladesh that threatens to destroy one of the world's largest mangrove ecosystems to hundreds of people at risk of displacement from a mega-sugar plantation in Sri Lanka, corporations and big business are often implicated in human rights abuses across Asia. Yet many of these crimes go unpunished. Companies are able to evade responsibility by operating between different national jurisdictions and taking advantage of corruption in local legal systems, not to mention the fact that many corporations are richer and more powerful than the states that seek to regulate them.

Across the world we observe the rise of autocratic populist leaders who are embracing "nationalism" and "country-first" slogans to gain and hold on to power.

After the election of Donald Trump, The Oxford Dictionary announced their word of 2016:

post-truth
Adjective
Relating to or denoting circumstances in which objective facts are less influential in shaping public opinion than appeals to emotion and personal belief.

THE DECLINE OF TRUST IN GOVERNMENT

If the collapse in public trust is greatest in the institution of government, we decided to better examine *why* that is.

In the USA, surveys like Gallup's *Values and Beliefs Survey*[9] reveal that Americans believe the *government is the greatest problem facing the U.S.*, with 20% naming some aspect of the federal government or its elected leaders as the nation's top problem.

Here are the top issues:

- Dissatisfaction with government
- Immigration/Illegal aliens

---

[8] "Can Asia (and the UN) Hold Corporations Accountable? *The Diplomat*
https://thediplomat.com/2018/10/can-asia-and-the-un-hold-corporations-accountable/
[9] "Americans View Government as Nation's Top Problem in 2017" *GALLUP*
https://news.gallup.com/poll/224219/americans-view-government-nation-top-problem-2017.aspx

- Race relations
- Economy in general
- Unifying the country
- Ethics/Moral decline
- Lack of respect for each other
- Healthcare/Hospitals
- Gun control/Guns
- Unemployment/Jobs
- Federal budget deficit/Debt
- International issues/problems
- Education

To quantify where Americans stand on the issues confronting our democracy, we turned to the Pew Research Center, and its survey on *The Public, The Political System and American Democracy* [10].

The survey reveals that at a time of growing stress on democracy around the world, Americans generally agree on democratic ideals and values that are important for the United States. But for the most part, they see **the country falling well short in living up to these ideals,** according to a new study of opinion on the strengths and weaknesses of key aspects of American democracy and the political system.

The following **democratic values** are important to the public:

- Rights and freedoms of all people are respected
- Elected officials face serious consequences for misconduct
- Judges are not influenced by political parties
- Everyone has an equal opportunity to succeed
- Republicans and Democrats work together on issues
- Balance of power between government branches
- News organizations are independent of the government
- Government is open and transparent
- Campaign contributions do not lead to greater political influence
- People are free to peacefully protest
- News organizations do not favor a party

---

[10] "The Public, the Political System and American Democracy" *Pew Research Center* https://www.people-press.org/2018/04/26/the-public-the-political-system-and-american-democracy/

- Military leadership does not publicly support a party
- Views of those not in the majority on issues are respected
- Tone of political debate is respectful
- People agree on basic facts even if they disagree on politics
- Government policies reflect views of most Americans

The survey finds that the public is deeply skeptical about partisan co-operation, the tone of debate, and the influence of major political donors.

According to the survey:

Some of the public's most negative judgements are reserved for values that are most squarely in the political sphere. Large majorities do not see partisan cooperation (80%) or respectful political debate (74%) as describing the country well. Similarly, 72% say the country is not well described as a place where people who contribute to campaigns do not have more influence than other people; 69% also say the phrase "elected officials face serious consequences for misconduct" does not describe the country well.

The USA is viewed as **falling short on a range of widely supported democratic values.**

Specifically, the public's ratings of government performance declined on the following issues:

- Ensuring access to health care
- Protecting the environment
- Responding to natural disasters
- Ensuring safe food and medicine
- Setting workplace standards
- Helping people get out of poverty
- Ensuring access to quality education
- Ensuring basic income for 65+
- Keeping the country safe from terrorism
- Maintaining infrastructure
- Strengthening the economy
- Managing the US immigration system

There is still significant **common ground** with regards to the government's role on a number of issues such as defending against terrorism, managing the immigration system, responding to natural disasters, maintaining infrastructure and ensuring safe food and medicine. For example, 67% of respondents say the government should have a major role in addressing poverty, up from 55% two years ago.

There is, however, a problem in terms of objectivity and **truth**. Evaluations of government performance vary widely based on party affiliation.

ASK: What factors have created the inability to identify the truth?

"TRUTH DECAY" – WHAT ARE ALTERNATIVE FACTS?

The RAND Corporation has published an insightful report titled *Truth Decay: An Initial Exploration of the Diminishing Role of Facts and Analysis in American Public Life*[11] by Jennifer Kavanagh, and CEO Michael D. Rich.

Truth decay is defined by a set of four interrelated trends:

- an increasing disagreement about facts and analytical interpretations of facts and data;
- a blurring of the line between opinion and fact;
- an increase in the relative volume, and resulting influence, of opinion and personal experience over fact; and
- lowered trust in formerly respected sources of factual information.

The report explores three historical eras — the 1890s, 1920s, and 1960s — for evidence of the four Truth Decay trends and compares those eras with the past two decades (2000s–2010s). It turns out that two of the four trends occurred in earlier periods: the blurring of the line between opinion and fact and an increase in the relative volume, and resulting influence, of opinion over fact. **Declining trust in institutions, while evident in previous eras, is most severe today.** And most importantly, **no evidence of an increase in disagreement about facts was seen in the earlier periods.**

Examples of this decay are all around us.

Vaccines have virtually eradicated diseases like smallpox, polio, and measles in the United States. Yet polling shows that fewer people support vaccinating children[12] today than a decade ago. A similar divide exists on

---

[11] "Truth Decay: An Initial Exploration of the Diminishing Role of Facts and Analysis in American Public Life" *Rand Corporation*
https://www.rand.org/pubs/research_reports/RR2314.html
[12] In U.S., Percentage Saying Vaccines Are Vital Dips Slightly, *GALLUP*
https://news.gallup.com/poll/181844/percentage-saying-vaccines-vital-dips-slightly.aspx

many other topics: Violent crime has been steadily decreasing[13], but many people believe the opposite. More Mexican immigrants are leaving the U.S.[14] than are coming in, yet the perception that they're streaming into the U.S. is used to fuel anti-immigration policies.

"This inability to agree on an established set of facts or to take into account expert analysis is as serious a threat to the United States as any adversary or terrorist group in the world today," says RAND CEO **Michael D. Rich**. The researchers also identify four main drivers of truth decay:

1. Polarization in politics, society, and the economy
Segregation across the American electorate along economic, political, and social lines contributes to the development of insular and isolated communities, each with its own narrative, worldview, and, increasingly, even "facts."

2. Competing demands on the educational system that challenge its ability to keep pace with information system changes
The growing number of demands and fiscal constraints on the educational system have reduced the emphasis on civic education, media literacy, and critical thinking. Without proper training, many students do not learn how to identify disinformation and misleading information, and are susceptible to disseminating it themselves.

3. Changes in the information system, such as the rise of 24-hour news coverage, social media, and dissemination of disinformation and misleading or biased information
The volume of information overall has increased dramatically — especially content based on opinion, personal experience, and even falsehood. At the same time, social media and search algorithms can create self-reinforcing feeds of information by winnowing out competing perspectives. Together, these changes drown out facts, data, and analysis.

4. Characteristics of human information processing, such as cognitive biases
Cognitive biases reflect mental patterns that can lead people to form beliefs or make decisions that do not reflect an objective and thorough assessment

---

[13] 5 facts about crime in the U.S., *Pew Research Center* https://www.pewresearch.org/fact-tank/2019/10/17/facts-about-crime-in-the-u-s/

[14] What we know about illegal immigration from Mexico *Pew Research Center* https://www.pewresearch.org/fact-tank/2019/06/28/what-we-know-about-illegal-immigration-from-mexico/

of the facts. For instance, people tend to seek out information that confirms preexisting beliefs and reject information that challenges those beliefs.

The result of this failure to agree on facts has led to our current situation, where, according to the researchers, **"the most damaging effects might be the erosion of civil discourse, political paralysis, alienation and disengagement of individuals from political and civic institutions, and uncertainty about U.S. policy."**

"Alternative facts" are lies.

The **agents** of this Truth Decay are identified as the media, academia and research organizations, political actors and governments, and foreign actors. What can be done? Researchers tells us that we'll need interdisciplinary research and cooperation among research organizations, policymakers, educators, and other stakeholders to develop a clearer understanding of the problem and devise possible solutions. Priority areas for attention include:

- educational interventions
- improving the information market
- institutional development and rebuilding
- bridging social divides
- harnessing new technologies
- behavioral economics, psychology, and cognitive science
- organizational self-assessment

Does this cooperation seem likely in our current climate?

Not without **brand activism**.

Keith Weed – former CMO at Unilever, the world's second largest advertiser – threatened to pull marketing spending from digital platforms that **failed to take a stand**[15] against **fake news** and **divisive content**. Reports[16] say that *Weed has stated that brands can no longer stand by while hateful content that promotes sexism, racism, and extremism infiltrates social media platforms.*

---

[15] "Unilever warns social media to clean up 'toxic' content" *TechCrunch*
https://techcrunch.com/2018/02/12/unilever-warns-social-media-to-clean-up-toxic-content/amp/
[16] "Advertising Giant Unilever Threatens to Pull Spending From Platforms That Fail to Combat Division" *RELEVANCE* https://www.relevance.com/advertising-giant-unilever-threatens-to-pull-spending-from-platforms-that-fail-to-combat-division/

The **Reputation Institute** publishes an annual study[17] of corporate reputation in America, and now, in 2018, the *US RepTrak 100*[18] reveals an average three-point decline in company reputation. This is the most significant downward trend since 2008, made even more startling because each point corresponds to $1 billion in market capitalization. All reputation dimension scores are down, says the report, because **there is a growing belief companies focus on *profits over people*.**

Stephen Hahn-Griffiths, the chief research officer of the Reputation Institute has said: *"It's not enough to just have a high-quality product and deliver results on Wall Street. Social activism, aligning with communities, what you do to make the world a better place—that's the metric."*

Another survey from **Marketing Sherpa** finds that the most broadly cited experience among dissatisfied customers was *the company not putting their needs and wants above its own business goals.*

THE FLYWHEEL OF CORRUPTION

For some time now we've been saying that the wheels have fallen off our democracy[19]. Things aren't looking good around the world. *The Guardian* reports the world's **26 richest billionaires own as many assets as half the planet**[20]. *26 plutocrats own as much wealth as 3.8 billion people.* Welcome to serfdom.

When billionaires like Ray Dalio[21] and Nick Hanauer[22] question capitalism, it's time for a gut check.

How did we get to this place?

[17] "America's Most Reputable Companies 2018" *Forbes*
https://www.forbes.com/sites/vickyvalet/2018/04/17/americas-most-reputable-companies-2018/#48870873294e
[18] "2018 US RepTrak' *Reputation Institute* https://www.reputationinstitute.com/us-reptrak
[19] "When the Wheels Fall Off Our Democracy" *The Huffington Post*
https://www.huffpost.com/entry/when-the-wheels-fall-off-our democracy_b_589f961ae4b080bf74f03d11
[20] "World's 26 richest people own as much as poorest 50%, says Oxfam" *The Guardian*
https://www.theguardian.com/business/2019/jan/21/world-26-richest-people-own-as-much-as-poorest-50-per-cent-oxfam-report
[21] "Why and How Capitalism Needs to Be Reformed (Parts 1 & 2)"
https://www.linkedin.com/pulse/why-how-capitalism-needs-reformed-parts-1-2-ray-dalio/
[22] "The Pitchforks Are Coming... For Us Plutocrats" by Nick Hanauer, *Politico Magazine*
https://www.politico.com/magazine/story/2014/06/the-pitchforks-are-coming-for-us-plutocrats-108014

American CEOs[23] are, apparently, also questioning the road we're on. How did the gap between the rich and the poor get so wide?

Democracy and capitalism can't seem to co-exist. Everywhere we look, **democracy is in decline**[24]. We have to **confront capitalism**[25].

The question we have to ask is: **why aren't our politicians working for us?**

We borrowed and adapted a business concept from **Jim Collins**[26] to explain what's going on: the **flywheel of corruption**.

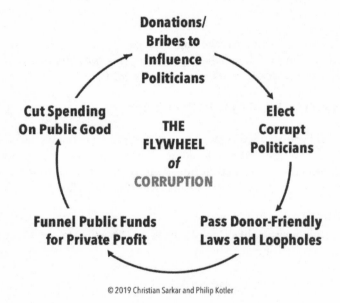

© 2019 Christian Sarkar and Philip Kotler

The answer?

Our **politicians work for their donors**, *not for us, the people.*

---

[23] "Why American CEOs are worried about capitalism" *Financial Times*
https://www.ft.com/content/138e103a-61a4-11e9-b285-3acd5d43599e
[24] Democracy in Decline: An Interview with Philip Kotler, *The Huffington Post*
https://www.huffpost.com/entry/democracy-in-decline-an-i_b_10369536
[25] http://www.confrontingcapitalism.com/
[26] "Turning the Flywheel" by Jim Collins, *THE MARKETING JOURNAL*
http://www.marketingjournal.org/book-review-turning-the-flywheel-by-jim-collins/

Small wonder that we feel like our politicians have been bought, that the system is *rigged*.

Corporations are "people." And campaign contributions are free speech. In every case, we find that private, **for-profit interests** win over the people's interests:

- Healthcare – for profit
- Drugs – for profit
- Education – for profit
- Infrastructure – for profit
- War – for profit
- Guns – for profit
- Water – for profit
- Environment – for profit
- Infrastructure – for profit
- Green New Deal – *sorry, no can do;* let's stick with fossil-fuel profits.

Just name the issue, and you'll find a donor, or perhaps group of donors, that are benefiting while the citizen's needs are neglected. **The Common Good is sacrificed on the altar of private profit.**

Is Capitalism working for *you*?

The answer to the question depends on who you ask.

With a few notable exceptions, if you ask America's **corporate executives**, their answer is that American Capitalism is working well and would even work better if there were fewer government regulations and if taxes were lowered.

If you ask America's **middle class**, their answer is that American Capitalism worked better in the past but now it is harder to finance a middle class life style given the high costs of sending students to college and taking care of their parents who failed to save enough money for their retirement. Healthcare and drug costs are out of control. In fact, healthcare emergencies are a leading cause of individual bankruptcy[27].

---

[27] "This is the real reason most Americans file for bankruptcy" *CNBC*
https://www.cnbc.com/2019/02/11/this-is-the-real-reason-most-americans-file-for-bankruptcy.html

If you ask **working–class Americans**, their answer is that they haven't improved their earnings since the 1980s but their expenses have risen dramatically and they can only survive with a credit card and rising indebtedness.

If you ask the 15% of our population living in **poverty**, their answer is that they can't find a decent job and they barely survive on food stamps, food kitchens, clothing handouts, and cheap housing or even homelessness.

Markets, left to themselves, do not always lead to efficient or equitable outcomes. Free-market capitalism can lead to monopolistic or oligopolistic industry domination–witness Google, Facebook, Amazon, and Apple. It inevitably leads to a growing concentration of income and wealth. The average income for the top 0.01 percent of households grew 322 percent, to $6.7 million, between 1980 and 2015. As of 2015, the data shows that half of all US income[28] went straight into the pockets of the top 10 percent of earners. **Thomas Piketty**, the economist, predicts that eventually 60 percent of income will go to the top 10 percent of earners.

Unfortunately, this pattern is a global phenomenon. Politicians work for their donor/masters. Many political systems are purpose-built for corruption.

And, despite what we keep hearing, government can't be "**run like a business.**" **This is one of the biggest fallacies in the current political debate.** We are told, time and time again, that a candidate for public office is qualified because he or she has run a business. The assumption is that this makes them fit for government service. One only has to look at the failure of Rex Tillerson in the State Department to see that even the CEO of ExxonMobil didn't have what it takes to do the job.

But to understand why this is, we need to look at what the job is.

What's the job of government? Who is the customer?

Let's answer this simply – **the job of government is to serve the public in the public interest, or Common Good.**

---

[28] " 11 Charts That Show Income Inequality Isn't Getting Better Anytime Soon" *Mother Jones* https://www.motherjones.com/politics/2016/12/america-income-inequality-wealth-net-worth-charts/

Unlike business, the government does not get to select which customer segments to serve and which segments to ignore. **The government must serve *all* its citizens and constituents.** When it fails to do so, it becomes dysfunctional.

Guess what – the dysfunction is by design!

Katherine Gehl and **Michael Porter** explain what's going on in *Why Competition in the Politics Industry is Failing America*[29]:

The starting point for understanding the problem is to recognize that our political system isn't broken. Washington is delivering exactly what it is currently designed to deliver. The real problem is that our political system is no longer designed to serve the public interest, and has been slowly reconfigured to benefit the private interests of gain-seeking organizations: our major political parties and their industry allies.

Take a minute to let that sink in: **The US political system does not serve the public interest (or the Common Good).**

The United Nations Convention against Corruption addresses the major manifestations of corruption, such as bribery and embezzlement, and the acts carried out in support of corruption, such as obstruction of justice, trading in influence and the concealment or laundering of the proceeds of corruption. The Convention covers not only corruption in private-to-public relationships (business relationships with public officials, including state-owned enterprises), but also private-to-private relationships (relationships among companies only).

The following is a list[30] of common manifestations of corruption. See if you recognize any (or all) of them:

- Bribery of national public officials;
- Bribery of foreign public officials and officials of public international organizations;
- Bribery in the private sector;
- Embezzlement of property in the private sector;
- Trading in influence;
- Abuse of function;

[29] "WHY COMPETITION IN THE POLITICS INDUSTRY IS FAILING AMERICA" by *Katherine Gehl and Michael Porter* https://www.hbs.edu/competitiveness/Documents/why-competition-in-the-politics-industry-is-failing-america.pdf
[30] An Anti-Corruption Ethics and Compliance Programme for Business: A Practical Guide http://www.unodc.org/documents/corruption/Publications/2013/13-84498_Ebook.pdf

- Illicit enrichment;
- Laundering of proceeds of crime;
- Concealment of proceeds of crime; and
- Obstruction of justice.

One can argue that in our current system, the only customer served by the government is the wealthy donor, and the corporations that fund candidates' re-elections. And, when they leave Congress, candidates are then employed as lobbyists for these corporations. According to Sourcewatch[31], "The government-industry revolving door puts industry-friendly experts in positions of decision-making power. Often individuals rotate between working for industry and working for the government in regulatory capacities, arrangements that are fraught with potential for conflicts of interest."

Of course, these conflicts of interest are often hidden behind closed doors.

Dark money groups also hijack the political process by ensuring that the needs and wants of their donors are positioned above the needs of society. Our government is in the business of diverting public resources to private interests – the influencers and special interests – mainly corporate entities – the corpocracy.

Let's look at a few examples:

Healthcare[32]. In 1912 the AMA declared that it was unprofessional for physicians to be under corporate control and in 1934 "condemned contractual arrangements whereby lay persons and entities directly profited from the services rendered by doctors." The theory is that "physicians need to be able to make medical decisions free from the interference of lay persons, particularly lay persons whose allegiance extends more to the bottom line than to the well-being of patients."

What changed? The downfall of the US healthcare system can be traced to President Nixon's choice (as a personal favor for his friend and campaign financier, Edgar Kaiser, then president and chairman of Kaiser-Permanente) to allow medical insurance agencies, hospitals, clinics and even doctors to function as for-profit business entities.

---

[31] "Government-industry revolving door," *Sourcewatch*
https://www.sourcewatch.org/index.php/Government-industry_revolving_door
[32] See https://freemarkethealthcareblog.com/2017/07/03/for-profit-entities-and-prices/

Education. According to *Hijacked by Billionaires: How the Super Rich Buy Elections to Undermine Public Schools,* an investigative report[33] by Network for Public Education Action, some of America's wealthiest individuals collaborate to hijack the democratic process by pouring millions of dollars into state and local races, often in places where they do not live. They don't believe in public schools. The agenda is to advance the privatization of public schools by whatever means necessary: by spending heavily on state referenda, on state school board elections, or on local school board elections. They want their allies to control state and local school boards so that more public schools will be closed and replaced by privately managed charter schools or even vouchers for religious schools.

Climate Change. *The Guardian* reports[34] that ExxonMobil, the world's biggest oil company, knew as early as 1981 of climate change – seven years before it became a public issue. Despite this the firm spent millions over the next 27 years to promote climate denial.

The Intergovernmental Panel on Climate Change (IPCC) has issued a grave warning to the public that there's a closing window to act to prevent a climate catastrophe. ExxonMobil's reaction? Pledging a $1 million contribution to a campaign for a carbon tax, a move that critics are calling "a scam."[35]

Gun Control. According to research by the Center for Responsive Politics[36], nearly all the 46 senators who voted against a measure which would have enforced background checks as a condition of commercial firearms sales received donations from the gun lobby. What chance is there that these public officials will ever vote in the public interest? Zero.

Prisons. It turns out that the immigration crackdown that ICE is pursuing has lifted shares of stock in the Geo Group and CoreCivic, two private, for-profit prison businesses. Why? Because they profit from a private system of jail-as-a-business[37] .

---

[33] *THE NETWORK FOR PUBLIC EDUCATION ACTION*
https://npeaction.org/wp-content/uploads/2018/09/Hijacked-by-Billionaires.pdf
[34] "Exxon knew of climate change in 1981, email says – but it funded deniers for 27 more years" *The Guardian* https://www.theguardian.com/environment/2015/jul/08/exxon-climate-change-1981-climate-denier-funding
[35] "This Is a Scam": ExxonMobil-Backed Carbon Tax Will Not Save the Planet" *FIXCapitalism.com* http://fixcapitalism.com/this-is-a-scam-exxonmobil-backed-carbon-tax-will-not-save-the-planet/
[36] Gun Rights vs Gun Control, *Open Secrets* https://www.opensecrets.org/news/issues/guns/
[37] "Prison and Profits" by *Christopher Brauchli* https://www.commondreams.org/views/2017/04/15/prison-and-profits

War. It is common knowledge that the US military budget is out of control. The US Army has accumulated $6.5 trillion[38] in expenditures that cannot be accounted for. According to reporter Dave Lindorff: "politicians of both major political parties are demanding accountability for every penny spent on welfare," and they have also been engaged in pervasive efforts "to make teachers accountable for student 'performance.'" Yet, he observed, "the military doesn't have to account for any of its trillions of dollars of spending . . . even though Congress fully a generation ago passed a law requiring such accountability."

By the way, did you know the Pentagon operates more than 170 golf courses[39] worldwide?

Voter Suppression. The Center for Media and Democracy (CMD) reports[40] that after Barack Obama swept into office in November of 2008 with the energized support of youth and African Americans, suddenly "voter fraud" became a deep concern for many in the Republican party -- despite no evidence fraud occurred in any statistically significant way. And when Republicans emerged from the November 2010 elections with new majorities in statehouses across the country, a total of 37 states saw strict voter ID laws introduced in 2011 and 2012. Many of those proposals contained elements of the American Legislative Exchange Council (ALEC) "model" voter ID act, which imposes new burdens on the right to vote by requiring voters show state-issued ID cards.

Coupled with an active gerrymandering[41] agenda this has significantly prevented proportional and descriptive representation[42], as the winners of elections are increasingly determined by who is drawing the districts rather than the preferences of the voters.

Foreign Influence. *The Huffington Post* reports[43] that Crown Prince Mohammed bin Salman, implicated in the alleged murder of journalist Jamal Khashoggi, could blunt criticism using the most sprawling foreign influence

---

[38] "Over Six Trillion Dollars in Unaccountable Army Spending"
https://www.projectcensored.org/2-six-trillion-dollars-unaccountable-army-spending/
[39] "The Budget Deal Is a Big Win for the Pentagon" *Mother Jones*
https://www.motherjones.com/politics/2013/12/pentagon-budget-deal-charts-cuts/
[40] "Democracy, Voter Rights, and Federal Power" *Center for Media and Democracy*
https://www.alecexposed.org/wiki/Democracy,_Voter_Rights,_and_Federal_Power
[41] https://en.wikipedia.org/wiki/Gerrymandering
[42]https://en.wikipedia.org/wiki/Representation_(politics)#Descriptive_representation
[43] "Saudi Arabia Wants Trump and Congress To Forget Jamal Khashoggi. Here's Its Likely Playbook" *The Huffington Post*
https://www.huffpost.com/entry/jamal-khashoggi-trump-congress-saudi-arabia-lobbying-arms-deals_n_5bc20a93e4b040bb4e82b65a

campaign in the U.S. today: "By directing billions of dollars of Saudi money into the U.S. for decades, Riyadh's ruling family has won the support of small but powerful circles of influential Americans and courted wider public acceptance through corporate ties and philanthropy." President Trump went on record blaming "rogue killers"[44] for the journalist's disappearance.

Corporate Influence. The late David Koch and Charles Koch – known as the Koch brothers[45] - were the right-wing billionaire co-owners of Koch Industries. As two of the richest people in the world, they were key funders of the right-wing infrastructure, including the **American Legislative Exchange Council (ALEC)** and the State Policy Network[46] (SPN).

ALEC is funded by corporations and corporate foundations and its agenda extends into almost all areas of law. Its bills:

- undermine environmental regulations and deny climate change;
- support school privatization;
- undercut health care reform;
- defund unions and limit their political influence;
- restrain legislatures' abilities to raise revenue through taxes;
- mandate strict election laws that disenfranchise voters;
- increase incarceration to benefit the private prison industry, among many other issues.

The Center for Media and Democracy CMD explains how ALEC works[47]: The Koch brothers and their network of billionaires are operating with a reach and resources that exceed those of political parties and they are using that power to erode the integrity of our elections and sap taxpayer dollars away from investments in public infrastructure, education, and healthcare to benefit narrow special interests and global corporations.

Since the CMD first exposed ALEC in 2011, more than 100 corporations have dropped ALEC, including Verizon, Ford, Coca-Cola, Wal-Mart, General Electric, and Google.

---

[44] Trump Says 'Rogue Killers' May Be Behind Jamal Khashoggi's Disappearance, *HUFFPOST* https://www.huffpost.com/entry/trump-says-rogue-killers-are-behind-jamal-khashoggis-disappearance_n_5bc4909fe4b040bb4e845d66
[45] Koch Brothers, *Center for Media and Democracy* https://www.sourcewatch.org/index.php?title=Koch_Brothers
[46] State Policy Network, *Center for Media and Democracy* https://www.sourcewatch.org/index.php/State_Policy_Network
[47] *Center for Media and Democracy PRWatch* https://www.prwatch.org/cmd/index.html

In *Manufacturing Consent* [48] Noam Chomsky told us: "At this stage of History, either one of two things is possible: either the general population will take control of its own destiny and will concern itself with community interests, guided by values of solidarity and sympathy and concern for others, or alternatively, there will be no destiny for anyone to control."

Now, the policies of Donald Trump have taken our existential crisis of democracy to another level.

Philip Kotler has noted in the *Huffington Post* [49] that what is most disturbing is the President's attack on the *idea of America*. **America is an idea, not simply a country.** Trump is succeeding in turning *e Pluribus Unum* into "every man for himself"; he is *Closing the American Mind* by using a strategy of polarization [50] – by politicizing every aspect of government and civic life. This is not an accident. What we see with Trump is a systematic targeting of all the institutions and policies that actually made America great. One can argue that the Trump administration (aided and abetted by the GOP) is like an institutional terrorist planting bombs to **blow up the pillars of our Democracy.**

In his book, *America: The Farewell Tour* [51], **Chris Hedges** describes the danger at hand:

The most ominous danger we face does not come from the eradication of free speech through the obliteration of net neutrality or through Google algorithms that steer people away from dissident, left-wing, progressive, or anti-war sites. It does not come from the 2017 tax bill that abandons all pretense of fiscal responsibility to enrich corporations and oligarchs and prepares the way to dismantle programs such as Social Security. It does not come from the opening of public land to the mining and fossil fuel industry, the acceleration of ecocide by demolishing environmental regulations, or the destruction of public education. It does not come from the squandering of federal dollars on a bloated military as the country collapses or the use of the systems of domestic security to criminalize dissent. The most ominous danger we face comes from the marginalization and destruction of

[48] *Manufacturing Consent* by Noam Chomsky https://www.amazon.com/Manufacturing-Consent-Noam-Chomsky-Media/dp/B0031DDI4I/
[49] "The 'Terrorist' in the White House" by Philip Kotler *The Huffington Post* https://www.huffpost.com/entry/the-terrorist-in-the-white house_b_58aa969fe4b0b0e1e0e20d50
[50] "Trump wants to boost defense spending by 10% and cut social spending, *Los Angeles Times* https://www.latimes.com/politics/washington/la-na-essential-washington-updates-201702-htmlstory.html#public-deeply-polarized-and-already-dug-in-on-trump
[51] America: The Farewell Tour by *Chris Hedges* https://www.amazon.com/America-Farewell-Tour-Chris-Hedges-ebook/dp/B075RTDPJ7/

institutions, including the courts, academia, legislative bodies, cultural organizations, and the press, that once ensured that civil discourse was rooted in reality and fact, helping us distinguish lies from truth, and facilitate justice.

Similarly, in *Read & Riot: A Pussy Riot Guide to Activism*[52], a courageous **Nadya Tolokonnikova** writes:

When Trump won the US presidential election, people were deeply shocked. **What was in fact blown up on the 8th of November 2016 was the social contract, the paradigm that says you can live comfortably without getting your hands dirty with politics.** *The belief that it only takes your one vote every four years (or no vote at all: you're above politics) to have your freedoms protected. This belief was torn to pieces. The belief that institutions are here to protect us and take care of us, and we don't need to bother ourselves with protecting these institutions from being eroded by corruption, lobbyists, monopolies, corporate and government control over our personal data. We were outsourcing political struggle like we outsourced low-wage labor and wars.*

The current systems have failed to provide answers for citizens, and people are looking outside of the mainstream political spectrum. These dissatisfactions are now being used by right-wing, nativist, opportunist, corrupted, cynical political players. The same ones who helped create and stoke all of this now offer salvation. That's their game. It's the same strategy as defunding a program or regulatory agency they want to get rid of, then holding up its resulting ineffectiveness as evidence that it needs to be folded.

Are there no limits to this corruption?

Apparently not.

What name should we give this phenomenon?

Crony capitalism? Predatory capitalism?

Corporate tyranny?

ASK: Are we subverting Democracy? What does a society without respect for the Rule of Law mean for our business?

[52] *Read & Riot: A Pussy Riot Guide to Activism*, Nadya Tolokonnikova
https://www.amazon.com/Read-Riot-Pussy-Guide-Activism-ebook/dp/B071NKV7M2/

9. THE END GOAL OF BRAND ACTIVISM

How do we make America great again? **By making sure the government serves the people and the public interest.**

Corporate interests must be managed in conjunction with the society. Anything less at this point means we are ready to embrace the corruption of a *mafia* economy – based not on merit, or equality of opportunity, but on tyranny and violence.

MAKE GOVERNMENT SERVE THE PUBLIC AGAIN

The rule of law cannot stand when its institutions are corrupted. In the current political climate, we see new proposals for change coming from various sources.

Katherine Gehl and **Professor Michael Porter** tell us that "the structure of the politics industry has created unhealthy competition that fails to advance the public interest." In a ground-breaking report titled *WHY COMPETITION IN THE POLITICS INDUSTRY IS FAILING AMERICA: A strategy for reinvigorating our democracy*[1], they point out:

Citizens are beginning to understand that something is deeply wrong with our democracy. Surveys of both Harvard Business School alumni and the general public identified the political system as America's greatest competitive weakness.

It wasn't always that way. America's political system was long the envy of the world. It advanced public interest and gave rise to a grand history of policy innovations that fostered both economic and social progress. Today, however, our political system has become the major barrier to solving nearly every important challenge our nation needs to address.

Why? Because the parties compete on ideology and unrealistic promises, not on action and results. The parties compete to divide voters and serve special interests, rather than weighing and balancing the interests of all citizens and finding common ground to move the country forward.

---

[1] WHY COMPETITION IN THE POLITICS INDUSTRY IS FAILING AMERICA by *Katherine Gehl and Professor Michael Porter*
https://www.hbs.edu/competitiveness/Documents/why-competition-in-the-politics-industry-is-failing-america.pdf

Another recent paper, *CSR Needs CPR: Corporate Sustainability and Politics*[2], by **Thomas P. Lyon** and colleagues argues that firms must become as transparent about their **corporate political responsibility** (CPR) as their **corporate social responsibility** (CSR).

On the political front we are going to see more proposals like the one put forward by **Senator Elizabeth Warren** whose proposed Accountable Capitalism Act[3] restores the idea that giant American corporations should look out for American interests.

The key points of her proposal include:

- Corporations with more than $1 billion in annual revenue would be required to get a **federal corporate charter**.
- The new charter requires corporate directors to consider the interests of **all major corporate stakeholders**—not only shareholders—in company decisions.
- Shareholders could sue if they believed directors weren't fulfilling those obligations.
- **Employees** would elect at least 40% of directors.
- At least 75% of directors and shareholders would need to approve before a corporation could make any political expenditures.
- To address self-serving financial incentives in corporate management, directors and officers would not be allowed to sell company shares within five years of receiving them—or within three years of a company stock buyback.

Warren's proposal has already stirred up the hornets[4]. We think that's because she's headed in the right direction.

To look the other way in the presence of evil is evil. Former Unilever CEO Paul Polman wrote this on his blog[5]:

---

[2] CSR Needs CPR: Corporate Sustainability and Politics, *Berkley Haas*
https://www.hbs.edu/faculty/Publication%20Files/Lyon_et_al_2018_CMR_f4406d48-0511-4f2a-a83f-7ee1e2952c8c.pdf
[3] https://en.wikipedia.org/wiki/Accountable_Capitalism_Act
[4] "Kevin Williamson's unhinged attack on Elizabeth Warren's corporate accountability bill, explained" *Vox* https://www.vox.com/2018/8/17/17698502/kevin-williamson-elizabeth-warren-corporate-accountability
[5] "Universal Human Rights – The Foundations of the Global Goals"
https://www.linkedin.com/pulse/universal-human-rights-foundations-global-goals-paul-polman/

...business can only flourish in societies in which human rights are respected, upheld and advanced. Safe working conditions, fair wages, protection from forced labor, and freedom from harassment and discrimination: these must become standard global operating conditions. Business has a responsibility and opportunity to be the driving force for the advancement of universal human rights.

It all comes down to ensuring dignity and equality – an enormous task central to many, if not all of the Sustainable Development Goals. An Oxfam report on inequality[6] revealed that 1% of the global population own more wealth than the other 99% combined. We must reverse this trend if we are to build a better future for all. And human rights are at the heart of the work desperately required to end poverty, reduce inequality and provide decent employment.

The question is simple: will business do the right thing?

Will it stand for the Common Good, or will it stand for political corruption, defined[7] as "the illegitimate use of public power to benefit a private interest"?

What issues are troubling to the Customer of the Future? The Employee of the Future?

We ask you to consider the following issues, and see how far you stand from your stakeholders – today and tomorrow:

- Income Inequality
- Climate Change & Ecocide
- Population
- Corruption
- Human Rights
- Black Lives Matter
- Healthcare
- Food Security
- Tax Loopholes
- Education
- Lobbying
- War Industries

---

[6] "62 people own same as half world" *Oxfam*
https://oxfamapps.org/media/press_release/2016-01-62-people-own-same-as-half-world-says-oxfam-inequality-report-davos-world-economic-forum/
[7] https://en.wikipedia.org/wiki/Corruption

- Digital Disruption
- AI & Robots and the Impact on Jobs
- Voter Suppression
- Gerrymandering
- Citizen's United
- #MeToo

Predatory capitalism is unnatural,[8] says **Umair Haque**. Here's how he sees it:

...there is nothing the remotest bit natural about capitalism. The bees are not stockpiling honey to sell at a profit. The trees are not charging the bees to build their hive. The soil is not leasing itself to the flowers. The sun is not sending bills to them all. None of these beings are trying to seek some kind of predatory advantage from the next. They are merely supporting one another. That is their nature. It is the essence of them.

Haque states it elegantly:

We are part of nature. But nature is not just a predatory machine. It is a place where, like the trees, sun, flowers, and bees, life flows from one to another, in a beautiful and wondrous and endless dance. Let us see ourselves that way—and then maybe we will love ourselves for our nobility, instead of despising ourselves for our ugliness.

As Philip as pointed out in his book *Confronting Capitalism*,[9] the current state of capitalism falls short because it:

- Proposes little or no solution to persistent poverty
- Generates a growing level of income inequality
- Fails to pay a living wage to billions of workers
- Not enough human jobs in the face of growing automation

- Doesn't charge businesses with the full social costs of their activities
- Exploits the environment and natural resources in the absence of regulation
- Creates business cycles and economic instability

---

[8] "How Life Under Predatory Capitalism Traumatized a Nation" by *Umair Haque*.
https://eand.co/how-life-under-predatory-capitalism-traumatized-a-nation-c90969df042d
[9] Confronting Capitalism: Real Solutions for a Troubled Economic System by Philip Kotler
https://www.amazon.com/Confronting-Capitalism-Solutions-Troubled-Economic/dp/0814436455/

- Emphasizes individualism and self-interest at the expense of community and the commons
- Encourages high consumer debt and leads to a growing financially-driven rather than producer-driven economy
- Lets politicians and business interests collaborate to subvert the economic interests of the majority of citizens
- Favors short-run profit planning over long-run investment planning
- Should have regulations regarding product quality, safety, truth in advertising, and anti-competitive behavior
- Tends to focus narrowly on GDP growth
- Needs to bring social values and happiness into the market equation.

Free-market capitalism has subverted our democracy. The growth of income inequality has undermined the American Dream. Increasing polarization has destroyed our unity as a nation. The plutocracy must end. We need to produce wealth for the many, not the few. We need to commit to improving life for those at the base, and middle, of the pyramid.

What about globalization? **Henry Mintzberg** raises an important point[10]:

The central problem is that what we refer to today as globalization is really economic globalization: It enables economic forces to prevail over social concerns and democratic precepts. In economic globalization, multinational companies play governments off one another in their quest for reduced taxes and suspended regulations, while local communities have to compete for jobs that can be no more reliable than the next better offer from elsewhere. There is no ensured, sustainable employment in this model. Globalization may connect us everywhere, but it is rooted nowhere.

The choice is between "Nationalism" and "Globalization" is a false choice. Mintzberg explains: "We need to keep globalization in its place, namely the marketplace, where it creates value, while keeping it out of the public space, where it has become increasingly destructive."

Thus, the end goal of Brand Activism must be to take responsibility for the system – to eradicate the corrupt alliance between government(s) and industry and promote a democracy that works for the public, *not* against it.

---

[10] "We Must Keep Globalization in Its Place" *MIT Sloan Management Review*
https://sloanreview.mit.edu/article/we-must-keep-globalization-in-its-place-the-marketplace/

It comes down to this: *we will never be able to fix major challenges like climate change, social security, and student debt without first addressing our broken democracy.* That is what ethical business must promote if it wants to be a good citizen – locally and nationally.

ASK: Do we respect and defend the Common Good? The public interest? Democracy?

COLLABORATIVE CAPITALISM AND THE COMMON GOOD

Capitalism must become a democratic, collaborative system that enjoys profits without harm to the future of society and the planet.

Business must seek consent, not just of the customer, but society as well.

The prevalent form of corporate organization is unsustainable. We've seen private enterprise, state-owned enterprise, but not enough of employee-owned enterprise. Slowly, we are seeing the emergence of new more democratic forms of business – the B-corp, Benefit corporations, cooperatives, and collaboratives.

The sharing economy must be democratically owned and controlled to be a sharing economy – otherwise it is exploitation. Uber and Airbnb are not about sharing at all. So collaborative capitalism must include co-ownership.

In India, the success of **Amul**, a collaborative dairy, has helped the country emerge as the largest milk producer in the world. For over 65 years, the Amul co-op has empowered the milk producers to control procurement, processing, and marketing, from village to district, to state, and to national levels. The farmers own the dairy, their elected representative manage the village societies and district unions, and they employ professionals to operate the dairy and manage the business.

Another example from the Basque region of Spain is **Mondragon Corporation**, a collaborative enterprise, made up as a corporation and federation of worker cooperatives. The tenth-largest Spanish company in it employed 74,335 people in 257 companies and organizations in four areas of activity: finance, industry, retail and knowledge. According to *Wikipedia*, at Mondragon, there are agreed-upon wage ratios between executive work and field or factory work which earns a minimum wage. These ratios range from 3:1 to 9:1 in different cooperatives and average 5:1. That is, the general manager of an average Mondragon cooperative earns no more than 5 times as much as the theoretical minimum wage paid in their cooperative. The wage ratio of a cooperative is decided periodically by its worker-owners through a democratic vote.

Compare this to the traditional US corporation where the pay-ratio of the CEO to the average worker can be as high as 1000:1.

On another note, does your business support the Green New Deal[11] ?

The American Sustainable Business Council (ASBC) does:

As responsible business leaders and investors in industries across America, we support the Green New Deal. By aligning with its brave vision and reality-based goals, American innovation can bring to scale *long-overdue* economic, *environmental, and social benefits. We can create* broad opportunity, *rebuild our deteriorated infrastructure, and combat the clear and present danger of climate change. At its core, the* Green New Deal offers a policy *direction that will result in better business results for all stakeholders and a more vibrant and resilient economy.*

ASBC represents 250,000 businesses – including Patagonia, Ben and Jerry's, and Seventh Generation – that believe government policy needs to change to reflect the triple bottom line: people, planet, and profit. Their stance comes from the understanding that **we are all in this together:**

The ideas of stewardship and wise investment to secure future prosperity is neither conservative nor liberal, neither Democrat nor Republican. It is a fundamental tenet of successful business and a core component of the American Dream.

What's holding your business back?

A recent article[12] in the *Harvard Business Review* proposes two broad and complementary opportunities for businesses:

1. **Supporting Green Initiatives:** Companies can help reduce the burdens of the energy transition by supporting economically sustainable low-carbon initiatives. How? By creating new economic enterprises where coal extraction previously thrived *and* being more proactive in their efforts to expand access to renewable energy.

---

[11] "H.Res.109 - Recognizing the duty of the Federal Government to create a Green New Deal" *CONGRESS.GOV*
https://www.congress.gov/bill/116th-congress/house-resolution/109/text
[12] "What Would the Green New Deal Mean for Businesses?" by Sanya Carley and David Konisky *Harvard Business Review* https://hbr.org/2019/02/what-would-the-green-new-deal-mean-for-businesses

2. **Develop Inclusive Business Models**: tailoring new business models for vulnerable populations. These include subscription-based community solar and energy service companies (ESCOs).

Of course, none of this happens in a vacuum. Federal, state, and local government will need to do their part, say the authors, to create incentives, or at least not put up barriers, as many are doing now, to facilitate the inclusivity of the energy transition. Is that too much to ask?

The risks of inaction far outweigh any ideological or political leanings your company has. Have you considered what the impact of severe climate change will be on society, your customers, and your industry?

Nothing lasts forever. Jeff Bezos, the world's richest man, told his employees that their focal job is to delay the time when Amazon dies.

Bezos is not only aware that companies inevitably die. He is keenly aware that planet earth will eventually die. Forever the optimist, Bezos is investing money in designing space ships where human life could continue. He differs from Elon Musk who sees human survival to depend on moving to and living on Mars.

The task of extending the earth's life is urgent. Scientists estimate that mankind has only 12 years to reduce our carbon footprint before the damage cannot be reversed. The Intergovernmental Panel on Climate Change concluded[13] In October 2018 that in order to limit warming to 1.5 degrees Celsius above pre-industrial levels, the world would have to reach net-zero emissions of carbon dioxide by the year 2050. Otherwise, mankind will face increasingly severe climate impacts.

Most of the world's worsening climate and pollution is manmade. Our automobiles, our buildings and our meat animals release gases and CO_2 emissions warming the earth. A warming earth leads to melting ice and water flooding of coastal cities, creating untold human and physical damage.

The United States is the only country whose leader calls climate change a hoax. In becoming the U.S. President in 2016, one of Trump's earliest moves was to renounce and withdraw from the Paris climate agreement. One of the world's major polluting countries decided to take no systematic steps to curtail pollution and climate change.

---

[13] "Summary for Policymakers of IPCC Special Report on Global Warming of 1.5°C approved by governments" *ipcc* https://www.ipcc.ch/2018/10/08/summary-for-policymakers-of-ipcc-special-report-on-global-warming-of-1-5c-approved-by-governments/

In the year 1776 when Adam Smith published the *Wealth of Nations*, our earth supported less than one billion people. Smith's vision of capitalism now much be revised for an earth that today has seven billion people. By 2050, the earth will need an economic system that can feed nine million people.

Only two billion of today's seven billion people enjoy a middle class or higher income. Citizens in developing countries look with envy at the middle class life style and want to achieve it. An increasing number of citizens are intent on leaving their own backward or dangerous country to enter Western Europe or the United States. Even if some succeed, the chance that most of them will achieve a middle-class lifestyle is small. It is estimated that we would need the resources of five earths to support seven billion people in a middle-class lifestyle.

There is not enough income and resources to deliver a middle-class standard of living. We would be smarter to aim for livable levels of income and resources for most denizens on the earth. Stop the steady preaching of "more is more," and replace it with E.F. Schumacher's *Small is Beautiful* and "less is more."

Actually, those who achieve a middle-class level of income know that it comes with its own set of problems. Citizens living in advanced industrial countries have to spend an increasing amount of time getting to and from their job. They sit longer in their slow-moving cars facing growing congested traffic. They need a car because public transportation is poor in most large cities. They own an expensive car that sits idle during most of the day and night.

Citizens living in advance industrial areas work 40 hours a week and may work much longer. Many employees worry that their company will fail or that their job will be turned over to a robot. They worry about a family member having an injury or illness that wipes out all their life savings.

Most companies adopt the twin goals of growing their sales and their profit. They plan to meet the growing consumption needs of a growing population.   .

But there is a problem. The earth has finite, not infinite resources. The earth's resources are inadequate to meet a growing population's needs and wants. Countries and companies need to give up on the idea of pursuing a Growth Economy. Environmentalists propose that a Growth Economy needs to be replaced by the concept of a Circular Economy. The aim is to build a closed loop system requiring few new resources. The work in a

Circular Economy will probably fall short of what is needed to meet climate change. We would still face a world of finite resources. A major step would be to aim for a constant and not a growing population. Families should be encouraged to have fewer children. Each child born consumes a certain level of resources over his/her lifetime. China adopted the extreme policy of limiting families to have only one child. Democratic regimes, however, have not imposed any limit. Several major religions push the idea of large families. Agricultural-based societies in poor countries strive for more children to do the work of planting and harvesting.

Democracies have based their hope on educating more women to join the work force. Working women have less time or appetite to spend their lives in producing and managing children.

The main challenge in a world of finite resources is to persuade people to reduce their consumption. Do citizens need as many clothing items that end up unused in overstuffed closets? Does the fashion industry need to carry out planned obsolescence so that people need to acquire the latest stylish garments? Do citizens need so many brands of cosmetics or cereals? Should the nation allow the building of many large mansions when so many people are squeezed into small and poor apartments?

Most democracies bury their heads in the sand rather than adjust to living in a world of finite resources. In the U.S., this problem of finite resources was finally addressed on Feb. 7, 2019. On that day, New York Representative Alexandria Ocasio-Cortez (AOC) introduced the Green New Deal in the House of Representatives. Senator Ed Markey of Massachusetts introduced a companion resolution in the Senate.

The Green New Deal outlined a comprehensive vision for how the U.S. might tackle limited resources and climate change over the next decade, while also creating high-paying jobs and protecting vulnerable communities. The Green New Deal proposed seven goals:

- Making every building energy efficient
- Growing the clean energy economy
- Ensuring a just and fair transition
- Clean air, water and healthy food as a human right
- Sustainable transportation
- Cutting carbon emission
- Moving to 100% renewable energy

The primary climate change goal is to reach net-zero greenhouse emissions in a decade. "Net-zero"[14] means that after tallying up all the greenhouse gases that are released and subtracting those that are sequestered, or removed, there is no net addition to the atmosphere. The goal, then, is slightly less ambitious than calling for no greenhouse gas emissions at all.

The goals seek reform in four areas: electricity generation, transportation, agriculture, and economic security.

Electricity generation. The goal is to meet "100 percent of the power demand in the United States through clean, renewable, and zero-emission energy sources." This would involve "dramatically expanding and upgrading renewable power sources" and "deploying new capacity." The proposal did not take a position on whether nuclear energy should be expanded or contracted. However, an FAQ (stands for Frequently Asked Questions) released by Ocasio-Cortez added that the right way to capture carbon is to plant trees and restore our natural ecosystems. The EPA (Environmental Protection Agency) estimated that generating electricity accounts for about 28 percent[15] of the nation's greenhouse gas emissions.

Transportation. For the country to reach net-zero emissions in a decade, emissions reductions must occur in transportation. Greenhouse gas emissions in transportation are responsible for about 28 percent of the U.S. total.

The Green New Deal requires "overhauling transportation systems in the United States to remove pollution and greenhouse gas emissions from the transportation sector as much as is technologically feasible, including through investment in (i) zero-emission vehicle infrastructure and manufacturing; (ii) clean, affordable, and accessible public transit; and (iii) high-speed rail."

The Green New Deal calls for reducing transportation emissions "as much as is technically feasible." It suggests building high-speed rail and zero-emission vehicles (electric cars), There is no mention of air travel, even though air travel releases a considerable amount of greenhouse gas emission. Perhaps it was not mentioned because it would generate considerable political opposition. FAQs suggested that high-speed rail and more public transit would greatly reduce the amount of needed air travel.

[14] "Global warming of 1.5°" *ipcc* https://report.ipcc.ch/sr15/pdf/sr15_spm_final.pdf
[15] Sources of Greenhouse Gas Emissions, *EPA*
https://www.epa.gov/ghgemissions/sources-greenhouse-gas-emissions

Agriculture. About 9 percent[16] of the nation's greenhouse gases stem from agricultural activities, including the release of nitrous oxide from soil and methane from livestock. The Green New Deal calls for "working collaboratively with farmers and ranchers in the United States to remove pollution and greenhouse gas emissions from the agricultural sector as much as is technologically feasible, including (i) by supporting family farming; (ii) by investing in sustainable farming and land use practices that increase soil health; and (iii) by building a more sustainable food system that ensures universal access to healthy food." Note that the resolution doesn't say anything about cows and the livestock emission of methane gas. Methane production from livestock accounts for almost a third[17] of the greenhouse gas emissions from U.S. agriculture, and more than a quarter of all methane emissions.

Economic security. A key goal in the Green New Deal is to "create millions of good, high-wage jobs and ensure prosperity and economic security for all people of the United States." The Green New Deal wants to guarantee "a job with a family-sustaining wage, adequate family and medical leave, paid vacations, and retirement security to all people of the United States." An FAQ sheet goes further and proposes guaranteeing economic security to "all who are unable or unwilling to work."

The Green New Deal is a plea to companies, citizens and communities (the 3 Cs) to change their behaviors in the interest of achieving better air, water and soil and reducing climate crises from hurricanes, tornadoes and floods.

The climate problem is worsening and one political party is busy denying it and not proposing any solutions. The quality of life in many U.S. communities is deteriorating and the same political party is without any real proposals of solutions. The Green New Deal comes along admittedly as an imperfect and imprecise set of remedies. Instead of viewing it as starting point for serious discussion and planning, the Republican Party prefers to satirize and clown about the proposals.

Here we end with a set of statements from persons who care deeply and wisely about mankind's future in a changing world.

[16] Sources of Greenhouse Gas Emissions, *EPA*
https://www.epa.gov/ghgemissions/sources-greenhouse-gas-emissions
[17] "Sources of Greenhouse Gas Emissions" *EPA*
https://www.epa.gov/ghgemissions/sources-greenhouse-gas-emissions

"Economic powers continue to justify the current global system where priority is given to speculation and the pursuit of financial gain. As a result, whatever is fragile, like the environment, is defenseless before the deified market." – **Pope Francis**.

"We should no longer measure our wealth and success in the graph that shows economic growth, but in the curve that shows the emissions of greenhouse gases. We should no longer only ask: 'Have we got enough money to go through with this?' but also: 'Have we got enough of the carbon budget to spare to go through with this?' That should and must become the centre of our new currency." – **Greta Thunberg**.

"Our economic system and our planetary system are now at war. Or, more accurately, our economy is at war with many forms of life on earth, including human life. What the climate needs to avoid collapse is a contraction in humanity's use of resources; what our economic model demands to avoid collapse is unfettered expansion. Only one of these sets of rules can be changed, and it's not the laws of nature." – **Naomi Klein**, author of *This Changes Everything: Capitalism vs. The Climate*

We need to recognize the threat that climate change poses to capitalism and our democracy. The Green New Deal serves as the **starting point** for our discussions and planning.

What will your company's future look like if you fail to act?

In *The Age of Surveillance Capitalism*[18] **Shoshana Zuboff** describes the power of **surveillance capitalism**[19] and the quest by powerful corporations to predict and control our behavior. Surveillance capitalism is a novel market form and a specific logic of capitalist accumulation. Zuboff characterized it as a "radically disembedded and extractive variant of information capitalism" based on the commodification of "reality" and its transformation into behavioral data for analysis and sales. She differentiated "surveillance assets", "surveillance capital", and "surveillance capitalism" and their dependence on a global architecture of computer mediation that she calls "Big Other", a distributed and largely uncontested new expression of

---

[18] The Age of Surveillance Capitalism: The Fight for a Human Future at the New Frontier of Power by Shoshana Zuboff https://www.amazon.com/Age-Surveillance-Capitalism-Future-Frontier/dp/1610395697
[19] https://en.wikipedia.org/wiki/Surveillance_capitalism

power which constitutes hidden mechanisms of extraction[20], commodification, and control that threatens core values such as freedom, democracy, and privacy (h/t *Wikipedia*).

According to Zuboff, surveillance capitalism was pioneered at **Google** and **Facebook**, in much the same way that mass-production and managerial capitalism were pioneered at Ford and General Motors a century earlier, and has now become the dominant form of information capitalism.

Zuboff identifies four key features of this surveillance:

1. The drive toward more and more data extraction and analysis.
2. The development of new contractual forms using computer-monitoring and automation.
3. The desire to personalize and customize the services offered to users of digital platforms.
4. The use of the technological infrastructure to carry out continual experiments on its users and consumers.

The excuse that companies have used for this unprecedented surveillance is "customer centricity."

We need your data in order to serve you better.

In China, the state has taken this a step further. In this article[21] in *The Atlantic*, Anna Mitchell and Larry Diamond describe the Chinese vision of surveillance:

Imagine a society in which you are rated by the government on your trustworthiness. Your "citizen score" follows you wherever you go. A high score allows you access to faster internet service or a fast-tracked visa to Europe. If you make political posts online without a permit, or question or contradict the government's official narrative on current events, however, your score decreases. To calculate the score, private companies working with your government constantly trawl through vast amounts of your social media and online shopping data.

---

[20] "How Silicon Valley Could Solve–Instead Of Cause–Income Inequality" *FAST COMPANY* https://www.fastcompany.com/3056209/how-silicon-valley-could-solve-instead-of-cause-income-inequality
[21] China's Surveillance State Should Scare Everyone, *The Atlantic* https://www.theatlantic.com/international/archive/2018/02/china-surveillance/552203/

TRUST ↓ ↑

SURVEILLANCE CAPITALISM vs COLLABORATIVE CAPITALISM

SURVEILLANCE CAPITALISM	COLLABORATIVE CAPITALISM
Centralized Power	Distributed Power
Profit is Purpose	Purpose beyond Profit
No Privacy	Privacy
Customer Data is Money	Customer Data is Protected
Value Extraction Model	Value Sharing Model
Community is Enemy	Community is Friend
Owner vs Customers	Customers as Owners
Owner vs Creators	Creators as Owners
Creates Inequality	Creates Equality
Creates Poverty	Creates Wealth
Performance is Profit	Performance is Satisfaction
Autocratic	Democratic
Command	Consensus
Unjust Profits	Just Profits
Opaque	Transparent
Excludes Society	Includes Society
Property Rights	Human Rights
Regressive	Progressive

© Christian Sarkar and Philip Kotler 2019

Why is this an issue for us? The authors explain:

China's experiments with digital surveillance pose a grave new threat to freedom of expression on the internet and other human rights in China. Increasingly, citizens will refrain from any kind of independent or critical expression for fear that their data will be read or their movements recorded—and penalized—by the government. And that is exactly the point of the program. Moreover, what emerges in China will not stay in China. Its repressive technologies have a pattern of diffusing to other authoritarian regimes around the world. For this reason—not to mention concern for the hundreds of millions of people in China whose meager freedom will be further diminished—democracies around the world must monitor and denounce this sinister creep toward an Orwellian world.

It can't happen here[22] ,you say. Well, in the US, we've all just learned[23] that the Federal Bureau of Investigation (FBI) and Immigration and Customs Enforcement (ICE) are exploiting state DMV records for facial recognition data without the knowledge or permission of drivers.

Is surveillance capitalism our future?

Collaborative capitalism must be based on consent and collaboration, which is the opposite of surveillance (state or private).

Can we bring democracy to the corporation?

Perhaps a democratic corporate structure with board representation for women and minorities, *and* the union, should be pursued, if not voluntarily, then by law. Groups like the Platform Cooperativism Consortium[24] are creating a space for **collaborative capitalism**. They are justifiably upset with **"platform capitalism"** because they view the Internet slipping out of ordinary users' control. Their point-of-view:

The power held by principal platform owners like Uber, Amazon, and Facebook has allowed them to reorganize life and work to their benefit and that of their shareholders. "Free" services often come at the cost of our valuable personal information, with little recourse for users who value their privacy.

The paid work that people execute on digital platforms like Uber or Freelancer allows owners to challenge hard-won gains by 20th-century labor struggles: workers are reclassified as "independent contractors" and thus denied rights such as minimum wage protections, unemployment benefits, and collective bargaining. Platform executives argue that they are merely technology (not labor) companies; that they are intermediaries who have no responsibility for the workers who use their sites. The plush pockets of venture capitalists behind "sharing economy" apps allow them to lobby governments around the world to make room for their "innovative" practices, despite well-substantiated adverse long-term effects on workers, users, the environment and communities. At the same time, in the gaps and hollows of the digital economy, a new model follows a significantly different ethical and financial logic.

---

[22] It Can't Happen Here by Sinclair Lewis https://www.amazon.com/Cant-Happen-Here-Signet-Classics-ebook/dp/B00DGZKU88/ref=onewwworldcom
[23] FBI, ICE plunder DMV driver database 'gold mine' for facial recognition scans, *ZD Net* https://www.zdnet.com/article/fbi-and-ice-are-using-dmv-gold-mine-for-facial-recognition-scans/
[24] A hub that helps you start, grow, or convert to platform co-ops, *platform cooperativism consortium* https://platform.coop/

Their goal is to foster **platform cooperativism** – a growing international movement that builds a fairer future of work, rooted in democratic ownership. Bottom line? The Internet *can* be owned and governed differently.

Is it any wonder that we are beginning to see a new wave of startups and businesses striving to do good, to create a **platform around purpose**? For example:

- Up & Go[25] offers professional home services like house cleaning, (and soon childcare and dog walking) by those who are looking for assistance with laborers from local worker-owned cooperatives. Unlike extractive home-services platforms which take up to 30% of workers' income, Up & Go charges **only the 5%** it needs to maintain the platform.
- Fairbnb.coop[26] is a **vacation rental platform** which **gives back 50% of its revenues to support local community projects** of your choice such as social housing for residents, community gardens and more.
- MiData[27] is a Swiss "health data cooperative," creating a data-exchange which will securely host member-users' medical records. MiData aims to out-compete private, for-profit data brokers and ultimately return the control and monetization of personal data to those who generate it.
- Gratipay[28] provides a free subscription-based patronage infrastructure for developers of open-source ventures, by enabling credit-card transactions at-cost, subtracting only the processing fees from users' subscriptions
- Ecosia[29] is a **search engine**, a social business, and the first German B-Corp. The profits generated from your searches are used to plant trees where they are needed most. As of this time, Ecosia has used over $9 million euros to plant over 61 million trees!
- MyCelia's[30] goal is to empower a fair, sustainable and vibrant music industry ecosystem involving all online music interaction services. They seek to unlock the huge potential for creators and their music related metadata so an entirely new commercial marketplace may flourish, while ensuring all involved are paid and acknowledged fully, and to see that commercial, ethical and technical standards are set to exponentially increase innovation for the music services of the future.

---

[25] *Up & Go* https://www.upandgo.coop/
[26] Community powered tourism, *fairbnb* https://fairbnb.coop/
[27] *MiData* https://www.midata.coop/en/home/
[28] *Gratipay* https://gratipay.com/
[29] *Ecosia* https://www.ecosia.org/
[30] *MyCelia* http://myceliaformusic.org/

- Brave[31] is an open source browser built by a team of privacy focused, performance-oriented pioneers of the web, led by Brendan Eich, the creator of JavaScript at Netscape. Brave blocks unwanted content by default, loads pages up to 8x faster than Chrome and Safari, and blocks the software that follows you around.

All of these companies are developing ecosystems and platforms built around connecting customers with the job to be done, for less, or for free. They are seeking to build a more equitable, **common platform** for value exchanges.

What this brings us to is the idea that we will soon see non-profit and **public exchanges** that enable value-exchanges between customers and creators that will build on community and local participation and more *democratic* and *inclusive* forms of governance and ownership.

Simone Cicero and **Stina Heikkilä** ask an important question: **Can public institutions be platforms[32]?**

Short answer: yes, they can, but it will take political and social activism.

What if there was a non-profit version of Facebook? What if your local post-office was a public platform for banking[33]?
"Move fast and break things[34]" may be a catchy phrase, but democracy is a fragile social construct. Stay tuned. Big disruptions are coming.

In Canada, there are **no political contributions from businesses or unions**. The will of the people trumps private interests.

Businesses can't be allowed to become monopolies, because monopolies stifle innovation and simultaneously create inequality. We have to get back to a level playing field.

---

[31] https://brave.com/
[32] Can public institutions be platforms? By *Stina Heikkilä*
https://stories.platformdesigntoolkit.com/can-public-institutions-be-platforms-c54e3cb633cf
[33] Post Office Banking: An Old Idea Getting New Life, *Nerdwallet*
https://www.nerdwallet.com/blog/banking/post-office-banking-2/
[34] The Era of "Move Fast and Break Things" Is Over, *Harvard Business Review*
https://hbr.org/2019/01/the-era-of-move-fast-and-break-things-is-over

Can the employee be a shareholder? An employee stock ownership plan (ESOP)[35] provides a company's workforce with an ownership interest in the company. What if an ESOP was also a B-Corp?

The future may not be capitalist after all. The capitalist market may increasingly be eclipsed, circumvented and overshadowed by an emerging Collaborative Commons[36].

At the heart of all of these shifts is what it means to be human and the values of humanity. **Activist brands must learn to collaborate, promote, and nurture the human family and the planet.**

Are you in?

---

[35] https://en.wikipedia.org/wiki/Employee_stock_ownership
[36] Post-Capitalism: Rise of the Collaborative Commons, *BASIC INCOME*
https://medium.com/basic-income/post-capitalism-rise-of-the-collaborative-commons-62b0160a7048

10. VOICES FROM THE FRONT LINE

In this section we speak to a cross-section of leaders – from business and beyond, to understand their work and contributions to making the world better.

We hope you enjoy these insights as much as we did.

- **Hanneke Faber:** The Future of Branding Is Activism
- **Scott Galloway:** Algorithms, Democracy, And Capitalism
- **Martin Whittaker:** Ranking America's Most Just Companies
- **John Elkington:** Beyond the Triple Bottom Line
- **Stephen Hahn-Griffiths:** From CSR To Corporate Reputation
- **Raj Sisodia:** From Conscious Capitalism to Healing Organization
- **John Ehrenreich:** Third Wave Capitalism
- **Nigel Sizer:** Will the Amazon Fires Wake Up the World?
- **Christopher Davis:** A Return to Activism
- **Stephen M.R. Covey:** The Trust Crisis: What Do Leaders Do Now?
- **Anjana Das:** Conscious Fashion
- **Hennie Botes:** The Challenge of Affordable Housing
- **Elsie Maio:** Does Your Business Have A Soul?
- **Stuart L. Hart:** Capitalism at The Crossroads
- **David Hinds:** Where There Is No Justice
- **Clark Fox:** Enough Is Enough
- **Hazel Henderson:** Some Prescriptions for Human & Planetary Health
- **Philip Kotler:** The War for The Soul of Capitalism

HANNEKE FABER
The Future of Branding Is Activism

Hanneke Faber is President, Foods & Refreshment at Unilever, and a member of the Unilever Leadership Executive. She joined Unilever in January 2018 as President of Europe and member of the Unilever Executive. In this role, she delivered strong results and accelerated the digitization of the European business. Hanneke spent most of her career in the FMCG and retail industry. Prior to joining Unilever, she worked at Royal Ahold Delhaize as Chief E-commerce and Innovation Officer, and member of the Executive Committee playing a key role in accelerating the company's e-commerce business. Between 2013 and 2016, she was Chief Commercial Officer & Member of the Executive Committee of Royal Ahold responsible for e-commerce, digital, innovation and customer branding. Hanneke started her career at Procter & Gamble where she became Vice President and global leader of three of P&G's top brands with a presence in over 180 countries. We asked her about the future of brand activism.

You have said that "brand builders need to take a stance, to create movements, to evangelize and even sacrifice." Can you explain what you mean?

I think it's really important that brands do three things to win, and I always use Ben & Jerry's as the example to illustrate those three things. At Unilever, they are our most purposeful, activist brand.

The first thing is they need to be *really clear on what their purpose is in life*, in the brand, so Ben & Jerry's purpose is phrased as "Peace, Love & Ice-Cream."

That's funny and easy to remember, but they're very serious about the peace and the love, as well as of course, the ice-cream – they make fabulous ice-cream. The ice cream is a given, but peace and love for them stands for issues such as inclusivity, a fair chance for everyone. They're concerned about justice in the criminal justice system, for example. They work for climate justice, because they figure that "ice caps, like ice cream, are best kept frozen."

They stand up for democracy, refugees, and fair trade. Peace building. Cleaning up the politics of influence. Equality for everyone, everywhere – from racial justice to marriage equality[37].

---

[37] LGBT Equality, *Ben & Jerry's* https://www.benjerry.com/values/issues-we-care-about/marriage-equality

The second thing a brand needs to do is to link that purpose to locally relevant issues that reflect the times. Twenty-five years ago, when Unilever bought them, peace, love & ice-cream meant something different. Today, peace, love and ice-cream means "Pecan Resist" which calls for peaceful resistance against the Trump administration's "regressive and discriminatory policies" targeting minority groups, women, people of color, LGBTQ people, refugees, and immigrants.

It's all about inclusivity, no walls, etc.

Pecan Resist supports four organizations that are working on the front lines of the peaceful resistance: Color of Change[38], Women's March[39], Neta[40], and Honor the Earth[41].

They've executed against their purpose in very different ways around the world. Local relevance is critical. In Germany there's also a refugee issue, not around a wall, but it followed Angela Merkel's *"wir schaffen das"* statement– which means we'll get it done. Ben & Jerry's is present at pro-immigration rallies – being very visible in the refugee debate.

The third point is that the brand must *talk about it*. You can't have a great purpose and do great things and then use old-fashioned TV advertising. So what Ben & Jerry's does is spend virtually all of its ad marketing money on activism – in events, in packaging, and in the store. All their money is spent on activism – on bringing their purpose to life. They *do* and then they *communicate*.

Has this been successful? Ben & Jerry's has enjoyed many years of double-digit growth here in Europe. I'm just trying to bring this on to more of our brands. Most of our brands had a purpose once upon a time when they started, but over time they've lost some of it.

How did you become a brand activist?

I grew up as a marketeer at Procter and Gamble – where it was all about superior product benefits. Tide washes whiter, and Pantene makes your hair shinier. That is important, but it's no longer sufficient in a time where

---

[38] *Change of Color* https://colorofchange.org/
[39] *Women's March* https://womensmarch.com/
[40] *NETA* https://netargv.com/
[41] *Honor the Earth* http://www.honorearth.org/

there's so much competition. Now you need people to love you not only for what you deliver, but also who you are. Just providing great ice-cream is not enough. Unilever has given me the license to be much more activist on individual brands.

From my own upbringing, my Dad led the massive European anti-nuclear movement in the 1970's and 80s, galvanizing almost 500,000 citizens to demonstrate in Amsterdam and London. He was a role-model. He also fought for human rights in Eastern Europe. I saw how activism can rally people and create a movement.

What do you say to critics who may feel that "purpose" is simply another marketing gimmick?

I will say you can't invent a purpose for a brand. You have to go back to the origin of the brand and ask where did it come from? What was the intent of the founder? The founders are critical. And then, you need to make that brand purpose relevant for today. We have brands which are over a hundred years old.

So, can a brand wake up?

The purpose of the brand will stay the same from when it was founded. But the local issue of today is likely to be rather different from a hundred years ago. A hundred years ago, Lord Lever was interested in hygiene – so children wouldn't die. Today, in the western world, the opposite may be true. Kids don't get dirty anymore, because they spend all their time playing on a screen. So now our job might be to encourage kids to get dirty, to go out and play, and yes, we'll help you clean up after. Dirt is good.

How can a brand purpose be brought to light?

What about the point of historian Rutger Bregman at Davos – who said that the rich just need to pay taxes, instead of avoiding them?

Well, he's right. We absolutely pay our fair share of taxes here in Europe. I think this is super important, because otherwise your 'say-do' gap become very high. If you're a tax dodger, you can't be serious about purpose.

And how do you feel about lobbying?

I don't think lobbying has to be a bad thing. At Unilever, we work with governments and NGOs to deliver on our company purpose ('to make sustainable business commonplace') together. To make real change, companies need partners.

But the tobacco industry lobbying, for example, that's another story. I've been lobbying in Brussels about plastics; as an industry, we produce a lot of plastic, and as Unilever, have committed that by 2025 all our plastics will be 100% recyclable, and we'll move to at least 25% recycled plastic. I would like to see incentives for all companies to be doing this. So, governments can play a role in helping companies do the right thing.

A lot of the plastic that's polluting the ocean comes from the single-use plastic *sachets* that were supposed to make products affordable for the base of the pyramid...

Yes. Single-use plastic sachets allow low-income consumers in developing countries to buy small amounts of quality products that would otherwise be unaffordable to them. These products tend to provide hygiene or nutrition benefits.

The problem is, these multi-layer flexible sachets are not currently recycled and have little or no economic value, so they leak into the environment.

We have invested in a new CreaSolv pilot plant in Indonesia, designed to recover polyethylene (PE), which accounts for more than 60% of the layers. We use this to produce high-quality polymers, which are then made into new sachets. Having proved the technology, we're now starting discussions with investors and other interested parties to develop a commercial plant.

Our industry has been a polluter, and we need to urgently take action, and be at the forefront of reducing that pollution. We have to be very careful that we do things for the *common good*, and not just what's good for our industry. So we want to collaborate with partners and governments to help them encourage businesses to clean up their act.

Are you planning on moving your offices to higher ground in the Netherlands, especially?

(Laughter)

How do you manage the balance between economic performance and social good? Are they mutually exclusive?

We don't see it as a balance. Purpose and profits are not opposed to each other. We believe more purpose leads to more profit. They are intricately linked. Companies with purpose last longer. Unilever has been around over a hundred years, and we want to be around for another hundred plus.

Brands with purpose grow faster than other brands. We have plenty of internal evidence of that. *70% of our growth comes from brands that we define as purposeful.* The purpose-brands have grown 46% faster than the other brands over the past three years. Our total shareholder return for the past 10 years has been really strong.

Finally, we also find that when our people can link their personal activism to the company's purpose, they are more engaged, more committed, do a better job, and stay the course. We attract the best people in the market – we're the no. 1 employer of choice in our industry in 44 countries around the world.

We've also saved money through waste and energy reduction. We have to disconnect growth from our environmental footprint. They don't have to go up at the same rate.

We have less risk – because we have more sustainable sourcing. We have less risk socially because of our commitment to human rights through the entire supply chain.

We don't see a trade-off, and if there is, we know it's temporary. We look for savings in other places in order to do the right thing, and we believe our customers will respond.

What do you see for the future of Brand Activism?

I think for the planet and for society, I hope it is the future. I don't think it's going to be easy for every brand. In our Unilever portfolio, we recently acquired a brand called the Vegetarian Butcher. Its purpose is *to free animals from the food chain* by offering a complete and delicious alternative to meat. They've done really well here in Holland.

Will the world go vegan by 2050? It may well be one of the most important things we can do as citizens to fight climate change.

SCOTT GALLOWAY
Algorithms, Democracy, & Capitalism

Scott Galloway is a Professor of Marketing at NYU Stern School of Business where he teaches Brand Strategy and Digital Marketing to second-year MBA students and is the author of the Digital IQ Index ®, a global ranking of prestige brands' digital competence. In 2012, Professor Galloway was named "One of the World's 50 Best Business School Professors" (Poets & Quants). Professor Galloway is also the founder of several firms including: L2, a subscription business intelligence firm serving prestige brands; Red Envelope, an e-commerce firm (2007, $100mm revs.); and Prophet, a global brand strategy consultancy with 250+ professionals.

Professor Galloway was elected to the World Economic Forum's "Global Leaders of Tomorrow," which recognizes 100 individuals under the age of 40 "whose accomplishments have had impact on a global level."

What was your reaction to NIKE's appointment of Colin Kaepernick as the face of their *Just Do It* anniversary campaign?

Colin Kaepernick. I think this was a *genius move*, regardless of what you think of the politics. NIKE just did the math. NIKE has a $35 billion-dollar business: $15 billion domestically and $20 billion abroad. Of the $15 billion, domestically, ten of it of it comes from people under the age of 35 who tend to skew urban, wealthy and progressive. So realistically, they probably only put 2-3 billion dollars at risk, that is, 20% of their domestic consumers might be offended. And if you look at the remaining $20 billion abroad, there's very few people abroad who think that America's got it right on race relations, or that we're headed in the right direction.

So, the calculus here is that this is an opportunity to come across as a leader, to do something bold, and strengthen your relationship with 90-95% of your customer base at the risk of alienating 5-10% - a good trade.

How has Trump changed "Brand America"? How does his behavior cost business in the future?

Trump has a very strong brand in the red states. You had 30 years of resentment at political correctness building up in red states where they became enraged by the current political narrative. And he came in and played that perfectly; the Trump brand has resonated in the red states. The

American brand via Trump has been strengthened in the middle of the United States at the expense of its brand equity on the coasts of the US and everywhere else.

Our alliances abroad have been weakened for political gain, and our enemies sense chaos. I don't think our enemies think the President's crazy, but they see the chaos, divisiveness, and weakness. In the past weeks, we've taken a real hit on moral leadership[42], where it has become obvious that the President would be happy to ignore murder as long it involved more tanks and more submarines being sold. I think the only person more upset than MbS as to how this has played out is the President.

We're trading off long-term moral leadership in exchange for short-term profits.

What should brands be doing now to solve society's biggest problems? Is this something they should pursue at all?

I'll start with CSR. Corporate Social Responsibility has largely been a failure. It's been vastly overestimated. Consumers today will largely buy the product that offers them the best value, the best trade-off. And the notion that consumers are so mindful…

There's always this hope that the more recent generation is more "woke" than the last generation, and then we look at the purchase patterns and it just doesn't bear out. They want Rolexes and BMWs regardless of those firms' behavior. Now there's probably a growing segment that pays more attention to this stuff, but I would argue that CSR, in the traditional sense, has not yielded the benefits that everyone thought it would.

Having said that, I will say this idea of corporations filling what we call the "moral void of capitalism" is not only an ideological or moral play, it's an economic play. The reason why is the following: *30% of America will elect 70% of our representatives*, so the red states are disproportionately represented, because they have no population – the cities have taken a ton of the population out of the ecosystem. In other words, people are moving from the farm to the city. You have this immense migration into the cities into the purple or blue states, so you have a funky dynamic. At the same time,

---

[42] "Silicon Valley's Saudi money crisis illustrates a decline of 'moral leadership' in America" *Vox* https://www.vox.com/2018/10/19/17998278/saudi-mbs-jamal-khashoggi-silicon-valley-kara-swisher-scott-galloway-facebook-portal-amazon-hq2

10% of the population is capturing 90 to 95% of the income gain. That 10% is neon blue.

When you're NIKE or Dick's Sporting Goods announcing that you're not going to carry assault rifles, it may be the right thing to do, but it's definitely the smart thing to do. Because educated, affluent moms and dads who have captured all of the incremental disposable income – they lean left.

So, the risk you're taking, traditionally, that if you enter the political fray, you're automatically alienating half the population – and that's still true. Now you're alienating 48%.

But you're only alienating, in some instances, 10% of the income growth. Because the Trump supporters, who I affectionately call "white and ignored" because the economy has failed them – they are angry, hardened, and a political force, but economically, it's never been better to be blue. The moment you look at income inequality – you see that the people making all the money, or incremental money, tend to be college-educated and tend to be in cities, which is *Latin* for Democrats. So a company entering the political fray and making moderate or progressive decisions or noises, no longer represents the dangerous calculus it used to. As a matter of fact, it may actually be the shareholder-driven thing to do. The people who burned their Nikes probably had to buy them on layaway. That population has been kicked in the nuts for the past 30 years. The reality is the political power has shifted right, while the economic power has shifted left.

So how can we fix this polarization? How do we bring people back together?

Mathematically, the biggest the space should be in the middle, but in terms of our political dialogue we have a coarseness, led by the President, where people now identify their friendships and relationships based on their political views. So I go on FOX once a week, because I want to get out of my echo chamber, at CNN we're in violent agreement, and when I'm at FOX, I like to think we learn from each other and have a little empathy for one another.

So the problem is there is no co-mingling – the rich kids go to private schools, so they have no empathy for the poor kids. Gerrymandering has caused our elected officials to be hard right or hard left, no middle ground.

And this is barely talked about, but we now spend more time on the phone screen than a TV screen, other than sleeping and working. The American public spends a majority of their time on algorithmically-controlled screens, more than any other activity except for sleep. That's a ten or twenty-year-old phenomenon.

The problem is that the content they are served is algorithmically driven, and the algorithm has been informed to maximize engagement – to drive as many clicks as possible – so that more Nissan ads can be served, and the owner of that algorithm can make more money and grow their shareholder earnings.

We bought into this false notion that connecting the world would be a good thing. Unfortunately, it's not. We, as a species, are tribal. And we immediately find people like us and enter into these hermetically sealed cohorts, where we don't pursue information like a judge trying to get to the truth, but instead we behave like lawyers, cherry-picking things that support our initial intuition or bias.

The result is that algorithms have figured out that the way to create more engagement and more clicks is to *foment rage*, embarrass the other side or point out the shortcomings of the other side.

If you look at the right rail on your YouTube channel, if you look at the Tweets that are served by the Twitter algorithm, or your newsfeed on Facebook, the moment they figure out you're a progressive, they'll show you video of a Senate intelligence panel making a fool of Betsy DeVos. If you're hard right, they'll immediately start serving you videos of Hillary Clinton saying stupid things.

The algorithm has figured out that the way to make more money is to drive us to a pole. We overlook the fact that these algorithms that determine the content in our lives have a profit incentive to create rage.

The monetization of rage? Wow.

You've written about the power of the four horsemen[43] - Amazon, Apple, Facebook Google. Can you explain how they threaten our Democracy, and what you feel should be done?

---

[43] "The Four Horsemen" – An Interview with Scott Galloway, *THE MARKETING JOURNAL* http://www.marketingjournal.org/the-four-horsemen-an-interview-with-scott-galloway/

I think we need to break them up. We're going to need DOJ action to break them up. We have to redefine anti-trust law. For the last 20-30 years, it's been all about whether a product is good for the consumer, and when a product is free, it's hard not to make that claim. What we need now is to look at anti-trust law and channel power – so if one company controls 93% share, is it creating an environment where small companies are having a hard time getting out of the crib? Are they stifling larger companies and euthanizing them prematurely?

So we're going to have to go to a new definition of anti-trust, something called Brandeisian anti-trust [44] – and once we have that, and I think we can have that, then we break these guys up.

The fastest way to curb Google's monopoly is to create a second search engine, and we have one, the second-best search engine in the world is YouTube. But right now YouTube and Google collaborate and coordinate instead of compete with each other.

Facebook, Instagram, WhatsApp, and Messenger, can all shrug their shoulders and say "you know there will always be bad actors, we can't guarantee the platform won't be weaponized," but if they were four separate companies, one of them would raise their hands in the effort to attract more advertisers, and say: "we're going to screen all our content, and guarantee that Russians aren't going to weaponize the platform."

I think the answer is competition. The answer is Capitalism. That for me is the key step because you want to thread the needle between curbing their power but at the same time maintain their stakeholder growth. You don't want to kneecap innovation and economic growth.

The danger is that for some reason we have decided that this is Capitalism. So people on the Left, like me, run to socialism, the attitude being "if this is Capitalism, I want out." But this is not Capitalism – this is surveillance Capitalism, an autocratic economy, that is totally fine-tuned to transfer wealth from the bottom 90% to the top 10% and that's not Capitalism.

---

[44] "The New Brandeis Movement: America's Antimonopoly Debate," *OXFORD Academic*
https://academic.oup.com/jeclap/article/9/3/131/4915966

Capitalism only works when you have a vibrant middle class. Capitalism that works has guardrails. It has regulations. It's thoughtful about how the engine of growth and the middle class thrive. So what I argue is that we don't have Capitalism – we need to restore Capitalism. This authoritarian economic rule must end.

MARTIN WHITTAKER

Ranking America's Most Just Companies

Martin Whittaker is the CEO of JUST Capital, an organization with the mission to "build a more just marketplace that better reflects the true priorities of the American people." JUST Capital ranks 1,000 of the largest publicly traded U.S. corporations on the issues Americans care about the most. In partnership with Forbes, they recently presented their 2018 list of America's Most JUST Companies [45].

How did JUST Capital come into being?

We can trace our origin back about six years ago, to conversations between Deepak Chopra, Rinaldo Brutoco who founded the World Business Academy, Paul Tudor Jones, and a couple of other founding board members who – as a result of an inquiry from one of Deepak's students at Columbia: *"how can companies and markets be more just, more fair, equitable, and balanced?"*– decided to see if they could create an organization, a non-profit, that could build a more just economy in America.

It appealed to those people because they were interested in exploring ways to train companies on becoming more just, and to channel capital to solve social, economic, environmental and health challenges. The definition of JUST, it was felt, should come *of, by, and for the people*, from the bottom up, so as to serve the interest of the public. This gave rise to the idea of polling the public to find out what matters the most to them.

The data, the rankings, are all derived in an open and transparent way. And this leads to a framework that companies could use to improve – to recognize best practices, and to learn what works – and to better align with all their stakeholders.

Today we find that 76% of working Americans said that when considering accepting a job, they would opt to work at a more just company, even if it paid less. In fact, the majority of working Americans say they would accept 20% less pay.

What did the latest survey uncover?

In 2018, companies in the JUST 100, compared to other Russell 1000 peers on average:

---

[45] 2020 Overall Rankings, *JUST Capital* https://justcapital.com/rankings/

- Pay their median workers 26% more.
- Pay a living wage to 12% more of their workers.
- Are 9 times more likely to have conducted gender pay equity analyses (69% vs. 8%).
- Are 4 times more likely to have PTO and parental leave policy disclosures (80% vs. 20%).
- Are nearly 2 times more likely to offer flexible work hours or day care (92% vs. 48%).
- Are nearly 4 times more likely to have diversity targets (31% vs. 8%).
- Recycle 8 times more waste (41% vs. 5%).
- Give 6 times as much to charitable causes per dollar of revenue (2.4% vs. .4%).
- Employ 2.4 times as many U.S. workers.
- Pay 99% fewer sales terms fines, 90% fewer environmental fines, 71% fewer worker safety fines, and 41% fewer EEOC fines per dollar of revenue.
- Have 4 times as many women directors (27% vs. 6%).
- Have a 5% higher return-on-equity (23% vs. 18%).

Topping the list was Microsoft[46], which performs exceptionally well on many of the issues defined by the American public – including Workers, the Environment, Customers, and Leadership & Shareholders.

See the complete JUST rankings at www.justcapital.com/rankings

What's the response been from the companies that are being ranked?

I would say cautiously welcoming, and the numbers support that. Three years ago, when we first opened up a portal for companies to submit their data, we only had a dozen or so companies that got involved. Last year it was about a 110, and this year its been over 335. So that's a good leading-indicator that companies support it.

What's important is that the companies that are engaged with us are not just the companies who do well in the rankings – they are companies from across the board, and all industries. There's been a frustration among companies with existing rankings and lists out there because some are "pay

---

[46] 2020 Overall Rankings, *JUST Capital* https://justcapital.com/rankings/

to play" others are "black box" methodologies, and some have a profit motive. All of this has helped us – we're a non-profit, and we want to transform capitalism in a positive way. Companies themselves, we see, want to be better on a whole raft of non-performance areas. We're trying to be as unbiased as possible – we don't have an ax to grind. So we see companies shifting from healthy skepticism to realizing we're providing them with real value, celebrate leadership and create a race to the top.

In the JUST rankings, what differences are you noticing between the leaders and the laggards?

Over the past five years, the JUST index, which is essentially the top 50% companies in every sector, has delivered 7% higher return on equity (ROE) on average than Russell 1000 companies not in the Index. And when you look at the JUST 100, you see a return on equity that's 5-7% higher than the rest of the field.

We haven't published this, but I can tell you that the top 20% of companies in every sector has outperformed the bottom 20% in live trading over two years in the region of 2000 basis points.

I think when we look at the quintiles – there's a real difference between the leaders and the laggards.

One of the vexing questions for both proponents and skeptics of sustainable investing is whether profitable companies perform better on ESG issues because they can afford to, or whether strong ESG performance can lead to higher profits. In other words, are profitable companies more just, or are just companies more profitable? We've run the Fama-French model and we find that 75-80% of the additional return is *not* explained by the traditional drivers of performance.

Without being naïve, we've identified an incredibly strong connection between companies that treat workers well, treat customers well, and make great products, reduce environmental impact, look after the communities in which they operate, look after shareholders, are well managed, all of those things – and their market performance. You know what, that's just common sense. It's completely intuitive that that would be the case, but we now have the data[47].

[47] LOOKING FOR STRONG RETURNS? ASK THE AMERICAN PEOPLE BY HERNANDO CORTINA & DOTTIE JONES, *JUST Capital* https://com-justcapital-web-

Are certain industries more progressive than others? Do you see practice sin one sector influencing the others?

In resource intensive industries, you see some best practice spread within the industry. And in the social dimensions – non-discrimination, paid family leave, diversity in boards, transparent leadership, etc. you may see more cross-industry spread. It doesn't matter what industry you're in to follow social best practices.

The benefits of having a strong, diverse, well-compensated highly engaged workforce – those are the areas where we see progress across the board. Companies recognize they can be better.

How does your polling get done? How do you decide which issues matter? Do you poll people on income-inequality, for example?

The public decides which issues matter. Right now, we're just focused on polling in the United States, although some of the issues are global. We poll tens of thousands of people using different types of polls.

The issues that arise are organized into 7 major themes:

1. How a company pays and treats its workers

2. How a company treats its customers

3. The nature of a company's products and services

4. The impact of a company on the environment

5. The support a company provides for local communities, in the U.S. and internationally

6. The impact a company has on the job market overall

7. A company's leadership and how well it serves its shareholders and investors

In terms of how we measure companies, we do see the deeper trends, and the underlying issues shine through. We are very mindful about income-inequality and inequality of opportunity, for example. We track how companies spend their tax windfall, how companies are investing in

v2.s3.amazonaws.com/wpcontent/uploads/2018/10/JUSTCapital_LookingforAlpha_10262 018.pdf communities, how companies are paying their executives vis-à-vis their lowest paid workers, living wages, etc.

So, taken together, we do get a picture of income-inequality, and how companies can intervene to do better. We have to be careful not to put our finger on the scale in terms of which issues get measured, but the good news is that all the critically important issues do come through from the public. We start with a blank sheet of paper, and we get back a lot of common sense.

Overall, people believe in business and they just want a fair shake. Political extremism happens when people don't believe the system works for them, or is rigged against them. That's what we're seeing with the rise of populism.

In 2018, as part of our annual survey effort, JUST Capital conducted a special poll of the American public, to better understand what people believe companies should be doing with their tax savings. When asked to indicate the percentage (ranging from 0% to 100%) of tax savings they thought should be allocated to each category, the results were:

24%	**Give back to workers in pay/benefits**
17%	**Create new jobs**
13%	Give back to customers in price reductions and/or additional benefits
12%	Invest in ways to reduce its environmental impact
12%	Create more and/or better products
11%	Give back to communities
10%	Pass savings onto its shareholders

The feedback is striking when looked at alongside our analysis. While Americans agreed that 24 percent of savings should go toward worker pay and benefits, worker issues account for just *six percent* of how companies are actually allocating their savings.

What are you finding when it comes to CEO-to-Average worker pay?

JUST Capital's breakdown of CEO-to-Median Worker Pay ratios for the top 1,000 publicly traded companies in America provides some fascinating context on the issue. Take the industry comparisons, for example. Ratios tend to be much "lower" (between 100 and 150:1) in technology fields, where workers are paid more on a relative basis and many tech CEOs are company founders with high ownership interest, tending to pay themselves less in salary. At the other end of the spectrum, in Retail and Automobile industries for example, a proliferation of lower skilled workers with lower pay results in very high discrepancies between the earnings of CEOs and workers, in some cases above 400:1.

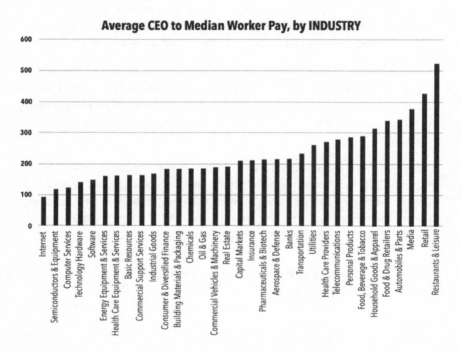

Based on our own studies, the increasing gap between CEO and employee pay in 2016 may actually be even greater than The Conference Board reports. SEC reporting rules for executive compensation require companies to report stock-based compensation in the year in which it's granted, not necessarily as its earned. For example, Apple CEO Tim Cook has earned an average of just over $7 million annually over the past five years, but he also received a $376 million bonus in 2011 that does not fully vest for 10 years.

Under JUST Capital's methodology, that bonus would then be spread evenly over 10 years and added to other annual compensation received during that span. Our numbers also include all executives who have held the title of CEO and/or Executive Chairman in a given year, while excluding all one-off cash payments (severance for departing executives and so-called "make whole" payments to new CEOs).

Using this methodology across the 728 companies in the Russell 1000 for which we have compensation data for both 2015 and 2016, median CEO compensation actually increased 9%, more than triple the average hourly earnings for employees in the private sector.

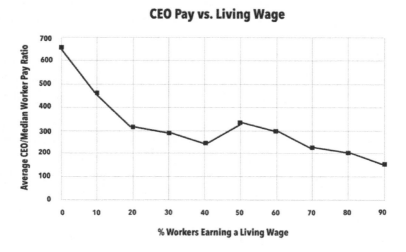

CEO Pay vs. Living Wage

We also took a look at how this ratio compares to other measures of worker pay. For example, we found that the companies that pay the majority of their workers a living wage tend to have a narrower gap between CEO and employee pay. Conversely, the gap is typically wider for companies that pay only a low percentage of workers a living wage. This stands to reason, as low-gap companies are in higher earning industries where more employees make a living wage.

Can you tell us about the JUST Scorecard?

We often hear from corporate leaders that they are looking for more tools and resources that can help them align their business practices with the values of the American public.

The JUST Scorecard[48] builds upon our survey results and the metrics we use to evaluate just business behavior in our Rankings, and creates a resource for companies to use in reviewing their own corporate practices. We hope businesses can use it as a guide with cross-functional teams to

---

[48] JUST Scorecard, *JUST Capital* https://com-justcapital-web-v2.s3.amazonaws.com/wp-content/uploads/2018/10/JUSTCapital_JUST-Scorecard_10262018-small.pdf

explore questions like: Where are we taking the lead on just business behavior? Where is there room for improvement?

What are you looking at for the future?

Corporate culture is going through a fundamental change – what people want, how they want to be treated, and their sense of purpose. The public is no longer ready to blindly accept authority – moral or otherwise – from business leaders. The whole area of human capital is changing.

We see issues like gender pay equity coming into the limelight – as companies work on fixing their policies and taking action to achieve real outcomes.

Surveillance and privacy are also becoming huge issues with the public. We see this in the controversy around leadership decisions around privacy. We could see an analogous situation to Big Tobacco – where technology and social media in particular begin to incur huge liabilities based on their current approach to privacy.

The bottom line is that companies that know who they are and what they stand for, and a North Star that helps them connect effectively with all their stakeholders will do better than those that don't. Significantly better, according to the data.

JOHN ELKINGTON
Beyond the Triple Bottom Line

John Elkington is a world authority on corporate responsibility and sustainable development. He is currently Founding Partner and Executive Chairman of Volans, a future-focused business working at the intersection of the sustainability, entrepreneurship and innovation movements. Back in 2004, BusinessWeek called John "a dean of the corporate responsibility movement for three decades." In 2008, The Evening Standard named him among the '1000 Most Influential People' in London, describing him as "a true green business guru," and as "an evangelist for corporate social and environmental responsibility long before it was fashionable." He is author or co-author of 19 books, the latest being The Breakthrough Challenge: 10 Ways to Connect Today's Profits with Tomorrow's Bottom Line, co-authored with former PUMA CEO Jochen Zeitz. He is a Visiting Professor at the Doughty Centre for Corporate Responsibility Cranfield University, Imperial College and UCL.

After 25 years you've "recalled" the Triple-Bottom Line (TBL) – the sustainability framework you brought to the world to examine a company's social, environment, and economic impact. Tell us why and what this means going forward.

As I said in the *Harvard Business Review* article[49], this is probably the first management concept subjected to a recall by the person who invented it.

So why recall it now? The Triple Bottom Line has failed to bury the single bottom line paradigm.

From the outset, the goal was *system change* — pushing toward the transformation of capitalism. It was never supposed to be just an accounting system. It was originally intended as a genetic code, a triple helix of change for tomorrow's capitalism, with a focus on *breakthrough change*, disruption, asymmetric growth (with unsustainable sectors actively sidelined), and the scaling of next-generation market solutions. Some businesses did move in this direction, as I point out, among them Denmark's Novo Nordisk, Anglo-Dutch Unilever, and Germany's Covestro.

---

[49] "25 Years Ago I Coined the Phrase 'Triple Bottom Line.' Here's Why It's Time to Rethink It" by John Elkington, *Harvard Business Journal* https://hbr.org/2018/06/25-years-ago-i-coined-the-phrase-triple-bottom-line-heres-why-im-giving-up-on-it

But we have a hard-wired cultural problem in business, finance and markets. Too many companies understood the concept as a balancing act, adopting a trade-off mentality. Profit first, then people and planet. Whilst CEOs, CFOs, and other corporate leaders move heaven and earth to ensure that they hit their profit targets, the same is very rarely true of their people and planet targets.

A much more comprehensive approach will be needed that involves a wide range of stakeholders and coordinates across many areas of government policy, including tax policy, technology policy, economic development policy, labor policy, security policy, corporate reporting policy and so on. Developing this comprehensive approach to sustainable development and environmental protection will be a central governance challenge – and, even more critically, a market challenge – through the 21st century.

How are B-corporations changing the equation. What can be done to get widespread adoption? What can be done with zombie management leading zombie companies?

They are a bright ray of hope. 2,500 businesses worldwide are now certified as B Corps. All are configured around the TBL — dedicated to be not just *"best in the world,"* but ***"best for the world."*** Companies like Brazil's Natura and Danone's North American operation are now B Corps, with other multinational corporations considering how to follow suit. But it's slow going. We are running out of time. In some countries, we see growing concern about 'zombie businesses,' propped up by government loans and spending all their cash on servicing debt— rather than investing in growth. But what if climate change created zombie economies? The 2013 World Economic Forum global risk report noted that the world economy is at growing risk as "persistent economic weakness saps our ability to tackle environmental challenges." Worst of all, is *zombie leadership* – leadership in business and government that is cynical about change – they have given up in a very practical sense. Business leaders can and must do much more to change the political *status quo.*

What is the Breakthrough Manifesto 1.0?

As WBCSD President and CEO Peter Bakker says, we need a revolution of capitalism. The Breakthrough Manifesto[50] says that we are now at the make-or-break in rebooting capitalism.

There are 7 points:

1. Breakdown is coming

2. Economic stimulus packages have skirted today's disasters

3. It's time to do the breakthrough politics

4. Business leadership is make-or-break

5. Financial markets are almost willfully blind to future risks—and opportunities

6. Disruptive change is needed

7. Join us

The time is almost past for going it alone. The nature and scale of the challenges now dictate that we work together.

Is capitalism, as it is practiced today, destroying the world? What are the barriers to breakthrough change?

"Extreme is the new normal," we are told, and this is an issue across all aspects and dimensions of our world. Key barriers include lobbying by those invested in the old order, ignorance (some of it willful), the complexity of the issues and responsibilities, the uncertainty that this complexity can induce, and the pervasive lack of political will. We have data on the barriers. Based on a survey of 1,660 experts in 117 countries, here's the list in order of priority:

- Lack of political will
- Vested interests in current approaches
- Complexity of issues/solutions/responsibilities
- Failure of markets to recognize future risks
- Misdirected financial incentives
- Regulatory gaps/constraints
- Poor economic performance of broad economy

---

[50] Breakthrough Business Leaders, Market Revolutions, *Volans* https://volans.com/wp-content/uploads/2016/02/breakthrough-business-leaders-market-revolutions.pdf

- Inadequate knowledge
- Lack of action by private sector
- Limitations of trade/international agreements
- Inadequate technologies

We have to build bridges, not walls. Business champions of breakthrough believe in capitalism, arguing that tomorrow's capitalism is the best cure for the ills of today and tomorrow. The problem is that we are seeing a deep-rooted shift in the nature and complexity of the challenges we face. One crucial tool in all of this, and one the World Economic Forum is developing is system mapping. This can help identify the key 'acupressure points' or levers of change.

You've described three scenarios for the future - system collapse, change-as-usual, and breakthrough. What must the C-level executive do to rise to the challenge?

System collapse comes in many forms. Some impending failures are easy to spot; others, involving systemic weaknesses, are harder to see coming. Breakdown mindsets often favor the 1% in the wealth spectrum over the 99%. At the same time, when we try to meet the needs of the 99%, we may also ignore crucial system conditions, like strains on resources or the natural environment, triggering different forms of breakdown.

Many Change-as-Usual approaches were semi- revolutionary when they began—including corporate social responsibility, socially responsible investment and sustainability reporting. Where they succeed in being adopted by companies and industry sectors, however, they often become diluted by wider priorities. There is a clear risk that CSR and even SRI leaders become too closely embroiled with those they support in the business world. The focus is often on rolling out current tools rather than on stretching towards tomorrow's breakthrough solutions.

The breakthrough scenario is an uncomfortable, high-risk zone. As Jeff Bezos of Amazon put it, "If you're inventing and pioneering, you have to be willing to be misunderstood for long periods of time." Most CEOs are not prepared to take that risk.

Unsurprisingly, then, incumbents don't make good insurgents, so the best place to look for the future is often at the fringes of the current system. But don't rule out all incumbents. The more nimble among them will find ways to link with insurgents to bring disruptive breakthrough solutions to scale.

Innovators, entrepreneurs, intrapreneurs, investors and—crucially— policy-makers work together to build a new economic and governance order, fit for purpose in a world of 7-going-on-9-billion neighbors. Progress is achieved through ventures that set ambitious targets and drive them through to change the market and political systems within which they operate.

What institutional innovations are required now to face the future?

The business of business is more than business. Increasingly, it is *change*. The focus must shift from short term profit to the long-term public interest. So our business models are flawed – they are part of the problem.

How do we get to a critical mass of Big Companies that act on this? The question now is whether CEOs and other business leaders will be content to remain part of the problem—or whether they have the will and the audacity to ride the rising breakthrough wave. It must be our business to ensure they have little choice in the matter.

What are you working on right now?

We're pursuing several breakthrough trajectories. They include the promotion of zero-based targeting in business and public policy, with our agenda outlined in *The Zeronauts: Breaking the Sustainability Barrier*, our involvement in initiatives pushing the boundary of science and technology, among them Biomimicry 3.8, founded by Janine Benyus, and cleantech venture fund Zouk Capital; plus C-Suite-focused platforms like The B Team, whose co-presidents are Sir Richard Branson and Jochen Zeitz, former CEO of PUMA. Jochen and I co-authored a book, *Tomorrow's Bottom Line*, exploring key dimensions of the system change agenda.

Is there a question you want to answer I haven't asked?

No. Great questions. Thank you. So perhaps less of a question and more of an observation. While we are working with corporations and businesses and governments to conceptualize and enact change, the world outside is taking matters into its own hands. The Earth's sixth major extinction is underway. Today livestock make up 60% of the biomass of all mammals on earth, followed by humans (36%) and wild mammals (4%). Our grandchildren will not see the world we saw.

STEPHEN HAHN-GRIFFITHS
From CSR to Corporate Reputation

Stephen Hahn-Griffiths is the Chief Reputation Officer at Reputation Institute[51]. He is a driving force in reputation thought-leadership, reputation risk management, corporate responsibility, integrated marketing communications, and brand purpose. As a champion of reputation intelligence and vanguard of RepTrak — Ri's proprietary reputation mining, measurement, and management framework — Stephen plays a pivotal role in spearheading best practices. In prior roles, he was as Chief Strategy Officer at leading multi-national agencies, including Leo Burnett, Mullen, and Saatchi & Saatchi. His academic credentials include an MBA from Stern, NYU. Stephen is an active public speaker on reputation and is often cited in leading media outlets, including Forbes, WSJ, USA Today, Financial Times, Associated Press, NPR, Bloomberg, and Lexis Nexis.

You've said that "reputation is less about Corporate Social Responsibility and more about a holistic approach to overall Corporate Responsibility (CR)" – can you explain what you mean?

Society is demanding that companies serve a greater purpose beyond their products and services. To earn and maintain a *strong* to *excellent* reputation, organizations must deliver in the areas of social, fiscal, environmental, and employer responsibility.

---

[51] https://www.reputationinstitute.com/

With these growing demands, we find that reputation is less about Corporate *Social* Responsibility and more about a holistic approach to overall Corporate Responsibility (CR). The social part, by itself, is restrictive. Yes, organizations are pressed to do the right thing across the social realm, but increasingly in other key areas as well.

Companies that lead in CR have earned greater levels of trust from stakeholders. CR helps companies establish foundations for mitigating, amplifying, and repairing trust. But the connection between trust and CR is yet to be established in the eyes of the general public and presents a unique opportunity for companies to impact their overall reputation while being genuine, responsible and trustworthy.

An example of a company that has significantly improved in corporate responsibility in recent years is **Adidas** AG. A top-20 performer in the 2019 CR RepTrak 100[52], Adidas has established itself as a leader in sustainability and an industry disruptor.

The concept of corporate responsibility (CR) has experienced an evolutionary process. What started as a focus on the environment — carbon footprint, recycling — and philanthropy is now a balancing act of business and society, thus intrinsically tied to profitability.

In other words, corporate responsibility is no longer just a measure of goodwill, **it's a measure of being a good business**. Investors and credit rating agencies increasingly rely on ESG (Environmental, Social, Governance) metrics, making corporate responsibility measures indispensable for the long-term success of organizations. For companies, that means delivering on CR is not optional, but a perquisite to profitability.

We know from our RepTrak studies that a lift in **corporate responsibility directly impacts a company's revenue** and other business KPIs.

For example, a 5-point increase in CR...

- increases **purchase intent** by 8.0%
- increases **advocacy** by 7.4%
- makes your company 4.7% more **crisis-proof**
- increases **trust** by 6.0%

---

[52] "Summary of Global CEO 2019 RepTrak study" *Reputation Institute*
https://ri.reputationinstitute.com/hubfs/_PDF/2019%20CEO%20RepTrak%20Summary.pdf

- helps **attract better talent** with a 5.1% increase

We define reputation as an emotional connection between organizations and their key stakeholders. Leaders in CR maintain a stronger emotional connection compared to performance in the 7 dimensions of reputation *(what companies do, rather than the emotion that they evoke).*

Today more than ever, employer reputation is a key business driver. For example, a company with a poor reputation spends at least 10% more per hire to be competitive vs its highly reputed rivals. That increases operating expenses and negatively impacts the company as being viewed as an "employer of choice."

Purpose and reputation are critical today to attract talent, it accounts for over 70% of the reason why talent choses a company over another!

CEOs are increasingly concerned about talent availability and core skills needed. But talent today seems to be looking elsewhere. Global employers are concerned of losing out to high-growth enterprises, but there's still a wide gap between beliefs and intentions and action. For example, 79% of business leaders think that purpose is central to business success, but only 34% say that purpose is a guidepost for decision-making.

That gap is telling.

What are the top companies getting right?

Two key points:

- ***Their messaging is aligned to corporate purpose.*** The top 10 companies in CR, have higher levels of brand expressiveness, with 41% of respondents who perceive the companies to be genuine in what they do and say, and with 32% who agree that the companies communicate in a relevant manner. Yet, there is a lot more opportunity to communicate corporate purpose with key stakeholders. Over 60% of the public are not sure or ambivalent to companies' corporate expressiveness and communication.
- ***They lead with responsibility and ethics.*** Among respondents familiar with CEOs, companies see a very significant 9.3-point lift in CR. Companies within the CR top 10 have CEOs who are seen to be responsible, behave ethically, and care about social causes. These CEOs have responsibility scores that are 5-points higher than companies that did not make the top 100.

How do you measure reputation? What are the 7 dimensions of reputation you've developed?

We built a research-based data driven means-end model by which to calibrate reputation. It's a Reputation Intelligence System that yields quantifiable and actionable insights along seven dimensions:

- *Products/Services*
  Do you deliver on a world-class experience? High-quality Products and Services can profoundly shape reputation.
- *Innovation*
  Is your company static or dynamic? Forward-thinking and creatively-inspired companies have a reputational advantage.
- *Workplace*
  Corporate culture directly impacts recruitment, retention, and talent acquisition. Positive perceptions of a workplace can help you achieve employer of choice status.
- *Governance*
  Can your company be trusted to do the right things when no one is looking? Practicing good governance is key in earning trust in times of crisis.
- *Citizenship*
  How does your company align with social values? Being a good corporate citizen has a positive impact that helps to make the world a little better.
- *Leadership*
  Companies with executives who align brand purpose with daily business activities outperform those focused solely on financials.
- *Performance*
  Financials matter, but it is important to link your financial success with positive social impact to maintain a license to operate.

RepTrak, as we call it, identifies which dimension is the most important to any given market, industry, or company in driving reputation and business results. We examine reputation by industry – Airline, Consumer, Energy, Financial Services, Pharma, Retail, and Technology etc.

What role does the CEO play? How does the CEO represent the brand?

CEOs are being judged by the merits of ethics and not just EBITDA, or share price. First and foremost, a CEO needs to be responsible and behave ethically.

Data shows that in driving CEO reputation, the perceptions of a CEO's ability to act responsibly, exhibit human empathy, and care about social causes matters most. Although it seems obvious, we should state it anyway: CEOs with strong reputations can elevate the reputations of their companies, while CEOs with weak reputations could pose a risk for their company.

The reputation of CEOs is shaped by four key dimensions:

- *Leadership*
  The CEO has a strong leadership image, clear strategic vision, and anticipates change.
- *Responsibility*
  The CEO acts responsibly, behaves ethically, and cares about social causes.
- *Influence*
  The CEO has good communications skills, a global perspective, and is viewed as highly influential.
- *Management*
  The CEO is an effective manager who understands the business and creates stakeholder value.

Fulfilling expectations in terms of Leadership, Management, and Influence are just table stakes. To be highly reputable today, a CEO needs to lead the way by doing what's right when no one is looking:[^]

- Act responsibly, and demonstrate a focus on social issues.
- Deliver on what matters and simply do the right thing.
- Meet elevated expectations for ethical behavior.
- Be empathetic and human while creating an emotional connection with stakeholders.
- Deliver assurance to those that matter most during a time of instant public judgment.

Can you name some of the leading CEOs in your 2019 rankings?

The CEOs who led the way in 2019 ranked highly based of the perceptions of taking responsible actions. These ten individuals took a stand on the things that matter to the stakeholders they serve:

Fabrizio Freda, The Estée Lauder Companies; Carsten Spohr, Deutsche Lufthansa; Ben van Beurden, Royal Dutch Shell; Michael Dell, Dell; Niels B. Christiansen, The LEGO Group; Ralph Hamers, ING; Chris Nassetta, Hilton Worldwide; Shuntaro Furukawa, Nintendo; Emmanuel Faber, Danone; David Holl, Mary Kay.

More and more CEOs are coming to us for an objective view of where they stand. We help leaders at the world's largest companies build credibility with the people that matter most — by delivering data-driven insights about how they are truly perceived.

What happens when things go wrong? Can you give us an example?

I don't think it's appropriate for me to publicly disparage any given company. But in general, when things go wrong, the data tells us that reputation recovery is especially driven by increases in perceptions of Corporate Responsibility – Workplace, Governance and Citizenship; but these are also some of the dimensions in which companies have the lowest scores, indicating a significant upside opportunity for all businesses.

RAJ SISODIA
From Conscious Business to Healing Organization

Raj Sisodia is a leading figure in the Conscious Capitalism[53] movement - he is the FW Olin Distinguished Professor of Global Business and Whole Foods Market Research Scholar in Conscious Capitalism at Babson College in Wellesley, MA.

Let's begin by asking: what is a conscious business? And what is conscious capitalism?

Conscious Capitalism is not a business strategy or business model. It is a comprehensive *philosophy* of doing business.

Too many businesses generate financial wealth at the expense of social, cultural, environmental, intellectual, physical, and spiritual wellbeing. They are *extracting* value rather than creating value. Conscious Capitalism is about doing business with a spectrum of positive effects, not having one positive "main" effect and many negative "side" effects. Conscious businesses spend money where it makes a positive difference. They don't waste money on unnecessary advertising, gimmicky promotions, and the revolving door of high employee and supplier turnover. They empower people and engage their best contribution in service of a higher sense of purpose. They make a net positive impact on the world.

Let's define this more clearly.

The four tenets of Conscious Capitalism are interconnected and build on important academic work relating to purpose, stakeholder management, leadership, and culture:

Higher Purpose: Recognizing that every business should have a higher purpose that transcends making money. It is the difference the company is trying to make in the world. By focusing on its Higher Purpose, a business inspires, engages and energizes its stakeholders.

Stakeholder Orientation: Recognizing that the interdependent nature of life and the human foundations of business, a business needs to create value with and for its various stakeholders (customers, employees, vendors,

---

[53] https://www.consciouscapitalism.org/

investors, communities, etc.). Like the life forms in an ecosystem, healthy stakeholders lead to a healthy business system.

Conscious Leadership: Human social organizations are created and guided by leaders - people who see a path and inspire others to travel along the path. Conscious Leaders understand and embrace the Higher Purpose of business and focus on creating value for and harmonizing the interests of the business stakeholders. They recognize the integral role of culture and purposefully cultivate Conscious Culture.

Conscious Culture: This is the ethos - the values, principles, practices - underlying the social fabric of a business, which permeates the atmosphere of a business and connects the stakeholders to each other and to the purpose, people and processes that comprise the company.

How do you recognize a conscious culture?

A Conscious Culture is captured in the acronym TACTILE:

- Trust
- Authenticity
- Caring
- Transparency
- Integrity
- Learning, and
- Empowerment

The word "tactile" also suggests that the cultures of these companies are very tangible to their stakeholders as well as to outside observers; you can feel the difference when you walk into a conscious business versus one that is purely driven by a profit motive and run just for the benefit of shareholders.

These four elements of Conscious Capitalism are mutually reinforcing, and describe a comprehensive systems perspective on business that is far richer and more complex than traditional machine metaphors.

Of course, we don't presume that the way we have defined Conscious Capitalism is the final word. What we have offered is a dynamic definition, one that will evolve as our consciousness grows.

How is a conscious business different from a traditional business?

Almost everything about a conscious business is different from traditional business.

A firm that uses financial incentives alone to attract and motivate a CEO will get precisely what it pays for: a CEO who is primarily motivated by money.

Such leaders are incapable of inspiring their employees to achieve extraordinary levels of engagement, creativity, and performance. The most effective leaders are those who transcend self-interest; they are primarily motivated by purpose and service to people.

We don't believe that a firm that treats its employees unfairly can prosper in the long-term in the transparent and incredibly connected world we now inhabit.

Good employees have a choice, and over time will migrate to firms that offer them not only fairness, but more importantly the opportunity to find meaning and purpose in their work. Companies cannot offer attractive, innovative products if they do not have engaged employees and high-quality suppliers.

This is an evolutionary process. Apple, E-Bay, Microsoft, Facebook, and H&M are all gradually moving towards a more conscious way of being, as are many other companies such as Wal-Mart, McDonald's, General Electric, and Procter & Gamble.

What about outsourcing?

Many companies do outsource production to low-wage locations to lower costs, and many lay off employees to improve their financial performance.

Our experience with conscious businesses is very different. Customers are increasingly aware that there are good ways and bad ways to lower costs. Conscious businesses lower their costs and offer attractive prices to customers by eliminating wasteful spending, not by squeezing their employees or suppliers.

There is nothing inherently bad about outsourcing. If it is done in a conscious manner, outsourcing creates opportunities in less-developed parts of the world and helps to lift people out of poverty. *However, if it is done purely to reduce costs without regard to its human consequences, it is no doubt harmful.*

When sales decline, conscious businesses do not automatically revert to layoffs in order to lower costs. In the recent economic downturn in the U.S., conscious businesses such as The Container Store and REI made it through by operating with a sense of *shared sacrifice*. Despite steep declines in sales, they chose to protect the jobs and pay of their most vulnerable employees: those who work part-time (referred to by The Container Store as "primetime" employees). Salaried employees took across the board pay cuts to get through the downturn. Such companies have emerged from the recession with stronger cultures and a deeper sense of shared purpose than they had before.

And what about financial performance?

Our research has found that conscious companies significantly outperform the market financially; in the first edition of my book *Firms of Endearment: How World Class Companies Profit from Passion and Purpose* (2007), we found a nearly 9-to-1 ratio of outperformance over a ten-year period. In the second edition (2014), the ratio was 14-to-1 over a 15-year period.

The financial dimension of corporate performance depends on a company's ability to grow its revenue and improve its efficiency. Conscious businesses are superior on both of these dimensions, because they are better aligned with the true needs of customers and are focused on investing money where it makes a difference (such as on rank-and-file employees and high-quality suppliers) and saving money in non-value adding areas (such as excessive marketing costs and high levels of employee turnover).

Currently, much of the growth of conscious businesses comes at the expense of their less-conscious competitors. If their competitors also become conscious businesses, such companies can still find healthy ways to grow by creating additional value through meeting the higher-level needs of their customers.

And, as competition among conscious businesses increases, it creates further impetus for innovation that benefits the companies and all of their stakeholders.

We have been working to understand how conscious businesses are able to operate with superior financial results while creating many forms of wealth and wellbeing for all of their stakeholders, including society. It boils down to something quite simple: *these companies knowingly operate with lower gross margins than they could achieve, but are still able to achieve higher net margins than their traditional competitors.*

Most companies try to maximize their gross margin by looking for the cheapest suppliers they can find, and then using whatever bargaining power they have to squeeze them as much as they can to get ever-lower prices. As a result, they end up with low-quality suppliers who struggle to stay profitable, and who can ill afford to invest in new technologies or anything else that will improve their quality or make their products more innovative.

Most companies also try hard to keep their payrolls down, minimizing what they pay to their rank-and-file employees, and are stingy with critical benefits such as health insurance. They try to use part-time employees as much as possible, keeping them under the threshold where they would qualify for any kind of benefits. They provide minimal training to their employees, and accept high employee turnover as inevitable.

Conscious businesses are very selective about their suppliers, looking for innovative, quality-focused companies that also operate in a conscious manner. They enter into mutually beneficial long-term partnerships with them. Suppliers are well paid, and in turn pay their own suppliers and employees well.

Conscious businesses also pay their rank-and-file employees very well, significantly above the industry norm, and are generous with benefits. Since their direct costs are higher, the gross margin of a conscious business is typically lower than average.

Conscious businesses typically have to spend very little on marketing. This is because they have legions of satisfied and delighted customers who are loyal and passionate advocates for the company. We have found that many conscious businesses spend as little as 10 to 25% of the industry average spending on marketing. This represents an enormous cost saving, at a time when marketing costs have been growing rapidly for most companies.

Conscious businesses typically operate with extremely low levels of employee turnover, thus saving greatly on new employee hiring and training. Turnover at The Container Store, a perennial on "best places to work" lists, is in the low single digits, in an industry where turnover often exceeds 100%. Employees at such companies are loyal, experienced, highly engaged and extraordinarily productive.

Such businesses take great care to hire people whose personal passions are aligned with the corporate purpose. At a time when overall employee engagement levels are shockingly low, conscious businesses have employees who are loyal, passionate, energetic, and creative. For them, their work is not just a job or a career, it is a calling. For example, REI is passionate about reconnecting people with nature, and all of its employees are outdoor enthusiasts for whom every day at work is deeply fulfilling because they get to help customers discover the joy and beauty of being with nature.

Conscious businesses have lower administrative costs because they continuously strive to eliminate non-value adding expenses, gathering ideas from their employees and suppliers about how to do so. They also look to control essential expenses such as health care costs, not through across the board cuts, but by devising creative ways to achieve win-win outcomes.

Conscious companies typically operate with much leaner management structures than do traditional businesses. They have created systems in which the right people are doing the right jobs and are given a great deal of autonomy. Most employees operate in the "value zone," where they are actively creating real value for customers rather than "managing" each other. These companies are designed to be largely self-organizing, self-motivating, and self-managing.

Finally, conscious companies operate in a system of very high trust between all stakeholders, and thus their legal costs are much lower than the norm. They understand their customers deeply, produce outstanding products (due in no small part to the fact that they have world-class suppliers), and thus have much lower levels of product returns.

What about executive pay?

The notion of pay equity at such companies is driven more by internal rather than external considerations. Senior executives at such companies are modestly paid relative to their peers at other companies. For example, Whole Foods Market has adopted a policy that no one can be paid more than 19 times the average salary (the typical ratio at large publicly traded companies are 350-400 times). The only way for executives to earn more at such companies is to raise the average salary of all employees.

What do you say to critics who question this "consciousness"?

Like humans, no company is perfect, and some companies that we identified as conscious businesses have stumbled in recent years. These companies have only to rediscover their own essence in order to get back on track.

Even the most conscious individuals sometimes act unconsciously. This does not negate the value of being conscious. The test of a truly conscious business is its ability to learn and grow from such experiences, and to emerge even stronger and more committed to a conscious way of being.

How does a business become conscious?

Obviously, it starts with the leadership. We invite business leaders to join us at our Conscious Capitalism CEO Summit in Austin in early October this year. It's designed for pioneering CEOs who conduct their business by focusing foremost on fulfilling the deeper purpose of their organizations and creating value for all of their stakeholders.

NOTE: learn more at www.consciouscapitalism.org

Now we switch to the latest book, co-authored with **Michael Gelb***: The Healing Organization: Awakening the Conscience of Business to Help Save the World.*[54].

What is a Healing Organization? And what made you and Michael Gelb write this book?

The Healing Organization says that done right, business can alleviate suffering and elevate joy in our lives – while still delivering extraordinary performance. For us, writing this book was a sacred undertaking. It was something we had to do. We want to alleviate the unnecessary suffering caused by the way in which business is done. It doesn't have to be this way.

The book is about the business as healing. The scope of our concern goes well beyond employees and their families. It includes all those whose lives are touched by your company, including the environment and indeed all life on the planet.

In our view, business can become a place of healing for employees and their families, a source of healing for customers, communities, and ecosystems, and a force for healing in society, helping alleviate cultural, economic, and political divides.

---

[54] The Healing Organization: Awakening the Conscience of Business to Help Save the World by Raj Sisodia and Michael J. Gelb https://www.amazon.com/dp/B07KDZ2SGF/

What's the difference between a traditional business and a Healing Organization?

A traditional business might say: "Here is an opportunity to make money by exploiting a need or gap in the marketplace."

A business with a slightly more advanced mindset says, "Here is an opportunity to make money by exploiting a need or gap in the marketplace, and we will initiate some corporate social responsibility initiatives and employee wellness programs to help mitigate the suffering we cause. And we will throw some money at a few charities."

A more evolved conscious business leader says, "Here's an opportunity to make a profit while serving customer needs and the needs of all stakeholders, including our communities and the environment."

A Healing Organization says," Our quest is to alleviate suffering and elevate joy. We serve the needs of all our stakeholders, including our employees, customers, communities, and the environment. We seek to continually improve the lives of all stakeholders while making a profit so that we can continue to grow and bring healing to the world."

Wow. So how does a company become a Healing Organization?

Sometimes businesses actually begin with this kind of noble healing purpose. In the book we talk about LifeGuides, a Public Benefit Corporation and how it was founded. Just as Match.com pairs people for love, LifeGuides connects people in need with those who can help.

In other cases, companies are transformed into Healing Organizations when the leader experiences an awakening.

Modern democracy and capitalism took root in the United States, evolved here, and then spread to other parts of the world. But now we are at an inflection point. This is a critical juncture in history. We must awaken our conscience and consciousness to meet the crises of our time.

This book is about how business is not only the cause, but also the solution of many of the world's problems.

How did we get to this point? We have been told that the purpose of business is profit. Is this narrative obsolete?

What is the purpose of business? It is not, as Peter Drucker wrote, "to create and keep a customer," and it is not, as Milton Friedman proclaimed, to make a profit. Creating and keeping customers and making profit are important measurements of success that are often mistaken for purpose. The purpose of business, now more than ever, must be to alleviate suffering and elevate joy by serving the needs of all stakeholders, including employees, customers, communities, and the environment.

We have to make a distinction between bad people and bad ideas.

The realms of business and corporate governance have been under the sway of many bad ideas for a long time, or at least ideas that are now obsolete. A short list of these bad ideas includes:

- Human beings are driven only by self-interest and are purely rational economic value maximizers.
- Business exists only to maximize profits for its owners.
- Work only matters in people's lives to the extent that it generates income.
- The best way to motivate people is to use a combination of carrots and sticks.
- The job of the leader is to motivate, pressure or coerce people into behaving in ways that achieve the leader's objectives.
- The world of work is separate and distinct from the world of our personal lives.
- The best way to increase profits is to squeeze employees and suppliers.
- It's acceptable to mistreat people and foul the environment if you donate lots of money to charity.

These ideas have been crystallized into theories and have become dogma for many business leaders. But when money-centric robots aren't programmed with moral responsibility, the result is often evil.

In the book you introduce three principles that define the Healing Organization. Can you mention them briefly? What is the Healing Organization?

The three principles are:

- *Primum non nocere*– first do no harm
- *Malus eradicare*– root out evil

- *Amor vincit omnia*– love conquers all

The premise of the Healing Organization is simple: when we understand and meet people's real needs, we help to heal them, while healing ourselves and generating abundance. Conversely, when we uncover and prey on their cravings, desires, fears, and addictions, we hurt them, and ultimately we hurt ourselves, our children, and our planet.

Let's go deeper – a specific example. Can you tell us about a specific Healing Organization?

Sure. In the book we highlight many companies that are making the transition.

Incorporated in the little Costa Rican town of La Florida in 1908, The Florida Ice and Farm Company (FIFCO) started as an agricultural and ice manufacturing business. Over time, the company evolved to focus primarily on brewing beer. It not only stopped polluting this natural treasure, but is now actively protecting it, while also showing other businesses around the world how to make more money by being better stewards of Pachamama, Mother Earth.

How did this transformation happen? It wasn't a sudden enlightenment but rather a gradual process that began with CEO Ramon Mendiola listening to his stakeholders, and eventually bridging the gap between business-as-usual and applying the values he learned from his parents.

What do we learn from FIFCO's experience in not only mitigating but in many ways reversing its environmental impact?

Here are six lessons:

1. Listening to and honoring all stakeholders to better understand the problem as well as participate in the solution.
2. Having a higher purpose that encompasses flourishing in all dimensions.
3. Taking a holistic approach to business, which looks at social, environmental, and financial performance simultaneously rather than sequentially.
4. Linking measurements and compensation to holistic goals. Forty percent of compensation for FIFCO leaders is linked to environmental and social goals, likely headed to 50 percent in the future.

5. Maintaining a visible, public commitment to tangible goals. This creates pride, enthusiasm, and optimism among employees and other stakeholders.

6. Collaborating widely. None of these challenges can be solved alone, especially the more significant ones. You need to partner with academia, civil society, and the government-not just locally but in many cases globally.

When he started listening to stakeholders' concerns around the company's footprints, Mendiola's consciousness was still very much rooted in fear. But after he started engaging with them, he began to see that the company could have a tremendous positive impact. Fear dissipated and was replaced by excitement and then joy.

He made a series of bold public social commitments, having to do with water, carbon, and solid waste. The company delivered on all of them on schedule, leading to a surge of pride in its employees. This was a great insight for the CEO: doing the right things makes people happy.

Even though the company's environmental and social initiatives were all externally directed, they found that the biggest impact was on people: "The engagement and commitment of my most important stakeholders, which are my employees, went up tremendously."

That creates a virtuous cycle: doing the right things leads to greater employee commitment and engagement, which leads the company to be even more effective at doing the right things.

JOHN EHRENREICH
Third Wave Capitalism

John Ehrenreich[55] is an American author, academic, and clinical psychologist who has published books on health policy, US social policy, and US history. He is the author of Third Wave Capitalism: How Money, Power, and the Pursuit of Self-Interest have Imperiled the American Dream *(2016).* [56]

How did you come to write this book?

I was a 60s social activist. The book came out of some contradictory feelings I was having about the state of the country. There was a sense of nostalgia for some of the good things about the America I grew up in that have now disappeared, combined with a realistic view of how bad things were for many people in the 50s and 60s - for African Americans, for women, for gay and lesbian men and women, for the poor. And there was the realization that we were losing the gains we had made through the sacrifices of so many - students, civil rights and feminist activists, the protests. I wanted to make sense of what is happening now. I asked myself is there a coherent, underlying narrative that explains why our schools are failing, why the improvements in the state of black Americans have halted, why the increased maldistribution of wealth, why the failure to reduce poverty, etc. Was there a pattern to this decline? What was it? That was the starting point for this book.

Let's look at a question you ask at the very beginning of your book: "How did we go from 'how lucky I am to be an American' to the 'American Dream is in trouble'?"

In many ways the United States of today is a far better country than that of the 50s and 60s. We are richer, healthier, better educated, and there certainly have been enormous gains for women, people of color, gay and lesbian and transsexual men and women. And yet despite the gains in wealth and well-being, our faith in the American Dream seems long gone. Our politics are gridlocked and impotent in the face of a faltering economy, climate change, increasing income inequality, and racism. Our public

---

[55] http://www.jehrenreich.com/index.php?p=1_4_About-John-Ehrenreich
[56] Third Wave Capitalism: How Money, Power, and the Pursuit of Self-Interest Have Imperiled the American Dream by John Ehrenreich (Author)
https://www.amazon.com/Third-Wave-Capitalism-Self-Interest-Imperiled/dp/1501702319

schools, once the wonder of the world, seem to lag behind those of a dozen other, poorer countries. Our healthcare system is the most expensive, yet least accessible and one of the least effective in the industrialized world. Racial inequities persist. The poverty level is a third higher than in 1973 and the middle class has slipped backwards - losing the gains made in the past. We may have a black president, but incarceration of black men (mainly for non-violent drug offenses) is five time that for white men, and sixty years after Brown vs Board of Education, well over a third of black students nationwide attend a school with fewer than 10 percent white students. We have re-segregated our schools.

My book is about all this - the changes that are part of what I call "Third Wave Capitalism."

Third Wave Capitalism? What is that?

Historical turning points are not always clear-cut, but in general, we can see three clear phases in the history of American capitalism.

The first phase - Industrial Capitalism - was the era of both small entrepreneurs and the robber barons and extended through most of the nineteenth century. It was a time when, the government's role in the economy was much less than now. This was a turbulent period for the United States, with widespread unrest, populist struggles, and battles between workers and their employers.

Then in the late 19th and early 20th century, we saw the emergence of Corporate Capitalism. Both government and corporations were forced to accommodate to some degree the needs of workers, farmers, and consumers. At the same time corporate leaders began to see the government as a mechanism that could directly serve their needs. The modern welfare state came into being, and business was increasingly regulated. Unions and other advocacy groups provided a counterbalance to the power of big business. There were big, industry-wide strikes that sometimes took on a "class struggle" tone, but after 1946, a general social compact emerged. Unions would accept the underlying class relationships of society, agree to long-term contracts that protected employers for the threat of frequent strikes, and give up the right to bargain over some issues, in exchange for employment stability, a steady increase in real wages, and health and pension benefits.

Since the 1970s, American capitalism has been evolving into a distinctive third phase - what I call "Third Wave Capitalism." This phase saw the dramatic growth of globalization - the rise of multinational corporations with global supply chains. Non-profit organizations became larger as well - now some 10% of the American population working for a non-profit - but the non-profits behave more and more like for-profit businesses.

Technological innovation transformed the workplace - from materials to electronics and automation, changing the workplace yet again. Around 1972, we also see a decoupling of productivity and wages. While productivity kept rising, wages did not. This is also when the rise in CEO pay began its dizzying ascent. Inequality grew.

How does Third Wave Capitalism destroy the "commons"?

There is also an ideological shift. There is a decline in the belief that we can solve our problems collectively. The government's role in providing for the common welfare lost out to free-market ideology and a belief in unbridled individualism.

Many social critics have documented a decades-long decline in the sense of community and a rise in rampant greed, litigiousness, consumerism, and belligerent egoism. Freedom seems to have become less about the absence of constraint than about freedom from obligations to one another.

The sense that individual problems and social issues are linked, the notion of public action for the public good has been lost, and in the case of conservatives, totally abandoned. For them government's not the solution, it's the problem. The gap in educational outcomes in poor neighborhoods is explained away with false characterizations about "grit" and character, instead of the impact of poverty - both directly on students and on their schools. Poor people are blamed for their own misfortune. Media attention focuses on street crime, the federal deficit, and gun-rights, instead of the real issues.

In Third Wave Capitalism there is the tendency for rewards to go not to those who create wealth, but to those who succeed in using their power over government and private institutions to grab a greater share of the wealth that would have been produced otherwise. This is what some are calling the "rigged economy." Economists call it "rent-seeking."

One of the best examples you have about how an industry becomes a third-wave system is the Healthcare industry. What's really wrong with our Healthcare?

The health care industry has followed a pattern of transformation now becoming common in other industries, as well.

In the 50s, a majority of decisions in the industry were made by individual doctors - who owned their own private practices. By the late 60s and early 70s, this had turned into a "medical-industrial complex., dominated not by the doctors but by giant "non-profit" hospitals, drug and medical equipment manufacturers, giant insurance companies, all more interested in "maximizing shareholder value" than in improving people's health. And the whole thing is heavily financed and subsidized by government.

The close relationships between the profit-driven pharma industry, the private health care organizations, and government policy dictated by lobbyists, together with systematic neglect of public health measures and of efforts to improve what are called the "social determinants of health" - housing, food adequacy, air and water pollution, waste disposal, and the like - have driven our effectiveness down and increased our costs. The result? The highest infant mortality rates in the industrialized world. A life expectancy several years less than in Japan and France. Mortality for women that has actually risen in 43% of our counties across the country. We still have 30 million people without healthcare insurance, despite Obamacare.

It is tempting to blame the overall poor performance of the US on aggregate measures of health status on the effect of poverty (though why that should count as an "excuse" I can't figure out). But even white, insured, college-educated, upper-income Americans have higher rates of heart disease, diabetes, cancer, and other problems than their counterparts abroad.

How is this possible? Third wave capitalism blames the victim for lack of discipline - for example, diabetes is viewed as the fault of the victim because he let himself get obese - while corporations that infuse our foods with unhealthy levels of salt and sugar and governments that tolerate sub-standard housing bear no blame.

You address poverty and racism and the retreat from social justice. Can you tell us what the impact of this has been on our economy and our society?

Let's focus on structural racism. Black communities have historically received less investment and fewer services from local governments. Social services addressing the needs of many people I the black community have been cut back. Lack of medical facilities, inadequate public transportation, infrequent trash pickup - are all factors that turn minority communities into slums. School budgets based on neighborhood property taxes mean that the poor are penalized for being poor - receiving fewer resources for education. For three decades, the tobacco industry targeted black communities, with obvious effects on health. We have backed away from any serious effort to end residential segregation. As a result, we have re-segregated our schools across this country. Banks also deliberately targeted minority communities in the early 2000s for the sale of sub-prime mortgages. As a result, black homeowners were more likely to lose their homes during the housing bust of 2008. And employment discrimination is certainly not a thing of the past.

I already mentioned the incarceration rates for black men.

Ideologically, our politicians (increasingly beholden to business interests) have backed away from programs to alleviate poverty, and have, in effect, criminalized poverty.

How is the professional, creative class under stress? What about the CEO class?

The CEOs have seen startling raises in their pay scale. In the mid 60s, the average CEO earned about 20 times what their employees earned. Now the ration is over 300 to 1. Meanwhile, professionals have lost ground. Writers, editors, teachers and professors, social workers, lawyers, even doctors have seen their autonomy undercut, their job security weakened, and their pay stagnating. The American Dream has slipped out of the grasp of most middle-class families. unless we change tracks, our children are faced with a worse standard of living than their parents.

What must be done? How can we the people reverse this decline? Where do we start?

For starters, we have to challenge the dominant narratives we are being fed by virtually all Republicans and, unfortunately, by many Democrats. Conservatives insist that our most pressing problem is our unbalanced budget. Higher taxes would burden the "job creators," and would threaten our international competitiveness, so we simply cannot afford to expand or even maintain government programs. They also tell us that the idea that complex social issues can be solved by government action is foolish. And to conservatives, big government is the enemy of freedom and prosperity. They insist that it is not government but the free market that solves social problems, and the only legitimate goals of public policy is to promote growth and serve the needs of businesses.

These narratives are all false. The same naysayers who tell us that government action is bad are happy to intervene on the behalf of their corporate sponsors - for bail-outs, exemptions, and tax loopholes. If taxes are raised to let Medicare subsidize an overly high salary of the CEO of a large hospital, or to permit a drug company to make outlandish large profits, or to let the Defense Department pay for $500 hammers, then yes, taxes are too high. But, if taxes are raised to provide you with drinkable water, or to protect you against the insecurity of unemployment, you have experienced a gain not suffered a loss. Despite the conservative refrain about Americans being overtaxed, taxes of the United States among the lowest in the world. As Oliver Wendell Holmes Jr. once said, "Taxes are what we pay for living in civilized society."

But the Left also has myths that have to be challenged. If we believe that self-interest - economic self-interest and group self-interest - is all there is to politics, we are badly mistaken. People also seek safety and stability, a sense of empowerment, a faith that the community will help take care of them if you need help, a coherent narrative about their own experience and that of their community, a need to ward off feelings of envy and shame, something to believe in, a pride in tradition. The Left has let the Trumps of the world get away with seeming to champion those needs, and if we don't address those needs, I fear what is to come.

Change will happen when people demand it. We need to support the messy and unruly movements that bring about change. That is democracy.

NIGEL SIZER
Will the Amazon Fires Wake Up the World?

Brazil has had more than 72,000 fire outbreaks so far this year, an 84% increase on the same period in 2018. According to The Guardian[57], the large number of conflagrations – set illegally to clear and prepare land for crops, cattle and property speculation – has prompted the state of Amazonas to declare an emergency, created giant smoke clouds that have drifted hundreds of miles, and sparked international concerns about the destruction of an essential carbon sink.

We caught up with the Rainforest Alliance 's[58] Nigel Sizer[59], to get his perspective on the situation.

The unprecedented scope of the fires across the Amazon seems to have woken people up around the world. What sort of pressure must individuals apply to make a real difference now?

We are seeing a reaction unlike anything we've seen before. People and businesses are contacting us to ask what they can do.

We responded on social media.

The first thing you can do is donate to frontline groups that are on the ground. We have pledged to redirect 100% of the funds donated in August via Instagram to frontline groups in the Brazilian Amazon, including the Brazil chapter of our Indigenous federation partner COICA and our longtime sustainable agriculture partner IMAFLORA (the other groups are the Instituto Socioambiental, Instituto de Pesquisa Ambiental da Amazônia (IPAM), Saúde e Alegria, and Imazon, Brazilian NGOs working to defend the Amazon and advance Indigenous rights). The response has been far above expectations. Our Instagram appeal raised $650K in three or four days. $500K is already transferred to Brazil.

The second thing you can do is communicate your concern directly to your grocery stores and your food companies, the Tescos, the Krogers, the Unilevers and Burger Kings. Tell them you want their assurance that the

---

[57] Amazon rainforest fires: global leaders urged to divert Brazil from 'suicide' path, *The Guardian* https://www.theguardian.com/environment/2019/aug/23/amazon-fires-global-leaders-urged-divert-brazil-suicide-path

[58] *Rainforest Alliance* https://www.rainforest-alliance.org/

[59] *Rainforest Alliance, Nigel Sizer* https://www.rainforest-alliance.org/bios/nigel-sizer

food they sell you isn't making deforestation worse. Ask them to work to promote green agribusiness.

Third, you can change your buying habits. Ask for more transparency – did the animal feed for your beef or bacon come from Brazil? Demand an ethical supply chain.

You can also eat less meat, or give it up entirely.

What is the Rainforest Alliance doing to bring institutions together to stop the madness?

We have been working on the Accountability Framework initiative[60] with collaborators like Greenpeace, WWF, Imaflora, The Nature Conservancy, the World Resources Institute, etc. to help multi-national companies seeking to eliminate deforestation from their supply chains. For companies and others committed to eliminating deforestation, conversion of natural ecosystems, and human rights violations from supply chains, the path forward isn't always clear. The Accountability Framework provides a practical roadmap, offering principles and guidance at each stage of this ethical supply chain journey.

The Framework is based on a consensus of leading environmental and social organizations – on the "best thinking and experience." It was developed through an open consultation process with stakeholders around the world over the past two years, and it reflects the collective experience of companies, NGOs, and governments about what "good" looks like for ethical supply chains.

The Accountability Framework is not a new certification standard, nor does it seek to supersede existing efforts—instead, it closes gaps between those efforts and creates a clear way forward for companies to fulfill their commitments on environmental and social responsibility. It helps progressive companies along the way, as they take the journey towards an ethical supply chain. The journey begins with a set of core principles[61] that define key elements of a strong company commitment related to the AFI's

---

[60] "Accelerate progress and improve accountability"
The Accountability Framework https://accountability-framework.org/

[61] Core Principles, The Accountability Framework
https://accountability-framework.org/core-principles/

environmental and social scope. The AFi provides operational guidance[62], he specific and practical details related to putting the core principles into practice.

How is this different from before? We've learned that since Bolsonaro took office at the start of 2019, deforestation in the Amazon has jumped by 67%.

Although global attention is now focused on the Brazilian Amazon, it is important to note that manmade forest fires are an ongoing phenomenon that threatens tropical forests around the world, from the Amazon and Indonesia to Guatemala and Mexico.

This should be of utmost concern to people around the world, since forests provide a powerful, natural climate solutions that, along with better agricultural practices, could deliver up to 37% of the greenhouse gas emissions reductions[63] required between now and 2030 to stabilize global warming below 2°C in a cost-effective manner. Research confirms that natural climate solutions are critical in mitigating climate change, thanks to their carbon sequestering and storage capabilities.

The problem in Brazil has been worse in the past – in the 90s and again in 2005. But this is different than before. The Brazilian government back then worked hard to reduce deforestation, bringing it down by 70%. They built their own monitoring technology using satellites, and created a leading, world-class approach to conservancy that was exported to Indonesia and Central Africa as a best practice. Now, the current Bolsonaro regime has dismantled that expertise and has encouraged deforestation – setting Brazil backwards on a path of irreversible harm.

Unlike arboreal forest fires in Siberia, for example, fires in the rainforest are not natural. They are set by humans. And this widespread fire across the Amazon is not natural by *any stretch of the imagination.*

It helps when world leaders step up to make a difference, like France's Macron did via Twitter:

---

[62] Contents of the Accountability Framework, *The Accountability Framework* https://accountability-framework.org/contents-of-the-framework/
[63] Natural climate solutions, *PNAS* https://www.pnas.org/content/114/44/11645

We all have to appeal to the world's leaders to take a meaningful stand.

**How can companies get involved to make a difference – even if they
haven't focused on the Amazon before?**

As I mentioned, we are getting requests from companies that are asking –
how can we help? Our employees want to contribute – what can we do?
To them we say:

- What are you spending your money on? Can you support the
  groups making a difference on the ground?
- How can you promote certification of an ethical supply chain?
  What access do you have to other business leaders in the
  community?
- How can you as a retailer educate the people on the issues? We
  have found that the public is confused about what's going on. Just
  allowing the news to get out and alerting the public to what is
  going on is not a bad way to start.

Ask also – what are we doing with our lobbying efforts? Are we helping
politicians make the right decisions for the common good? Are you
supporting the communities your company's impact?

Will we go back to business as usual, or is this a tipping point for a global green awakening?

I hope it is, but I don't think it will be. We have seen this sort of thing before. Remember Deepwater Horizon[64] ?

Already the headlines have changed to the trade war with China. The DNC voted down a Climate Change debate for the Democrats. Unfortunately, the media still isn't paying attention.

What will it take for people to wake up to the reality of Climate Change? I am guessing it will be something even more drastic. A die-back across an entire region, a collapse of food security, a series of national weather calamities, unless we are able to communicate the seriousness of the issue now, before it's too late. It's not like we have a lot of time left.

What do you think of Climate Change and the political situation in the US?

I am hoping that all our candidates will be more serious about Climate Change. If there is one issue that is an existential threat, this is it. It's time for us to work together to bring the world back from the edge of disaster. And we urge people to vote for candidates who understand the urgency of the climate crisis and are willing to take bold action.

[64] https://en.wikipedia.org/wiki/Deepwater_Horizon

CHRISTOPHER DAVIS
A Return to Activism

Christopher Davis *is the international director of sustainability at The Body Shop[65]. He's responsible for developing and overseeing the implementation of The Body Shop's corporate responsibility and campaign strategy across 65 countries.*

So many of us felt that The Body Shop lost its soul when it was sold to L'Oreal. Now, under Natura, the first publicly traded B-Corp, how are things changing?

The big moment for us when the founders of Natura visited the office and reminded us that business is a change agent – the world needs good business to face the challenges ahead. For me this connects the past – the legacy of our founder, Dame Anita Roddick – with the present – the passion of Natura's Founders, especially Guilherme Leal who is a real visionary thinker in sustainable business. They share the same tone, and the zeal of the founder. It was then many of us felt that The Body Shop was back. We remember what Anita said: "The Body Shop is not afraid of what is new and risky. We want to be a socially responsible business that carries on breaking new ground."

What is the company doing to resurrect the brand?

We are hearing words in a vocabulary and spirit that we have missed for ten years: triple bottom line, activism, conscious business, mindful leadership. Once again, we are conscious of the fact that activism – as force for change – must be built into the product. The revival has begun. The past years have been hard. At times, the culture was tough, but the core team worked hard to keep the Roddick DNA alive regardless of the risks to their own careers! Now we have a chance to work again on the issues we hold so dear – awareness, impact, political change, human rights, and a ban on animal testing.

Today, our CSR program includes a number of exciting initiatives where activism plays a key and driving role. Our *Forever Against Animal Testing* campaign to end animal testing in cosmetics worldwide. It's the biggest campaign in our company history. Its the biggest global campaign against animal testing ever. We took our petition with 8 million signatures

---

[65] www.thebodyshop.com/en-us/

to the United Nations and our store managers spoke at a roundtable in the UN calling for change. We believe we should use the power of our brand to change politics – alongside our customers and other partners including other companies and we remain dedicated to ending animal testing in cosmetics for good.

Activism is also alive and kicking in our Bio Bridge program where we are building bio-bridges all over the world to help protect animals and their natural habitats. 'Bio-bridges' are restored wildlife corridors in damaged landscapes that help endangered species to reconnect, breed and thrive again. As well as making financial contributions, we have also used our voice to work with government to advocate for long term protection and support which has proved really effective across the world.

Moving forward, as part of Natura & Co we are accelerating our actions. We are working with the non-profit organization the Future Fit Foundation, we've created a plan for systemic improvement that is *not* incremental, but much broader and impactful than the traditional CSR activities businesses are familiar with. The approach considers all our impacts across every element of our business and commits us to take action to run our company in accordance with planetary and societal needs rather simply looking at business through our own business lens

How do employees feel about your activism?

For are activists so the business is a reflection on their own beliefs. Our best people don't change when they walk through the company doors – they bring something of themselves to work. Work is an expression of who they are which – I believe – is when you get the best out of people. There is a tendency to define activists as extreme extraverts (We have these, many of them, especially in stores!) but that's not the case here. Many colleagues working behind the scenes in areas like finance or IT are big thinkers, dedicated to creating change. Our new chief technology officer is as vocal in pushing our agenda as our marketing teams. Which is where we need to be.

Is the Body Shop going to become a "B-Corp"? What are the benefits?

My team has been speaking with B Lab and B Corp for years and really admire the movement. The biggest benefit I have observed from being an outsider but speaking to B Corporation certified companies is their openness to sharing their experiences and learning. There is a genuine desire to create a collective of companies who are really driving change. Natura are – of course – one of the world's largest B Corporations and it is something we are looking at. When we do it, we will do it well so it takes a little preparation. More news soon.

What's next?

Lots! But my mind turns to my biggest priority – the integration of the business framework developed by Future Fit[66] - the Future Fit Business Benchmark – into our business. Simply put – it sets 23 end goals or destinations we need to reach to ensure we never undermine the wellbeing of people or the planet and then – we hope – surpass so we make a positive impact. It's a long-term plan and a big ambition. It requires deep though and for us to look at our company in a different way. It's not a reporting standard but it is a guide and a way of tracking progress. That is our biggest focus from today until 2020, when we will share the new program and our plans with the world.

---

[66] https://futurefitbusiness.org/

STEPHEN M.R. COVEY
The Trust Crisis: What Do Leaders Do Now?

Stephen M. R. Covey is a New York Times and #1 Wall Street Journal bestselling author of **The SPEED of Trust—The One Thing That Changes Everything**. *He is the former CEO of Covey Leadership Center, which, under his stewardship, became the largest leadership development company in the world.*

How is "trust" a key leadership competency in this fast-pace world of ours? And what can we learn from the trust-crisis at Facebook?

For business, today's global marketplace puts a premium on true collaboration, teaming, relationships, partnering, and all these interdependencies require trust. Partnerships based on trust outperform partnerships based on contracts. *Compliance does not foster innovation, trust does.* You can't sustain long-term innovation, for example, in a climate of distrust.

It was Einstein who said that "every kind of peaceful cooperation among men is primarily based on mutual trust and only secondarily on institutions such as courts of justice and police."

There's a French proverb – "Fish discover water last" – which is a way of saying that fish take water for granted – they're unaware of its existence, until it becomes polluted or it evaporates.

So it is with trust.

Trust is an integral part of society. We trust that people will follow traffic laws, that the water we drink and bathe in is safe, that our schools will teach our kids and prepare them for the future. What happens without this public trust? Without it, society closes down and ultimately self-destructs.

Trust is built from the inside out. Whatever trust we are able to create in our organizations or in the marketplace is a result of the credibility we first create in ourselves, in our relationships, in our organizations, in our markets, and in society.

The 5 Waves of Trust

SELF TRUST
RELATIONSHIP TRUST
ORGANIZATIONAL TRUST
MARKET TRUST
SOCIETAL TRUST

In issue after issue, the data is clear: high-trust organizations outperform low-trust organizations. Total return to shareholders in high-trust organizations is almost three times higher than the return in low-trust organizations. So, we assert that trust is a key competency. A competency or skill that can be learned, taught, and improved and one that talent can be screened for.

Trust is the one thing that affects everything else you're doing. It's a performance multiplier which takes your trajectory upwards, for every activity you engage in, from strategy to execution.

As the *Economist* article says, Facebook is not about to be banned or put out of business, but the chances of a regulatory backlash are growing, and distrustful users are beginning to switch off. Network effects can actually work in reverse. Facebook is worth $493bn, but only has $14bn of physical assets. Its value is intangible. A large part of that value is built on public trust. And that's why businesses must preserve and nurture public trust, in addition to the fact that it's the right thing to do.

Unfortunately, the climate we are in now is hurting this trust.

The distrust we see all around is *suspicion*, a response to the corporate scandals and vicious downward cycles of cynicism. But when a company focuses on the principle of *contribution for all stakeholders*, that becomes good business. Executives need to understand the economic benefits of this trust dividend, especially when the behavior is real, not artificially or superficially created as PR to manipulate trust.

Leaders must lead in creating trust and the job of the leader is to go first. Someone needs to go first, and that's what leaders do—*leaders go first.* PepsiCo believes in "performance with purpose[67] " and CEO **Indra Nooyi**

---

[67] "Helping to build a more sustainable food system"
https://www.pepsico.com/sustainability/sustainable-food-system

shows us that business plans and strategy must include products, people and the planet!

In a recent interview[68], Merck's CEO **Ken Frazier** says that "…businesses also exist to deliver value to society. Merck has existed for 126 years; its individual shareholders have turned over countless times. But our salient purpose in the world is to deliver medically important vaccines and medicines that make a huge difference for humanity. The revenue and shareholder value we create are an imperfect proxy for the value we create for patients and society."

We will see more and more leaders and companies moving in this direction because it makes economic sense, period. Plus, it's the right thing to do.

How do you identify a high-trust or low-trust organizations or institutions?

Trust is a powerful accelerator to performance and when trust goes up, speed also goes up while cost comes down — producing what we call a *trust dividend.* How do you know if you have a high trust culture? By observing the behavior of your people. In high-trust institutions we observe the following behaviors:

- Information is shared openly
- Mistakes are tolerated and encouraged as a way of learning
- The culture is innovative and creative
- People are loyal to those who are absent
- People talk straight and confront real issues
- There is real communication and real collaboration
- People share credit abundantly and openly celebrate each other's success
- There are few "meetings after the meetings"
- Transparency is a practiced value
- People are candid and authentic
- There is a high degree of accountability
- There is palpable vitality and energy—people can feel the positive momentum

---

[68] "Businesses Exist to Deliver Value to Society." by Adi Ignatius, *Harvard Business Journal* https://hbr.org/2018/03/businesses-exist-to-deliver-value-to-society

Another very visible indicator is the behavior of your customers and suppliers. What is your customer churn rate? Do you have a history of long-term customer and supplier relationships? What is your reputation or brand equity in your marketplace?

Conversely, when the trust is low, there's a ***trust tax*** which changes your trajectory downwards. In our work with organizations, we find that low-trust, low-performance organizations typically exhibit cultural behaviors like:

- Facts are manipulated or distorted
- Information and knowledge are withheld and hoarded
- People spin the truth to their advantage
- Getting the credit is very important
- New ideas are openly resisted and stifled
- Mistakes are covered up or covered over
- Most people are involved in a blame game, badmouthing others
- There is an abundance of "water cooler" talk
- There are numerous "meetings after the meetings"
- There are many "undiscussables"
- People tend to over-promise and under-deliver
- There are a lot of violated expectations for which people make many excuses
- People pretend bad things aren't happening or are in denial
- The energy level is low
- People often feel unproductive tension—sometimes even fear

Sound familiar? These behaviors are all ***taxes on performance***.

The work we do is to establish trust as your organizational operating system. That's a high-tech metaphor, but it's appropriate. We know how trust works, how to measure it, how to establish it, grow it, extend it, and sustain it – with all stakeholders.

Why is trust such a hidden variable to many otherwise competent managers?

Unfortunately, too many executives believe the myths about trust. Myths like how trust is soft and is merely a social virtue. The reality is that trust is hard-edged and is an economic driver.

For instance, strategy is important, but trust is the hidden variable. On paper you can have clarity around your objectives, but in a low-trust environment, your strategy won't be executed. We find the trust tax shows up in a variety of ways including fraud, bureaucracy, politics, turnover, and disengagement, where people quit mentally, but stay physically. The trust tax is real.

There are many myths about trust, and in my book, I present them in a table your readers may find helpful:

MYTH	REALITY
Trust is soft	Trust is hard, real, and quantifiable. It measurably affects both speed and cost
Trust is slow	Nothing is as fast as the speed of trust
Trust is built solely on integrity	Trust is a function of both character (which includes integrity) *and* competence
You either have trust or you don't	Trust can be both created and destroyed
Once lost, trust cannot be restored	Though difficult, in most cases, lost trust can be restored
You can't teach trust	Trust can be effectively taught and learned, and it can become a leverageable, strategic advantage
Trusting people is too risky	Not trusting people is a greater risk
You establish trust one person at a time	Establishing trust with the one establishes trust with the many

So trust is measurable? Quantifiable?

Absolutely, trust is measurable. Smart organizations measure trust in three key ways: 1) actual trust "levels"; 2) the "components" or dimensions that comprise trust; and 3) the "effects", or impact, of trust.

We have found that one very simple way to measure trust levels is to ask one direct question and roll it up and down throughout the organization. For internal stakeholders ask: "Do you trust your boss?" to employees at all levels of an organization. For external stakeholders, like customers or suppliers, you might ask them: "Do you trust our sales representative or account manager?" These are simple, direct questions that tell us more about our culture than perhaps any other question we might ask.

Now, wouldn't it be great if "trust" showed up on the financial statements as either a 'tax' or a 'dividend'? Organizations would then use resources to eliminate the tax or create a larger dividend! Although a high trust or low trust culture doesn't literally show up on financial statements, it does show up in the following ways, which are measurable, observable and economically relevant (all of which make a strong "business case for trust"):

The 7 Low-Trust Organizational Taxes	The 7 High-Trust Organizational Dividends
1. Redundancy	1. Increased value
2. Bureaucracy	2. Accelerated growth
3. Politics	3. Enhanced innovation
4. Disengagement	4. Improved collaboration
5. Turnover	5. Stronger partnering
6. Churn	6. Better execution
7. Fraud	7. Heightened loyalty
	(The opposites of the 7 Organizational Taxes are also Dividends)

What are the competencies, the behaviors that build trust?

Trust too often has been pigeonholed as based on character and integrity alone. There's nothing wrong with that, and that is clearly the foundation, but it's insufficient.

Trust is a function of both character and competence. Of course, you can't trust someone who lacks integrity, but hear this: if someone is honest but they can't perform, you're not going to trust them either. You won't trust them to get the job done.

That's one reason why trust has a soft image- because it has been severed from competence and results.

So how does one apply trust to branding?

When I look at a brand, a brand is nothing more or less than trust with the customer, trust with the marketplace. The principle behind a brand is reputation. The brand stands for a promise and the ability to deliver on that promise. And in that promise is a company's character *and* competence, its reputation.

From the character-side you start with *integrity*—honesty, congruence, humility and courage.

The courage to be open, to stand for something, to make and keep commitments. Then there's *intent*—is there a genuine concern for people, purposes and society as a whole or is profit your sole motive? What's the company's agenda? And how does it behave? Sometimes poor behavior can simply be bad execution of good intent.

On the competence side, you start with your *capabilities*—talents, skills, the ability to deliver. Is your company staying relevant, are you continually improving, do you have the right technologies to stay ahead of your competition? Brands need to reinvent themselves from time to time to stay relevant. Finally, look at your *results*. Your company and your brands are constantly measured based on past performance, present performance and anticipated future performance.

These four dimensions—integrity, intent, capabilities and results—make up the credibility and reputation of your brand. When the trust is high, you get the trust dividend. Investors invest in brands people trust. Consumers buy more from companies they trust, they spend more with companies they trust, they recommend companies they trust, and they give companies they trust the benefit of the doubt when things go wrong. The list goes on and on. On the Internet, a trusted brand versus an untrusted brand—the differences could not be clearer, you only give your credit card number to those you trust. And look what happens when a brand gets diluted or polluted or compromised, we see how fast consumers, and investors, turn away. They quit buying.

These same principles apply equally to companies and individuals.

What about the social responsibility of business? Is this part of the trust equation?

Initially many companies may move into this arena for PR purposes. More out of fear of not being in the arena, than really participating with their souls. But there are huge benefits that flow from this – the difference it makes with your employees first, then your customers, your suppliers, your distributors, your investors.

Trust varies by geography, as you've pointed out in your book. How do companies build trust globally?

Principles are universal; practices are local. The principles for building trust—focusing on Credibility and Behavior from the inside out—apply everywhere but their practical applications are heavily influenced by the cultural context. But trust itself is clearly a global principle. And there's no question that trust issues are global issues. Just like there might be an industry tax or dividend, there might also be a country tax or dividend. The Edelman Trust Barometer tells us, for example, that trust is often based on country of origin, as you cited from the Edelman study at the beginning of our interview. That data showed, for example, that trust in companies based in Canada and Switzerland were effectively getting a dividend while trust in companies based in Mexico and India were effectively paying a tax, with the US suffering the biggest decline in the past year.

Trust can be rebuilt. So how do you rebuild trust?

By your behavior. We've identified 13 behaviors which build trust. These apply to individuals, businesses, and governments.

1. Talk Straight

2. Demonstrate Respect

3. Create Transparency

4. Right Wrongs

5. Show Loyalty

6. Deliver Results

7. Get Better

8. Confront Reality

9. Clarify Expectations

10. Practice Accountability

11. Listen First

12. Keep Commitments

13. Extend Trust

Companies need to have a strong promise, because the promise builds hope. Keeping the promise is what builds trust.

My father had an expression: *"You can't talk yourself out of a problem you behaved yourself into."* So it is with trust.

Sometimes it takes a little time, but you can accelerate the process by declaring your intent and signaling your behavior, so others can see it.

People and companies can learn these behaviors. It's not a simple process which happens overnight. But it is a systemic, cultural process which can happen one leader at a time, one division at a time, one company at a time, and you can see the behavior shifting toward authentic, real trust-building behaviors as opposed to the more common counterfeit behavior of spin and hidden agendas and the like which tend to dissipate and diminish trust.

Is there a danger in being too trusting or even gullible?

One thing about trust is that everyone's for it.

However, there are three big objections which come up. The first one is that trust is a social virtue, to which I say no, it's much more than that; it's a hard-edged economic driver. Secondly, and we hear this all the time: "we can't do anything about trust, it's either there or it's not there." This too is a fallacy. Trust is a competency. It's something you can get good at. It's a strength you personally, and your team *and* your company can master. Being good at it will elevate every other strength you have.

The third complaint goes along these lines: "We've been burned before. We can't trust everyone. Are you suggesting we trust everybody?" That's where I suggest you exercise what I call "Smart Trust." Most leaders have been burned before, so they become distrusting. Our society is that way.

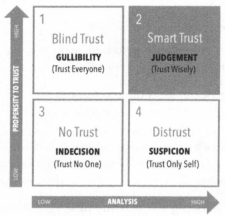

If you're not trusted, you tend to reciprocate with distrust. That's how the vicious cycle of mistrust starts and spirals downward.

There is a risk in trusting people, but the greater risk is not trusting people.

Smart Trust says you look at the opportunity, the risk and the credibility of the people involved. And you add to that verification and analysis. So you trust *and* verify. As opposed to *verify, then trust!*

Let's look at Berkshire Hathaway and Warren Buffet. I mention them in the book as an example of a high-trust company, about the acquisition they made based on a hand shake without due diligence.

But did you know that's how the entire company operates? They have 377,000 employees from some 60 different wholly-owned companies. How many people do you think work at corporate headquarters? A mere 25! Why? Because they choose to operate in a "seamless web of deserved trust" as Berkshire Hathaway Vice Chairman Charlie Munger calls it.

This is real. *It's not blind trust, but smart trust.*

ANJANA DAS
Conscious Fashion

*Founded in 2006 by **Anjana Das**, White Champa[69] is a global brand that bridges cultures to build a conscious fashion ethic. The company is based in Berlin, New Delhi, and Manila, and strives to create an aesthetic vocabulary for independent women across the world. We caught up with Das at a coffee house in Germany.*

What led you to create White Champa?
From an individual perspective, I didn't appreciate the fact that I had to have two different wardrobes – one for Asia, and one for Europe. My goal was to create a wardrobe that fulfills the dress needs for women in all

---

[69] www.whitechampa.com

cultural contexts across the many worlds that women inhabit – from home, to work, to socializing. I studied Japanese, Thai, Indian, and Filipino textiles and used my research findings to inform the cuts, shapes and ornamentation of my designs.

White Champa is where the *beauty of the drape meets the bravery of the cut*. We combine the Indian sense of fabric folding itself around the body with the European sensibility of fitted garments with darts and sizing.

Our philosophy is that the garment is a story, a narrative, in which the protagonist is the wearer. They create their own history through their personality and accomplishments. Their fashion choices should enhance their story.

What this means for fashion is that the customer creates their own sense of what fashion means for them. They express themselves through their choice of clothes. The woman wearing a White Champa garment in Berlin is connected to the maker of the fabric in the Philippines and the tailor in India.

Issey Miyake said it beautifully: *"The joint power of technology and manual work enables us to revive the warmth of the human hand."* We strive to create a product that is design driven yet reflects the rare and special human talents our master craftsmen contribute.

What were the branding challenges when you first started, and how have they changed?

When I first started this business in India, I knew what I wanted to achieve, but it was hard to challenge women to rethink what fashion means – for example, we are conditioned towards excessive ornamentation and "dressing to impress." In some ways, this mindset defeats itself because it actually diminishes the personality of the woman.

In India, women now want to buy clothes in department stores, like they do in the west, but this ignores the diversity in hand crafted textiles and makes artisans jobless. So progress in fashion in India does not necessarily translate to progress for the makers of Indian fashion. Globalization conducted this way destroys local industries.

White Champa had to establish itself as *the brand for women who were not afraid to challenge existing norms.* Our customers are leaders – they are citizens of the world. Many of them are creative forces in their own right – writers, artists, dancers, even academics and professional women.

What has changed is how we are now finding global acceptance for our design philosophy. More and more we see western women seeking us out.

White Champa has a reputation for conscious management practices. Can you tell us how that relates to the brand?

We are beginning to feel the harsh effects of the industry's unsustainable practices. The fashion industry is second only to Big Oil in terms of the destruction visited upon the planet. The average consumer is now purchasing 60 percent more items of clothing compared to 2000[70], but each garment is kept half as long.

Secondly, while many iconic brands are enjoying increases in revenue, the workers – generally women – are trapped in a cycle of poverty.

When we started White Champa in 2006, we decided to eliminate these issues[71] as part of our operations, first by paying our workers and suppliers above "living wages" – and second by creating a ***slow fashion*** mindset. Our customers are connected to us not as a product, but as a way of living. Our supply chain is part of our company – that is we manufacture the clothes with our own employees and partners that we are closely connected with. So we enjoy a relationship of trust and fairness that isn't the norm in our industry.

We also don't want our customers to keep buying stuff. Rather, we want them to wear our creations throughout their lives. We offer a free service to adjust the size of your clothes as you gain or lose weight over the years. In fact, we designed the White Champa Universal Sizing System to do just this.

A global sizing system?

The idea behind a global sizing system was an early innovation in our design process. We found that the size differences between body types in the West and Asia were significant. So we created a system that took into account the variance in waist-to-hip ratios and created the White Champa

---

[70] "Style that's sustainable: A new fast-fashion formula"
McKinsey & Company https://www.mckinsey.com/business-functions/sustainability/our-insights/style-thats-sustainable-a-new-fast-fashion-formula
[71] Where do the big brands stand in the race to a living wage? OXFAM Australia
https://whatshemakes.oxfam.org.au/company-tracker/

Universal Sizing System. The benefit of this system is that it accommodates different body types without the need to radically change our production values.

You studied Indology and political science and German Literature. How has that impacted the way you view your company?

When I was at the School of Oriental and African Studies in London, I studied the History of Art of the Indian subcontinent. This gave me a historical and political perspective on clothing – the rich cultural craft traditions that are neglected by today's industry.

I also worked as a designer for Jean-François Lesage when they started their work in South India. This helped me gain an appreciation for embroidery and the mastery of Indian craftsmanship. We continue to be inspired by the skill of the age-old tradition of hand embroidery in India.

What's next?

I want to introduce consumers – starting with the Europeans – to the idea of *bespoke slow fashion*, and what that entails: a lifelong relationship with your trusted brand.

HENNIE BOTES
The Challenge of Affordable Housing

Hennie Botes founded Moladi[72] in 1986, after building a global business as an entrepreneur and inventor. His ability to think outside the box has led him to found a company that is revolutionizing the affordable housing market through ethical design, innovation, and good-old fashioned ingenuity. We learned about Moladi during the $300 House Project [73], and it has recently been recognized by the World Economic Forum in their Future of Construction[74] initiative.

Can you tell us about how Moladi came about? How did you come up with the concept?

I think it starts with Abraham Maslow and food and shelter. Without the basic needs of life, little else can happen. So that's why housing is priority - across Africa and across the developing world.

But let's start at the very beginning. As it happened, my first invention was a plastic baby bath that fit across the bathtub and gave young mothers an easy and safe way to bathe their newborn children. The design was sold all over the world, and gave me the freedom to found Moladi.

Moladi was the result of my own difficulties with building with brick and mortar.

In South Africa, and many developing countries, we suffer from a colonial mentality. Our education system does not teach us how to plant and grow food or build things. And that is a tragedy. Africa will have to uplift itself, and learn how to build things itself.

The challenge for so many local housing developments is the lack of skills. We know how difficult it was to put bricks on top of each other in a straight line, and, once the wall is built, to plaster it.

Moladi was a way I saw to build a construction system which could evolve into a job-creation tool itself, since it *does not require skilled labor* - in fact, over 90% of a construction team on a Moladi housing site consists of unskilled laborers.

---

[72] www.moladi.net
[73] www.300house.com
[74] https://futureofconstruction.org/case/moladi/

My first attempts at building the right mold was not exactly a success but the geese on the farm got a dam as result. Gradually, and this is the way with all innovation, you learn from your mistakes. The result was the Moladi building system.

You say system, and not house. What do you mean by that?

We're a system, a way of thinking, not simply a product, and that is why we are different.

The Moladi building system, which incorporates green technology and sustainability also happens to provide the best solution to address six key challenges that hinder the successful implementation of low-cost housing projects in Africa:

- lack of sufficient funds
- shortage of skilled laborers
- lack of resources
- work flow control
- time constraints
- wastage

So the Moladi building system involves the use of a unique removable, reusable, recyclable and lightweight plastic formwork mold which is filled with an aerated SABS (South African Bureau of Standards) approved mortar to form the wall structure of a house in just one day.

The process involves the assembly of a temporary plastic formwork mold the size of the designed house with all the electrical services plumbing and steel reinforcing located within the wall structure which is then filled with a specially formulated mortar mix to form all the walls simultaneously.

We use Moladi technology as a means to alleviate many of the cumbersome and costly aspects associated with conventional construction methods without compromising on the quality or integrity of the structure. When we first started, people would say things like Moladi structures won't last. Now we have some that have been around for 30 years. From the very start, we were focused on solving the problem of affordable housing.

I thought the world would chop a path to our doorway asking for the solution, but it hasn't been that easy.

And why is that?

The masonry industry likes to protect its knowledge and its interests. Change has never been easy. But now things are changing. Whether through necessity or because of desperation, we are seeing more and more interest from private partners and governments that view us as a building block for the country's future.

We work hard to gain social acceptance from the local communities we work in. That is something that makes all the difference. Add to that the fact that we are cost effective, we create local jobs, and we are environmentally sustainable, and you understand why we are now growing at a much faster pace. We've also added toilet systems, window and door systems, and kitchen systems to the Moladi system, all at a much lower cost than the hardware store. Now we are in a position to say that we're world leaders at building entire village housing ecosystems.

Are you finding interest for Moladi extends beyond Africa?

Yes, that is most definitely the case. We have been in Mexico, in Panama, in Haiti, across Africa, and now we are in talks in Nepal. Moladi is currently deployed in 18 countries, reaching 20 within the next three months by adding India and Sri Lanka to our list.

You know, all materials used in the construction of Moladi homes, other than the formwork, are sourced and supplied from within the local community. Other than contributing to the local economy, this drastically reduces the need for additional and unnecessary transport and handling of goods and building materials. This follows from the logic that the fewer the number of operations, the higher the quality of the product, resulting in a predictive timeline and ultimately cost savings.

Can you tell us about the local benefits of building a village with Moladi?

For starters, the local impact is immediate. We are a major job-creation strategy at the local level. But most important is the change in the lives of Moladi customers. A house is still a castle. It is an asset for wealth creation and empowerment.

We see three types of developments - upgrading informal settlements, green-field development, and rural village development – the Moladi Smart

Village. Governments now understand how critical infrastructure and housing is for a prosperous future, for lifting citizens out of abject poverty.

That's really why we do this.

You mentioned sustainability. How are Moladi houses more eco-friendly than traditional building techniques?

We have found that we are about 61% of the CO_2 footprint for the same size of a house built with traditional brick and mortar. That's because we don't use bricks at all, and two, we recycle our molds which are used to build 50 houses out of one set of molds.

Add to that the fact that a house is built in a day, and you significantly reduce material wastage. That in itself adds to both cost effectiveness, cycle time, and sustainability.

What are your plans for the future?

We are expanding across the world. And we are not just housing for the poor. We think that decent, beautiful houses don't have to be the province of wealthy citizens. That is why design and aesthetics are important as well. We want our houses to fill residents with joy and pride.

It is not an accident that developers in the richer countries protect their markets from competition. But the world is getting smaller every day, and the tide is shifting. We want to partner with private companies across the globe, creating new business for them as well as us.

Despite all the bad news you hear about in the news, I feel optimistic about the future, and the real impact Moladi is having on the war on poverty.

ELSIE MAIO
Does Your Business Have a Soul?

Elsie Maio[75] has guided leaders in the Fortune 100 for over 25 years to achieve specific business goals by managing their brands strategically. She is an alumna of McKinsey & Company as well as strategy-practice leader at premier corporate identity firms. Since 1997 her own firm has helped CEOs prepare for what she then identified as "the coming tsunami of corporate accountability." Her firm – Humanity, Inc. is the successor company to Maio & Co, which emerged in 1994, born from three consulting disciplines: business strategy, brand strategy and values-led operations.

What message do you have for the CEO of a company embarking on the values journey?

Well, I have some tough love for that CEO. There's no time for a values journey now.

To begin with, your workforce is ahead of you. They are already animated by their sense of humanity and system identity. In fact, they are impatient for you to catch up and empower them to put those values to work to help restore equilibrium in society and the natural environment.

Other groups also think business can and should take that on now. For example, at Google's storied walkout last year organizers first made their point about the trigger event, a lack of accountability for sexual harassment. Then they announced this issue was only the beginning, and called for a shift in management's worldview. Even employee surveys in the traditionally conservative financial services sector exhort leadership to catch up and visibly demonstrate system-supportive behaviors. The population bulge of millennials and Gen Z are notorious for their intentional system-supportive choices. And, even in the general population of 28 countries in 2017, three out of four people surveyed have said that business could simultaneously increase profit and improve social and economic conditions in their communities.

Second, the Board needs you to make that authentic pivot, too. Heavyweight investors are pressuring them to mind the Governance risks associated with your company's impacts on Social and Environmental systems. The big four asset managers have publicly threatened to pull

---

[75] *Soul Branding* http://www.soulbranding.com/

portfolio companies who do not adequately address such ES+G risk factors. And a group of institutional investors doubled the list of traditional investment screening criteria with a set of granular system-friendly indicators, calling them NextGen investment criteria.

Last, you may never have another chance like this to bring a company into a generative new paradigm just ahead of an existential crisis, with so much support. Key constituents already want some kind of change, and VUCA operating conditions necessitate it.

Even the biggest whale of the financial conglomerates, meeting with fellow veterans of the Predators' Ball this week talked about a need to 'change capitalism'. The oligarchy is deeply spooked by the flammability of social disequilibrium today.

But I disagree with what Jamie Dimon reportedly said there, at Milken's latest conference. *Democratic* Capitalism is elastic enough for this challenge. We just have to put the *demos* back on its throne. I'm talking about shifting the prime directive of business from maximizing shareowner value to profitably generating wellbeing for each. Anything short of that is a provocation to "Let them eat cake." And we know what that led to last time.

Sure, the risks of maintaining the status quo catalyze action. But the pivot also opens you to an unlimited commercial opportunity for the human family to solve existential problems and nurture a virtuous circle of wellbeing with the web of life. As a frame of reference, think about the $12TR starting estimate for the 17 Sustainable Development Goals.

So that's the context, the meta journey worth taking now. Where can you, one leader, start? Pioneer cohorts have built a trail of outposts with lessons learned, pitfalls to avoid, data sets to mine and resources continuously refreshed over the past 25 years. Start your pivot there.

What did you observe when you first worked with Anita Roddick?

My first impression of Anita in person was, fire and ice. Anita was a fierce warrior for the soul of humanity. That's still a hallmark of new paradigm leaders, in my view.

To be clear, I spent only a few days with Anita, and more with her team. It was 2000 and I had just dedicated my company to social-impact. We were refining the SoulBranding℠ process by researching best practices of the most authentic pioneers in the field. The Body Shop was a visible one.

What I observed is the congruence of Anita's soul with her business. Back then, the personal care, cosmetics and women's fashion vibe was all about varnished, luxury brand name glamour. They were selling status. The Body Shop was selling a woman her own naturally empowered self in a ripe, natural world.

The Body Shop products were sensual, luscious, fresh smelling concoctions that celebrated the voluptuousness of nature — and the dignity of living systems at the same time.

Center stage in the retail shops were the humans who grew and gathered those exotic gifts of the jungle forests. The shops featured public campaigns to honor and support specific members of the indigenous tribes who collected and provided those ingredients. Anita was among the first to initiate fair trade programs in the supply chain. The urban office of The Body Shop was a cross between a lodge in the forest and a local community center, full of cogent flyers and calls to action to switch local utility service to the renewable energy provider. At that time, she had an autobiography out but she was on fire for the activist workbook she'd published, "Take It Personally."

The Body Shop was her magnet, a catalyst to reawaken the System Soul in consumers. As it did in me.

Her book was explicit about that, teaching readers to trace that throughline from the heart and soul to 'globally sound' decisions at the checkout counter. For her, motivation mattered and she called out business and policy makers to move on from their fear and greed. She embodied her values; they animated her.

Your readers are interested in activism, Christian, so my contrarian point of view might be interesting for them here. Because what I perceive as Anita's stance is opposite to what became the dominant trend, sustainability.

The ambiguous meaning of that word itself can shield a very different motivation from Anita's, and mine. For one thing, sustainable is not the same as flourishing. It is a stage of consolidation. And for another, companies often will define their sustainability by one particular issue, and ignore impacts on other nodes in their ecosystem.

Here's an example of a company we know well. They are the pioneer in one category of FMCG, environmentally sensitive household products. Everyone there was passionate for the wellbeing of the natural world. So much so that they were among the first to install a 'green roof', which was not core to their operation, per se. More a symbol of their commitment to the living natural system. Their employees were incentivized to cycle to work. Their products were the first of their kind to scale into broad international distribution. And they were proud to be such sustainability leaders.

But in their SoulBranding℠ Self Audit, they discovered an unintended consequence of their narrow focus. They left out the part of the living system that is human. Their HR policies and practices scored as unjust and dismissive. The culture respected the environment but not the people. That diagnostic was a rude awakening. But it allowed them to address the incongruence and restore integrity with employees. It was an object lesson in how unconscious bias is revealed when we relate through the lens of 'the other', the lens of whole-system reality.

In fairness, we've all become somewhat habituated to the ubiquitous if ambiguous sustainability norm. And it has led to at least one of society's existential crises, in my view. But the pain of those crises is rousing us to the fact that we live in a systems reality, hyperinterdependent with every aspect of life so dynamic and complex that it's impossible to wall off impacts. Our only hope is to collectively steward its holistic equilibrium.

What is a Soul Brand?

That's a good question. I may have a blind spot there. We don't really talk about soulbrands *per se* but think of it as an aspirational state.

Instead, we stand with the leader while they discover how to align the organization's actions profitably with the soul of humanity, with the wellbeing of the web of life. And we help build their internal competence to shepherd that process when we're gone.

In my experience, it's one of the most valuable skills our relational world today, calibrating what you say you stand for and the impact of what you do on other people and living systems. And it's tough to pull off in silo-ed leadership teams. But it's crucial. It's the place where operating effectiveness goes off the rails and it's the place where trust goes to die.

In these fraught times, trust barometers are flirting with negative territory, that is, people expect to be hurt by some of their own institutions, rather than trust that their interests are being considered. So it's particularly important now for activists of all types to be internally congruent with the stance they may take on any one issue.

In your earlier book *Inclusivity: Will America Find Its Soul Again*, Christian, you laid out the case for inclusion and diversity as part of the virtuous circle of value-creation in our systems world. The richer the inputs, the richer the solutions. But also, the more dynamic and challenging to maintain equilibrium: with inclusion comes diversity of stakeholders' interpretations, priorities, needs and ultimately perceived value.

So I'm not comfortable labeling a soulbrand. For me it's a constant discipline of managing that wobbly line between your implicit promise and its perceived delivery. That's why we put an –ing at the end of it in 1997: SoulBranding^SM.

What should companies do to take the long-term view?

There's really no model for the breadth and depth of transformation we are talking about here. I wouldn't underestimate the magnitude of the pivot from 'he who has the gold rules' to 'The Golden Rule'.

But there are parallels I can think of. Many of the leaders we've worked with or observed closely radically changed the direction of their large organizations and consortia. The main thing is to formalize and resource the process. Beyond that, some insights to help readers get off on the right foot.

The rule of thumb is, *You do it first.* Be the change, model system consciousness.

In this case we're talking about a pivot from the old paradigm egoic self into a *felt* experience of being one of many equals in a system of systems. You'll find your humanity. You'll see the world differently. You'll find a different center of personal gravity, and eventually of equilibrium. Your heart will likely open. You may feel vulnerable. Explore this state of being. Imagine what's possible for the world when everyone relates to each other and other living systems from this felt experience. Spend a few days exploring it, notice how different your body feels. Imagine what different choices you would make in your life, in your organization from this mindset, this state of being. There's a highly developed industry of trustworthy professionals ready to help you cultivate and operationalize it.

Let the opportunity lead.

When you have some idea of the pace of emerging trends and other exogenous forces at work, you might begin to socialize the question of what's possible for your company from this big pivot. You have your own protocols to explore appetite for change of course. Typically, it would start with confidantes on your team and maybe on the Board, before widening the conversation circle to an inclusive discovery group.

In any case, start the conversations with yourself already somewhat informed and intrigued by what's possible. To paraphrase Bucky Fuller: rather than tell people what not to do, give them a more attractive alternative. The wellbeing of all living systems is the prime objective of the new paradigm. That opportunity is not only inspiring but it's virtually unlimited.

So back to your question, in the long term the chance to hop on the virtuous spiral of wellbeing for the web of life — is well, as big as the web of life. And for now, environmental crises and the gaps between wellbeing and the human condition are daunting problems but a compelling focus for meaningful work. One way to parse these problems is into the 17 Sustainable Development Goals; estimated conservatively as a $12TR commercial opportunity. Plenty to do, and with growing financial incentives to do it. The SDG-finance sector is cohering rapidly to create a market for private investment. And even the conservative institutional investment community is nudging its portfolio companies in this direction albeit, from the risk management perspective, ES+G.

You have to transcend silos and egos with shared fate early on.

I remember one client organization was keen to identify how it could boost the effectiveness of various sustainability initiatives spread around 10 country markets. An internal team followed the SoulBranding[SM] process to map the throughline from the company's soul values to company competences, and data on the meta problems keeping populations up at night in that culturally diverse 10-country region.

Using the Core Mutual Value framework (it's demonstrated in the video on our homepage) they found the intersection of that region's existential pain and their unique ability to address it commercially.

234

Data is a powerful consensus builder, but it can also reach the heart. We used a similar methodology with an island nation looking to focus the resources of three disconnected sectors — its philanthropies, the corporates domiciled there and local service charities – on some pressing social issues. The collective pain of all 65,000 residents crossed class, economic, racial divides in that first quantitative survey. That inclusive reading of their nation's problems defined the three sectors' shared fate and established the platform for their fruitful collaboration.

Typically, it takes 4 to 6 years to operationalize a culture change program. This transformation is bigger than that. There are entire system-skillsets yet to be discovered no less developed. Models of profitable social impact to be scaled. All in a dynamic, disruptive environment. The comfort is in this systems world, we're all in the same boat, and we could have each other's back.

What role do you see for women as leaders?

That topic is central to restoring equilibrium. But it always triggers my internal stop sign: How can I hold this question without reinforcing the old paradigm binary, dualistic mindset? I don't think I'm alone in that self-inquiry, it's part of our learning how to honor individuality in an inclusive system of equality.

First, half the world is missing from the decision room. That greatly impairs the creativity and relevance of those decisions. Chaordic, complex systems such as we are part of generate better solutions the richer the inputs.

Second, women enhance the performance of the systems they actively participate in. Whether it's nature, nurture, cultural permission, personal agency or some combination of the above, women tend to exhibit behaviors that are especially well suited to system dynamics.

A close look at Grameen Bank in 2000 closed that debate for me. And for many others years later when Mohammed Yunis' economic model of women-centered microfinance very publicly won the Nobel Prize. Why? When Grameen put money in the hands of rural women they elevated the wellbeing of their entire communities through team-entrepreneurship. That was after testing the model with men, who spent it on themselves.

And that inclination of women to nourish the greater good shows up in big organizations and countries, too. Something about how women lead correlates with the higher profits and growth they bring to corporations, the lower performance risks to companies whose Boards they sit on, and outperformance on other important metrics.

So to answer your question, the role I see for women as leaders is to do it in a way that works for them. Because if a leadership role works for them and their own well-being, they will do it more often, with more confidence, and in more circumstances. That will benefit all of us.

I know many women who have opted out of leadership roles in toxic corporate cultures. That's a good thing; they are modeling the consciousness of their own system wellbeing. Like the airlines say, in the event of an emergency, put your own mask on first. Until society provides leadership roles that work for women, it will have limited access to the system wellbeing they naturally generate.

What are you personally working on that gets you excited about each morning?

It's good to step back and reflect on that. Thanks for the question.

Every day the sun rises and burns off a bit more of our collective trance. I'm excited each morning to chronicle society's awakening to system reality and news of its latest step toward embracing a new paradigm of system wellbeing.

I monitor this progress in the financial services and investment sector in particular. Brand activism has influenced Wall Street when it translates into profit risk, as I said earlier. I'm also encouraged by the substantive collaborations and myriad financial vehicles being developed to 'create markets' for the SDGs.

I'm excited to see the financial establishment wake up, one at a time, in their own way. To see rebels like Anand Giridharadas' walk into *The Economist* conference on impact investing and tell us to put it on a six month hiatus until we can figure out how to keep philanthrocapitalism from retarding the big pivot that's really needed. Truth to power.

What gets my attention are the strategic inflection points of that system change. What drives my diverse portfolio is where I can make the most difference and what lights me up. Right now,

I'm excited to wake up and coach activist entrepreneurs and local citizen groups, human beings embracing their agency, at an immediate level changing their worlds.

I'm excited by the warriors for humanity whose funds outperform the vulture capitalists. One of them, Tine Ward at Rockflower uses her unique 'Mothering' process to pick 8 out of 10 winners. The vultures on the other hand pick 8 losers out of 10.

I'm excited to support renewable energy visionaries like Bluenergy whose inventions are now breaking through into scaled operations after 30 years of their nursing the market.

I'm excited by the women who are making waves. I'm active on a couple of Boards and women's committees, at Hazel Henderson's Ethical Markets and at the fashion-industry disruptor esa New York, and am coaching cohorts of intergenerational women each so enlivened by their individual flavor of systemic impact. Some are VCs, founders of environmental movements, tech entrepreneurs, and a networking guru.

I'm excited to see higher education move toward systems disciplines especially in technology, and to have helped curate the business program at the first Peace Engineering Conference of global engineering deans and educators which featured Kim Polman and Bill McDonough talking about The Golden Rule and Waging Peace Through Commerce.

That's exciting, and then there's morning joy: Watching the dolphins and occasional whale from my New York City terrace. They came back to Harbor waters when equilibrium was restored.

STUART L. HART
Capitalism at the Crossroads

Stuart L. Hart is an American academic, writer and theorist and the founder of Enterprise for a Sustainable World, a non-profit dedicated to helping businesses make the transition to sustainability. Hart has published over 50 papers and authored or edited five books.

With C.K. Prahalad, Prof. Hart wrote the 2002 article "The Fortune at the Bottom of the Pyramid", later expanded into a book of the same name. He is author of the book **Capitalism at the Crossroads: The Unlimited Business Opportunities in Solving the World's Most Difficult Problems** *as well as several scholarly articles and publications. According to Bloomberg Businessweek, he is "one of the founding fathers of the "base of the pyramid" economic theory"*

A Fortune 100 consultant, Hart is one of the world's leading authorities on the implications of sustainable development and environmentalism relative to business strategy.

As someone who helped launch the sustainability movement in the business world, what do you see happening today? Is Capitalism still at the crossroads?

Businesses are learning that they do not need to accept trade-offs when it comes to societal and economic performance. You must meet both criteria. The future demand it, your customers demand it, and your conscience demands it.

In my book, *Capitalism at the Crossroads*, I presented new strategies for identifying sustainable products, technologies, and business models that will drive urgently needed growth and help solve social and environmental problems at the same time. I also argue that corporations are the only entities in the world today with the technology, resources, capacity, and global reach required.

What we're now experiencing is a transformation to a more sustainable form of capitalism—and ultimately, a more sustainable world. This transformation began in the 1990's with the "eco-efficiency" revolution when, for the first time, it became clear that reducing waste, emissions, and pollution can actually save money and lower risk.

In the past decade, two exciting new commercial developments have burst onto the global scene. One revolves around the commercialization of new green technology; the other around better serving and including the poor at the base of the income pyramid. Both are exciting, but the problem is that they have evolved as separate communities. The green techies say, "Just give us the venture capital, and we'll invent the clean tech of tomorrow," as if it will then spring magically into reality.

Proponents of the base of the pyramid approach seek to address poverty and inequity in developing countries through a new form of enterprise. They say, "How do we innovate business models, extend distribution, and become embedded in the community to build viable businesses from the ground up?" But such "pro-poor" business advocates often lose sight of the environment, as if all this new economic activity will automatically create a sustainable form of development at the base of the pyramid. Tragically, that way of thinking could take us all over the cliff, if we end up with 6.7 billion people consuming like Americans.

The challenge of our time, therefore, is to figure out how to bring these two worlds together to enable a global "Green Leap." Indeed, emerging clean technologies, including distributed generation of renewable energy, biofuels, point-of-use water purification, biomaterials, wireless information technology, and sustainable agriculture hold the keys to solving many of the world's global environmental and social challenges.

Because these small-scale green technologies are often "disruptive" in character, the base of the pyramid is an ideal place to focus initial commercialization attention. China's towns and small cities, Brazil's favelas, and India's rural villages present such opportunities. Once established, such technologies can then "trickle up" to the established markets at the top of the pyramid—but not until they have become proven, reliable, affordable, and competitive against the incumbent infrastructure.

In my view, the Green Leap is a key point of leverage in transforming the global economy toward sustainability. If I am right, this holds important implications for policy-making. Rather than circling the wagons and seeking to build a Green Fortress America (or Europe, or Japan), the best thing we could do is get our most promising technologists and entrepreneurs out of the US (and the rest of the developed world markets) and into the rural villages, urban slums, and shantytowns of the world where 4 billion plus people currently reside. It is here that the Green Leap will take place. And, it is here that the corporations of the 21st century will be born.

How does the Green Leap compare to "reverse innovation"? What are the dangers?

One area of important learning has been the potential for incubating disruptive innovations and business models starting in the underserved space at the base of the pyramid and later having some of these innovations move up-market.

Clay Christensen and I wrote about this over a decade ago (2002) in an article entitled "The Great Leap: Driving Innovation from the Base of the Pyramid[76] ." The idea has caught on. Over the past decade, a whole slew of new terms and buzzwords have arisen to describe this phenomenon, including trickle-up innovation, frugal innovation, and the latest incarnation—reverse innovation.

A key difference between reverse innovation and the earlier work on base of the pyramid strategy is the promise—even expectation—of large and profitable up-market migration for the innovations incubated in the underserved space: GE's hand-held ultrasound device, for example, has "trickled up" to the US and other developed markets and now constitutes one of the fastest growing and profitable businesses for GE's Healthcare business.

There is some good news and some bad news regarding this trend. First the good news: Reverse innovation provides an attractive internal logic for undertaking such innovation initiatives within large corporations: Rather than simply focusing on the possibility of opening up new markets among the world's poor and underserved, reverse innovation offers the potential for having your cake and eating it too—by incubating innovations in the underserved space that can migrate up-market bringing new, disruptive, affordable, and (potentially) more environmentally sustainable products and services. Witness the growing "trickle-up" success in point-of-care medical devices, mobile telephony, and distributed energy technologies, for example. Exciting stuff, to say the least.

But now for the bad news—there is a potential dark side as well: The risk that corporations gradually come to view the world's slums and rural

---

[76] "The Great Leap: Driving Innovation from the Base of the Pyramid" by Stuart L. Hart and Clayton M. Christensen, *MIT Sloan Management Review*
https://sloanreview.mit.edu/article/the-great-leap-driving-innovation-from-the-base-of-the-pyramid/

villages primarily as laboratories for incubating innovations for the rich. The poor, in other words, come to be seen more as guinea pigs than as underserved people and communities with special needs and requirements—a place for corporations to force cost constraints on their innovation process enabling even higher returns in the eventual (ultimate) market at the top of the pyramid.

Should this scenario come to pass, it would represent a double tragedy. Not only would this damage corporations' reputation and continuing right to operate, but the evidence is also mounting that few innovations incubated in the base of the pyramid space can easily travel up-market without significant modification, threat of imitation, or competitive reaction: Frugal designs must be upgraded to appeal to the wealthy; low-cost innovations can often be easily imitated, and competitors with lower cost structures can enter as fast seconds after the pioneers have incurred all the development costs.

Allow this to serve as a cautionary tale to all those large, incumbent corporations thinking reverse innovation is the magic bullet: Focus on first things first—better serving and lifting those underserved at the base of the income pyramid. Should some of these disruptive, lower cost, or environmentally sustainable innovations eventually lend themselves to application in the up-market, that is great news for the Corporations and the World. But let us not look back in ten years and view reverse innovation as yet another classic example of the Law of Unintended Consequences[77].

What can business do to embrace this transformation? Do you find a sense of urgency?

For the most part, the *Corporate Sustainability Advisory Council (SAC)* is now part of the standard apparatus for most major corporations.

The first SACs were launched in the 1990s; and with a few notable exceptions, they were used primarily as PR tools to curry favor with increasingly vocal environmentalists and other troublesome social stakeholders. Back in the day, members of SACs (myself included), were typically engaged to review (what were then new) Corporate Responsibility/Sustainability Reports, serve as judges for staff sustainability awards, and provide advice on specific CSR or environmental initiatives by

---

[77] "On Creating Smaller Problems" *Voice of the Planet*
http://stuartlhart.com/blog/2011/08/on-creating-smaller-problems.html

the company. Sacs typically met once or twice a year and members were almost always prominently featured on the corporate website, but seldom compensated, other than covering travel expenses and accommodations. This was presumably done to avoid the appearance that members were being "bought" but in reality, it was a statement about the perceived value of these councils: Meetings were usually run by CSR or environmental management staff. The CEO might make a symbolic appearance at the beginning or end of the meeting, but generally no senior executives or business leaders were engaged in the work of the SAC. It was a largely symbolic initiative convened for external appearances and social legitimacy. That was then.

This is now: The days of the Symbolic SAC are rapidly coming to an end: As social and environmental challenges become increasingly material, gaining serious advice on these matters is no longer a luxury. *Increasingly corporations are seeking to elevate the SAC—to make it an integral part of the strategic process of the company.*

What are the best ways to do that?

In my experience, there are five keys to taking the Sustainability Advisory Council to the next level:

1. *Encourage Free Speech.* Include only the highest quality people from diverse backgrounds with stellar reputations and strong views. And then encourage them to speak their minds. The last thing you need is a polite group of advisors willing to rubber stamp CSR initiatives. SAC members should be encouraged to ask hard questions and introduce variety, not provide cover for existing practices and strategies.

2. *Make it Real.* Don't waste valuable time on peripheral activities like Sustainability Reports, Websites, and Staff Awards. Instead, engage the SAC in the real stuff—the strategic and operating challenges that are most significant to the company's future. If SAC members have not signed NDAs there is something wrong.

3. *Engage the C-Suite.* Cameo appearances by the Chief Executive no longer cut it. If the SAC is tackling serious strategic issues, then the CEO and other key C-Suite Executives need to be active participants in the deliberations. Deep dialogue and mutual learning can only happen when people spend time together and get to know each other.

4. *Interact with the Board.* The past separation between the SAC and the Board of Directors must come to an end. In tomorrow's world where sustainability and strategy are joined at the hip, the Board cannot govern effectively without access to the SAC's expertise, and the SAC cannot gain the necessary perspective without knowledge of the Board's concerns and priorities. Hold at least one joint meeting (or overlap the two meetings) each year.

5. *Compensate Appropriately.* Members of the Board of Directors are paid serious money for their year-round engagement in the company's governance. Nothing less should be expected from SAC members. This means that pro-bono appointments and token honoraria must give way to compensation commensurate with the new expectations. Bottom line: Don't skimp on SAC member compensation if you expect them to prioritize SAC work over the myriad of other opportunities and obligations on their plates.

How do you help corporations begin the journey?

It starts with the mindset. After working with scores of corporations and executive leaders over the past twenty years on matters relating to business and sustainability, I have come to the conclusion that there are fundamentally four distinct mindsets of executives when it comes to this challenge: *Deniers, Avoiders, Camouflagers,* and *Transformers.* Not surprisingly, the sustainability strategy (or lack of one) in any given company is driven by the prevailing mindsets. Allow me to describe them for each type:

Deniers are executives who either refuse to face facts or willfully deny the existence of a problem despite the existence of overwhelming evidence to the contrary. Whether the issue is climate change, poverty, inequity, or loss of biodiversity, deniers consistently discount scientific evidence as "biased" or align themselves with a fringe minority of "experts" who expound the opposing view. For deniers, climate change is a hoax and poverty is due to laziness or lack of aptitude. Context and circumstance matter little to deniers. Belief is absolute, not unlike religious dogma. For those working in companies led by Deniers, it is virtually impossible to be an effective sustainability change agent since these concerns are literally dismissed out of hand by senior leadership.

Avoiders are executives who may actually understand the social and environmental challenges we face, but either postpone serious consideration or seek to avoid engagement of the issues in the company altogether. The classic Avoider is in his or her early 60s or only 2-3 years away from retirement or being packaged out with a large financial windfall. Their primary motivation is selfish—to "kick the can down the road" so that they don't have to invest the time and emotional energy in the few years they have remaining. For the Avoider, the serious challenges of global sustainability can wait, so they become someone else's problem. Patience is required if one seeks to be a change agent or sustainability champion in a company led largely by Avoiders.

Camouflagers are executives who wrap themselves and their companies in the jargon of sustainability but fail to take decisive action or launch initiatives that would fundamentally alter their strategic path. They take on the "protective coloration" of sustainability by investing in incremental initiatives that continuously improve existing operations and strategies. Camouflagers want their cake and eat it to: external validation for their progressive stance but little in the way of strategic risk or change. Companies led by Camouflagers typically publish elaborate Sustainability Reports with lots of charts and graphs showing how eco-efficiency and corporate responsibility have reduced emissions, lowered costs, or built brand image. Those seeking to become engaged in sustainability in companies led by Camouflagers had best get their Six Sigma Black Belt or demonstrate a passion for corporate volunteerism.

Finally, **Transformers** are executives who are willing and able to stake out a new direction for their companies—one which will disrupt current industry structure and "leapfrog" toward a more sustainable world. Transformers are not afraid to take unpopular positions within the current industry; they often withdraw from industry associations, defund lobbying designed to preserve the status quo, and make preemptive investments that threaten to unseat industry incumbents. Not satisfied with incremental improvement, Transformers seek creative destruction. For those really interested in using the power of business to drive us toward a more environmentally sustainable and socially inclusive world, companies led by Transformers are the place to be.

But where does the learning come from? How can business accelerate the shift?

It has been 30 years since I completed my Ph.D. degree. Over that time, I've served on the faculties at three different "top 20" business schools—Michigan (Ross), University of North Carolina (Kenan-Flagler) and Cornell (Johnson) and started Centers focused on sustainable enterprise and inclusive business at all three. I've watched the "American" business school model—with its emphasis on scholarly publishing and functional core courses in the MBA program—spread across the world. And as I start on my fourth decade of professional life, I have come to a conclusion: *The dominant model of business education and entrepreneurial development is broken.*

We desperately need new models of business education and entrepreneurial development appropriate to the challenges we face in the 21st century, which include epidemic inequality, ecosystem degradation, and a looming climate crisis. We need transformative change and revolutionary new business models, not just adjustment around the edges. We need a focus on the skills required to imagine, co-create, launch and scale game-changing new ventures that simultaneously lift the poor and leapfrog to new environmentally sustainable ways of living.

I've joined forces with the University of Vermont to create a new Sustainable Entrepreneurship MBA program. In essence, we're doing something about the "saddlebag"[78] approach to sustainability that has permeated academic world for so long. Together with my colleague and friend **Dean Sanjay Sharma**, who I first met more than 15 years ago, we're taking action on our article, "Beyond 'Saddle Bag' Sustainability for Business Education" (Organization & Environment). It chronicles the history of how business schools have incrementally added courses in sustainability, corporate social responsibility and ethics in response to evolving societal demands. What we're doing represents a bold new venture where a major university has sought to fundamentally reinvent business education and the MBA degree by addressing the environment, ethics, entrepreneurship, poverty and inequality.

Our aim is to build and nurture a global, action-learning ecosystem[79], enabling us to develop the next generation of leaders who will build, disrupt, innovate and reinvent sustainable businesses and enterprises in a world that demands it.

---

[78] "Beyond "Saddle Bag" Sustainability for Business Education" by Sanjay Sharma, and Stuart L. Hart, *SAGE*
https://journals.sagepub.com/doi/abs/10.1177/1086026614520713?rss=1
[79] "Create a Business Ecosystem: Think Like a Mountain" *Stuart L. Hart*
http://stuartlhart.com/blog/2012/11/create-a-business-ecosystem-think-like-a-mountain.html

What advice do you have for the CEO who is trying to get the ball rolling?

I'd ask them a few questions:

Where will the company's disruptive and leapfrog technologies come from?

Significant attention has been paid to the challenges of business model innovation, co-creation, and organizational innovation in facilitating BoP business venturing. Less attention has been paid to where the technologies and innovations that drive such ventures come from and how they might be best developed. Businesses are beginning to focus on the three primary sources of new technology for driving inclusive and sustainable business development and how they are best driven from the bottom up: Exponential technology, shelf technology, and grassroots/indigenous technology.

Is there a way for BoP business logic be applied to the developed world?

For the past decade the primary focus has been on the challenges of building successful BoP businesses in the impoverished rural areas and megacity slums of the developing world. Comparatively little attention, however, has been paid to how innovation from the bottom up might create opportunity and better serve the growing underclass in the US, Europe and other parts of the Rich World.

How do we move beyond silos? How do we apply systems thinking to improve BoP Sustainability?

Most BoP ventures to date have been focused on the sectors and industries that define business at the top of the pyramid: water, energy, transportation, telecommunications, food, housing, health, and education, to name just a few. Yet increasingly we see that the world's challenges, particularly those at the base of the pyramid, do not fit neatly into traditional sectoral or industry compartments. Instead, they cross boundaries and require broader ecosystems of partners to succeed. How do businesses understand and take on the challenges and opportunities of systems thinking, boundary spanning, ecosystems and interconnections in creating and scaling BoP innovations?

So yes, we are still stuck at the crossroads. **Given our short tenure on this planet, we humans are a bit like the crash test dummies** from the Auto industry, moving in slow motion: The changes that we see around us seem gradual enough that they do not seem particularly out of the ordinary— we've always had hurricanes, tornadoes, floods, droughts, and wildfires. So, maybe we are just in a bad stretch. Or even if this is the new normal, perhaps it won't be that bad: warmer temperatures mean longer growing seasons…etc.

But when we view this video in "real time"—that is in *geologic time*—then the changes that are happening are occurring in the blink of an eye, like the actual crash of the crash test dummies. As far as we can tell, the atmosphere and the climate of the earth have never changed this quickly before, in the history of the planet. Not even close. *Sure, the climate has fluctuated wildly over the billions of years that life has thrived on our planet.* But the changes took place over millennia, not decades. There was time for life to adapt. We, unfortunately, are driving ourselves into the proverbial wall, but we can only see it happening in slow motion. Time to clean out the head gear, humanity, or the next generation of dummies will not like how this crash video turns out.

What about the future of Corporate Social Responsibility?

There is a long-standing narrative in the field of management that goes something like this: Executives are hired to maximize profits, not social welfare: Spending shareholders' money on socially responsible but unprofitable endeavors is irresponsible.

Indeed, as stated in a recent *Wall Street Journal* editorial: "In cases where private profits and public interests are aligned, the idea of corporate social responsibility is irrelevant: companies that simply do everything they can to boost profits will end up increasing social welfare." But, the author argues, "in most cases, **doing what's best for society means sacrificing profits**…If it weren't, {society's pervasive and persistent} problems would have been solved long ago by companies seeking to maximize their profits." **The ultimate solution**, the author argues, **"is government regulation."**

There is a familiar ring to this argument. Indeed, *The Economist* dedicated a special section[80] to the topic as far back as 2005. However, most realize this perspective can be traced to **Milton Friedman's** famous dictum: **"The social responsibility of business is to increase profit."** While many

---

[80] "The good company" *The Economist* https://www.economist.com/special-report/2005/01/22/the-good-company

have demonized Friedman for his stance, it turns out–ironically–that he was right!

As Friedman asserted in his classic 1970 article[81] by the same title, it makes little sense for corporate managers to spend the shareholders' money on pet philanthropic projects that have little or no connection to the company's work. In fact, **the core premise of "corporate social responsibility" (CSR)–profit spending for the "greater good"–is fundamentally flawed.** While individuals can choose to donate their private wealth in any way they choose, corporate executives are paid to put the shareholders' capital to productive (i.e. profitable) use.

Even under the best of circumstances, it is simply not possible for companies to give away enough money to have a material impact on the world's growing list of social and environmental ills. CSR is like trying to bail out a sinking ship with a teaspoon. And as Maimonides made clear more than eight centuries ago, real philanthropy means giving anonymously. By this standard, **most CSR programs today are little more than self-serving public relations gambits designed to assuage corporate guilt.**

Where **Friedman was wrong**, however, was in **assuming that corporations cannot understand societal problems or environmental challenges**, which he viewed as the exclusive responsibility of elected governments. It is true that corporations are not democratic institutions designed to reflect the broad "public interest." But increasingly, it seems that the broad "public interest" is really an illusion–an abstract ideal created by enlightenment thinkers preoccupied with the design of rational and representative forms of government.

Ironically, **today's representative governments, captured by monied interests and powerful players, have become all but incapable of addressing society's real challenges.** The power of "incumbency" has rendered government a conservative (rather than progressive) force, protecting the interests of those seeking to perpetuate "yesterday's" solutions. It should come as little surprise, for example, that **Dick Cheney's** now infamous "energy task force" included no one from the renewable energy or conservation sectors. Nor should it be a surprise that efforts by the Obama Administration to reform the financial system,

---

[81] "The social responsibility of business is to increase profit" by *Milton Friedman* http://umich.edu/~thecore/doc/Friedman.pdf

reinvent health care, or craft a sensible climate policy were met with stiff resistance.

National governments are self-interested by design, concerned first and foremost with the security and well-being of their citizens. Tragically, **preoccupation with the "national interest" makes government less and less relevant in a world characterized by trans-boundary challenges** such as climate change, loss of biodiversity, and international terrorism. It is not at all clear today that the sum of "national interests" equals the "public interest" of the world. The relative ineffectiveness of the United Nations system over the past five decades stands in mute testimony to this fact.

Ironically, then, the for-profit corporation may turn out to be our best hope for a "sustainable" future—economically, socially, and environmentally.

Increasingly, corporations are global in scope, making them ideally suited to address trans-boundary problems and international challenges. It is not by happenstance, for example, that some multinational companies have led initiatives to address climate change (e.g. the US Climate Action Partnership), loss of marine fisheries (e.g. the Marine Stewardship Council), and sustainable development (e.g. the World Business Council for Sustainable Development).

Even more significantly, corporations may be better positioned than governments to understand—and respond to—emerging societal needs. Not the broad and abstract "public interest" trumpeted by enlightenment thinkers, but rather the fine-grained, on-the-ground, "micro" interests of actual individuals, families, and communities (human and natural). Getting "close to the customer" is, after all, the stock and trade of the corporate world. The profit motive can accelerate (not inhibit) the transformation toward global sustainability, with civil society, governments, and multilateral agencies all playing crucial roles as collaborators and watchdogs. **Through thousands (or even millions) of business-led initiatives, we can innovate our way into tomorrow's "clean" technology, and welcome the four billion poor at the "base of the pyramid" into the global economy.** The competitive process will weed out the bad initiatives—those that work neither for people, nature, nor shareholders. And like the industrial revolution two centuries ago, this commerce-led revolution will need no central administrator.

The end is nigh for the notion of "corporate social responsibility."

Emerging in its place are a new generation of **corporations that actually solve social and environmental problems through their core strategies**—and *profit in the process*. It's called **sustainable value**[82].

Where does your company fit in?

---

[82] "Sustainable Value" by Stuart Hart and Mark Milstein
http://www.stuartlhart.com/sustainablevalue.html

DAVID HINDS
Where There is No Justice

*Musician **David Hinds** is the founder and front-man for **Steel Pulse**, the world's leading reggae band. In 1978, race relations in Britain were in crisis.*

The National Front was gathering power and immigrants lived in fear of violence. But that year saw the birth of a campaign - Rock Against Racism (RAR) - aimed at halting the tide of hatred with music - a grassroots movement culminating in a march across London and open-air concerts across England and even in France. The campaign involved groups like The Clash, Steel Pulse, Buzzcocks, X-Ray Spex, The Ruts, and others, staging concerts with an anti-racist theme, in order to discourage young people from embracing racist views.

For over forty years, the band has brought conscious music and a message of equality to fans all around the world.

Steel Pulse has had a long history of fighting for social justice. How has that challenge shifted over the years?

I've never really been asked this kind of question before. But come to think of it, our message has transcended the national boundaries of the British

Isles, where several other countries, including the USA, the French
territories, the Caribbean and the entire African diaspora, who have been
affected by colonialism, have recognized and embraced our cry for justice
and equality. Our message has gone as far as having countries and regions
using us as a political tool to gain independence; something we were
completely unaware of at the time while it was happening. At that time, we
were given the impression that it was just another regular concert in a
faraway land, totally oblivious to the political undertones that awaited us.
And so, the answer is yes, this course has meandered over the years and it is
amazing to know that the whole "rocking against racism"[83] situation has
come 360 degrees.

Equality and justice are not abstract concepts. From the very beginning, we
decided to stand for people whose voices were not being heard – the
sufferah, as we say. Yes, things have changed, times have changed, but the
war for justice is still being fought every day. We started by singing about
injustice in our neighborhood of Handsworth, but that message resonated
around the world. Now our message is universal and our fans stand with us
around the world. Justice stands for all.

**What are the main issues facing the world today, and how do you
address them in your music?**

There are too many critical issues in this world today. All of them have
become critical because they initially started as things that were either not
taken seriously, or, where all of us thought that the problems will be solved
by laws, legislations and with time; not realizing that often times it's the
ones that have been administering laws and legislations, are the ones that
are responsible for creating the problems in the first place. I did brush on
racism and how the band has played an active role which began on our
home turf, but there are more issues besides racism, like human-trafficking
for instance. Many seem to believe that slavery was just a one-time thing
that ended over a hundred and fifty years ago. Now, with the age of the
Internet we are able to be informed far more accurately about the situation.

Steel Pulse has gone to the extent of recording such sentiments on our
latest album, "Mass Manipulation."

---

[83] https://en.wikipedia.org/wiki/Rock_Against_Racism

What is the new album about, and why now? Why the title "Mass Manipulation"?

Well, look at the times. We are probably in the worst place that humankind has ever been. The planet burns, and our politicians look the other way. We had to do something. And that's what this album is about. It's about waking people up to the predicament we face, as individuals, as communities, and as a planet.

Mass Manipulation is about the state we find ourselves in – and by we, I mean all of us. Turn on your television or check your Internet. Almost nothing about the dangerous predicament the Earth is in. No mention of the failure of our governments and public institutions to check the climate crisis. Instead, we're off to another war. That's what this album is about. We explore the various themes of injustice – the rise in hate around the world. And the media? Fake news everywhere. We could never trust the corporate media, but now everything must be fact-checked – twice.

So what's the answer? Can music make a difference?

Of course. Music is a part of our cultural life – and it has always been a channel to get a message through. The radio is dead – almost everything on the airwaves is morally and intellectually bankrupt. But that doesn't mean we can't sing our songs and get them out to the fans. Over the years we have built huge grassroots following – and these fans stay with us through thick and thin. Music is a way to give meaning and purpose to our everyday lives – not just through melodies, but also through the conscious message. That's what we have tried to be about, these past forty-five years.

So you are marketing justice and peace?

That's a funny way of saying it, but yes, we feel like that's the point. *Everyone must become an activist now.* Or we lose our future. Just take a look at Australia. The prime minister denies climate change and pushed the coal lobby. See what that gets you?

Add to that the message of hate we see politicians pushing across the world. White nationalism, bashing immigrants. What is the point of this? America was built on immigration, sadly. And now the government there continues to roll back all environmental-friendly laws to continue the rape of the Earth. Why? Tell us why, Mr. Politrickster? They sold the planet and our future, for a few pieces of silver. Should we, the people, just sit there and accept this future? Of course not.

Let's talk about the songs and the themes on this album. You cover revolution, racism, poverty, police brutality, human trafficking – and end with a positive plea for a "Higher Love." What went through your mind when you planned this album?

An album like this is not an overnight thing. It took shape over the years. Of course, we have always been about love, peace and justice. Without love there is no justice, and without justice there can be no peace. That has been a fundamental thread that runs through all our work.

We start with a song called "Rize." You can't make the world better by sitting on the couch. Get up, meet up with others, get organized. If you want **True Democracy**, you will have to fight for it.

So much for fallen soldiers
Don't let them die in vain
So much for freedom fighters
It's now that we feel your pain
So much for so called justice
A martyr's sacrifice
Got gunned down during the protest
Demanding our equal rights, equal rights, hey

The *world's gone mad*. That's what it seems like – and it won't fix itself.

The album was nominated for a Grammy?

(Laughs) Yes. We hope to stimulate the minds of all, to care more about the exploitation of so many across the planet. Prison reform has been one of the biggest "cop outs," in existence right now. How can reforms possibly work, if there are financial incentives to build more prisons?

Unfortunately, religion has also been used as a tool of manipulation.

And when you hone in on the situation, the bottom line is racism, once again. The surfacing of Brexit and its concepts run parallel to what is happening in the United States, where one is led to believe that their life style will be compromised by "foreigners." It is a cynical ploy foisted on a sleeping public. These are all hallmarks that have spawned the rebirth of factions such as the KKK. Nationalism and anti-immigrant sentiments fuel hate, brought to us by politicians and movements designed to divide us.

Then there's also the concern for safety, especially in public environments, with children losing their lives in schools during these mass shootings. All forms of terrorism, everywhere.

Global warming is also an issue that one should continue to address. Far too many creatures are on the verge of extinction because of this. We see a calamitous climate shift across the continents – from the melting snowcaps, to monster hurricanes, the desertification of vast areas of land, and the release of methane from the permafrost. Add to that the population problem, and leadership structures that don't look out for the needs of the people.

Music might not be the best solution to all of this but at least it's a medium that people of all ages and aspects of life, can share the same engagement. We know that for every thousand that listens to conscious music, maybe 10 might go on and act upon it. That one percent is better than zero percent, don't you agree? And it's always the people who care the most who make that significant difference – that's who we aim to reach with our messages.

The music is the message and the message is: ***without love there is no justice, and without justice there is no peace***.

At the end of the day, we share many things in common.

And that's what we must focus on. Do we want a world of brutality? without life? without hope? That's where we are going, if we don't rise up. Smoking ganja isn't going to increase justice in the world. You have to ***act***.

The narrative is simple. Without respect for all forms of life, we won't have a future worth living. The kids know this, and that's why we have **Greta Thunberg** and friends standing up. The **First People** show us the way – they are struggling to save the Earth from destruction – around the globe – from the Amazon to Australia to Hawaii. We must heed their warnings or perish. The rebellion is here and now. On the social justice front, we see **Colin Kaepernick** fighting and sacrificing everything for the truth. The NFL has failed.

Thank the rebels. Without them there is no progress. What is needed now is something ***more***.

We can't keep polarizing people. Reggae is about unity – and that's why we did the remake of "Higher Love" – the **Steve Winwood** song. By adding the "Rasta Love" vibe, we feel the song is more relevant than ever.

What do you think businesses need to be doing at a time like this?

Business and governments must serve their customers, the people. Build society instead of breaking it. Become conscious. Think of the long term. Where there is no justice, there will never be true prosperity. With all these issues, business corporations should seize the opportunity to get on board to promote positivity and prove to the populace that they are not all about grabbing the consumers' money.

Take Colin Kaepernick for instance, he was ostracized for taking a peaceful stance against the various kinds of injustice in the US. But on a humanitarian level, there was nothing wrong with what he was trying to relay to both his country and the world. So it was on this type of platform that Nike launched a brand new kind of a publicity campaign. I know PUMA is also doing something with Tommie Smith, so we are hoping to see more campaigns along these lines.

We still have plastic pollution and contamination to address, so why not make these bottled water entities design plans and ways of disposing this surplus of waste? Better still, have consumers play an active role to cut this pollution.

Prisons... How can these projects work to make sure that a prisoner, once released, has a secured job to come out to, which can work in accordance to the prisoner's academic and physical ability? I am talking about really helping them get their lives back on path. The list goes on as to the many goals and targets that can be set by business corporations.

Do you want peace and prosperity and a world in which Nature still has a place? Then what should you be doing differently? If one has a negative mind, then one can see a bleak future. Here are the words of the Emperor, Haile Selassie, that have helped me to live a life of hope and to put things into perspective:

"Throughout history, it has been the inaction of those who could have acted; the indifference of those who should have known better; the silence of the voice of justice when it mattered most; that has made it possible for EVIL to triumph."

We've got to continue to build a positive foundation for the generations to come.

What next?

We take our own advice. Get on the road[84] and try to spread the word – it's time to take back our Planet. To promote justice not war. Democracy is hard won, but easily lost. Keep the faith, and fight for it.

---

[84] *Steel Pulse* Tour Dates https://steelpulse.com/tour

CLARK FOX
Enough is Enough

Clark V. Fox [85] *(aka Michael Clark 1946) is a highly acclaimed, award winning American master artist with a Native American heritage. He spent the early part of his career as a second-generation Washington Color School painter in the 60's along with Sam Gilliam. They were the only two minority artists in that group of painters. He then moved to New York and began creating conceptual pop-art with a twist. That twist was a message of rebellion. Works by Clark Fox are included in more than 42 museum collections including the Yale University Art Gallery, National Gallery of Art, The Metropolitan, American University Katzen Museum, Phillips Collection, The Dorothy and Herbert Vogel Collection, Philadelphia Museum of Art, Smithsonian American Art Museum, and more. Clark earned his undergraduate degree at Pratt Institute and the Corcoran School of Art, although he admits he is self-taught. He founded and ran the not-for-profit art space called MOCA DC for over 14 years where he became known as the "Godfather of Modern Underground Art." This claim came from his participation in the new Street Art movement supporting the likes of Ron English and Sheppard Fairey in the 1990s. Clark is considered by none other than James Harithas as "one of America's greatest artists."*

---

[85] www.clarkfox.com

You've been compared to Warhol with one notable exception. You didn't sell out. Can you tell us about how you started painting?

(**Laughs**) I lived art history. I studied with Unichi Hiratsuka at the Japan-American Society of Washington DC, took figure drawing class with Lennart Anderson, and studied color with Irwin Rubin (Josef Albers assistant) at Pratt. I produced all 50 ***Popsicle*** paintings for the conceptual project called the Gene Davis *Giveaway* in 1969, and worked for and studied with Thomas Downing. I hung out with Rivers, Rauschenberg, Mary Heilmann, Jo Baer, Julian Schnabel, and Warhol.

My church is art, and I still feel it's a sacred trust.

Your art is political and relevant. How do you stay connected to the issues?

How can you not stay connected to the issues? Look at what's going on in this country, in the world. Right now we have a disgusting election season with the prospect of yet more war when the dust settles. The corporations are continuing their relentless march for profits, marginalizing the middle class and exploiting the poor. Mr. Peanut is eating our democracy for lunch. That's why I'm involved with **Move to Amend**- we must overturn *Citizen's United* for starters.

I can't look the other way.

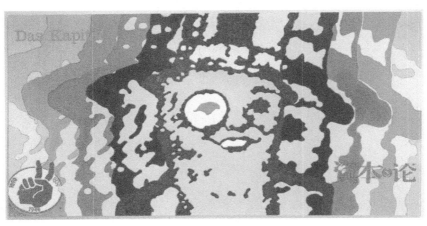

Who is Mr. Peanut?

Mr. Peanut seems like a real nice guy, but under his thin peanut shell he represents *all* capitalists with their relentless warmongering, profiting motives whose business profits from the death of the innocent and destroying our precious biosphere. Our history has rewarded greed, and the military-industrial complex shows no sign of weakness. Our democracy – alas – has been stolen. We kill for money. And we, the people, fund this madness. Mr. Peanut is my disdain for war profiteering and the exploitation of the masses and of mother earth.

What about the NAFTA Oranges? That's also a heavy political statement, is it not?

(Laughs) Not sure how heavy it is, but the NAFTA Oranges represent the trade deals made to benefit a few transnationals at the expense of the citizens of both sides.

I began just after the North American Free Trade Agreement went into effect – all modeled after fruit I bought from a Mexican guy on the side of the freeway. NAFTA has helped nothing except create more income inequality.

How has your Native American heritage shaped your work?

It has been the driving force behind my works. George Washington was not my President. His Native American name was ***Conotocarious*** meaning **Town Destroyer**.

Being a stranger in our own land has been the fate of the Native American and continues to this day. Just look at the situation with the Standing Rock Sioux and the Dakota Access Pipeline business. How is it that today we are still fighting the same battle and enemy all over again?

Is nothing sacred but profits?

Don't get me started. The *Lakota* are standing up for our sacred mother Earth and for the generations yet to come. And on the other side we have a militarized response from the state, private police, and serious threats to put journalists behind bars.

I mean, what does freedom mean? The freedom to plunder the earth's biosphere?

We have 10 years left to save the human species from extinction and these fools are worried about next quarter's earnings?

Collective human action is required to stabilize the Earth. There should be a global Marshall plan put in place now. Once the feedback loops start rolling there is no way to reverse the tipping points. We are presently in the Anthropocene, the 6th largest extinction of species on the planet. The Native Americans understand this very well. And on top of that we have the return of widespread racism, the KKK and confederate flag-wavers who know nothing besides hate. Our water is being poisoned by the fracking lobby, plastic pollution, geo engineering, runoff, and radiation from the Fukushima spill in 2011. The police are being completely militarized, we have lost our civil liberties, and we have a lunatic, robber-baron misogynistic demagogue for a sitting President.

And that's just in this country. Look at the rest of the world.

What message do you have for the world of business today?

Enough is enough. I have been reading a book called *Giants: The Global Power* by Peter Phillips. It is a must read if we are going to figure out who among this group will help influence the others. He suggests that we outlaw the billionaire class. I don't know what business solution is best because I am an artist.

Mother nature will equalize everything so we have to get off this unsustainable paradigm and get a new sustainable equitable paradigm fast. The Polar ice caps are melting as we speak and the huge category 4 and 5 hurricanes are coming. How many fires can we take? And there is a food and water shortage that no one is talking about. How is that good for your business?

Elon Musk may be crazy, but he's doing something. Why can't you?

Do the elites think that they can go away to New Zealand and be safe? There won't be anything left for their kids and grand-kids. Why is this so hard to understand? What can you do to solve our problem with government? Can we ban lobbying? Can we ban campaign contributions like they do in Canada? Why have we made bribery legal in this country?

We need business leaders that think. Think what you can do to help this country and this planet. We must come together to solve our complex problems. No time to waste. We need a global plan and we need it now.

HAZEL HENDERSON
Some Prescriptions for Human & Planetary Health

Hazel Henderson is the founder of Ethical Markets Media, LLC[86], a certified B-corporation, and the creator and co-executive Producer of its TV series. She is a world-renowned futurist, evolutionary economist, a worldwide syndicated columnist, consultant on sustainable development, and author of The Axiom and Nautilus award-winning book Ethical Markets: Growing the Green Economy[87] (2006) and eight other books. She co-edited, with Harlan Cleveland and Inge Kaul, The UN: Policy and Financing Alternatives, Elsevier Scientific, UK 1995 (US edition, 1996), and co-authored with Japanese Buddhist leader Daisaku Ikeda, Planetary Citizenship (2004). Henderson started Ethical Markets Media, LLC, to disseminate information on green investing, socially responsible investing, green business, green energy, business ethics news, environmentally friendly technology, good corporate citizenship and sustainable development by making available reports, articles, newsletters and video gathered from around the world.

A leading proponent of Earth Ethics[88], Henderson has been one of the critics to point out that the definitions of reality devised by natural and social scientists often pertain to the realities they are paid to study — raising questions as to who has funded these investigators and theoreticians, and why? Who deems certain research grants to be worthy of funding? Which questions crop up in the first place? Henderson believes that the various threats to peace, community security, and good environment have led us into a new era in which we are obliged to look for values, information, and know-how that we seemed to be able to do without until recent decades.

How ethical are markets today? Can a few bad actors destroy the planet?

Yes, we live in a world globalized on narrow economic textbooks which claim to be value free, but state that human nature is greedy, selfish and competitive! These theories also tell us that taking care of children, elders, sick and households, volunteering in the community is "un-economic." In reality, these so-called "economic laws" are bogus and mostly wrong, but they have institutionalized incentives that condone the most primitive kinds

---

[86] www.ethicalmarkets.com
[87] Ethical Markets: Growing the Green Economy by Hazel Henderson
https://www.amazon.com/Ethical-Markets-Growing-Green-Economy/dp/1933392231
[88] "Beyond Economism: Toward Earth Ethics" by *Hazel Henderson*
http://www.earthcharterinaction.org/invent/images/uploads/ENG-Henderson.pdf

of human behaviors, described in many religious traditions as "the Seven Deadly Sins" (greed, selfishness, competition, jealously, envy, love of money and materialism)!

REPERTOIRE of HUMAN BEHAVIOR

Conflict ← Competition Cooperation → Sharing

GAME THEORY

PSYCHOLOGY

SOCIOLOGY

ANTHROPOLOGY

INFORMATION/DECISION/THEORY

MARKET ECONOMICS

Thus, businesses around the world and in many countries have been able to over-ride more cohesive communities and values and been allowed in economic accounting protocols to simply "externalize" from their balance sheets social, environmental and human costs their operations frequently incur and burden future generations.

So a few bad actors, whether corporations manufacturing weapons of mass destruction or handguns, those promoting nuclear power, as well as militaristic governments, scientists, lone actors and terrorist groups … can indeed cause planetary-level destruction.

What must be done to accelerate the good?

To accelerate and incentivize the good in human societies, leaders at all levels and sectors need to promote and exemplify higher standards of behavior, based on "The Golden Rule" and teach higher levels of awareness of human interdependence. We humans now need to evolve as a species toward maturity and accept the scientific knowledge of how our home planet functions in relation to our "Mother Star" the Sun, and our interdependence with all other life forms in the biosphere. See my essay – *The Politics of Connectivity*[89].

---

[89] "The Politics of Connectivity" by *Hazel Henderson*

What signs do you see that business is taking sustainability more seriously than before?

Due to public pressure, building up since the 20th century, people suffering the damage from corporate activities began to organize and demand reforms. Today, these protests have increased, forming global movements (e.g: 350.org, Greenpeace, Friends of the Earth, WWF and the global children's strike led by Greta Thunberg). Thousands of laws and international protocols convened by the United Nations, the EU and other international bodies, as well as national governments are forcing corporations to begin internalizing all those "externalities" in new holistic accounting models. Since the 1970s, socially responsible investors and asset managers have also pressured corporations with their screen and ESG investing models, divesting from fossil fuels and irresponsible companies' stock, as well as engagement with management, naming and shaming publicity and damaging their brands and reputations. This is why we at Ethical Markets support your work with Philip Kotler!

Elections have consequences. How does the politicization of policy hurt the future?

Politics is finally catching up with the current faulty model of economic globalization based on "externalities" and GDP-measured growth. These public pressures led 195 members of the United Nations to ratify the new model for progress: The Sustainable Development Goals (SDGs) in 2015.

In 2019, in the USA, 90 members of the 116th Congress launched the Resolution for a Green New Deal, which our decade of Green Transition Scoreboard ®[90] research buttresses, that would transition the US economy from fossilized sectors to 100% renewable energy by 2030.
So-called "populist" revolts against the narrow corporate and finance sector led globalization must be addressed by requiring corporations, governments and finance to internalize all the "externalities" within their accounting systems and adopt the "6 Forms of Capital"[91] (finance, built, intellectual, social , human and natural) promoted by the International Integrated

---

https://www.ethicalmarkets.com/the-politics-of-connectivity-by-hazel-henderson/
[90] "2018 Green Transition Scoreboard" by Hazel Henderson, LaRae Long, Timothy Jack Nash http://4a5qvh23tbek30e0mg42uq87.wpengine.netdna-cdn.com/wp-content/uploads/2018/04/GTS-2018-Full-Report-1.pdf
[91] "Get to grips with the six capitals" *Integrated Reporting*
https://integratedreporting.org/what-the-tool-for-better-reporting/get-to-grips-with-the-six-capitals/

Reporting Council[92]. They must also repeal all subsidies to fossil fuels and fossilized sectors, while levying fines and taxes on all forms of pollution, including CO2.

What do you feel the business community needs to do now?

The business community worldwide needs to reform all business models to conform with all these new full-spectrum accounting standards and phase out polluting methods and products, as we and the Biomimicry Institute[93] prescribe in our *Principles of Ethical Biomimicry Finance*[94] which provides a one-stop knowledge system for asset managers and investors.

[92] International Integrated Reporting Council https://integratedreporting.org/
[93] "The Promise of Biomimicry" https://biomimicry.org/
[94] "Principles of Ethical Biomimicry Finance"
http://ethicalbiomimicryfinance.com/methodology.html

PHILIP KOTLER
The War for The Soul of Capitalism

Philip Kotler [95] is the "father of modern marketing." He is the S.C. Johnson & Son Distinguished Professor of International Marketing at the Kellogg School of Management at Northwestern University.

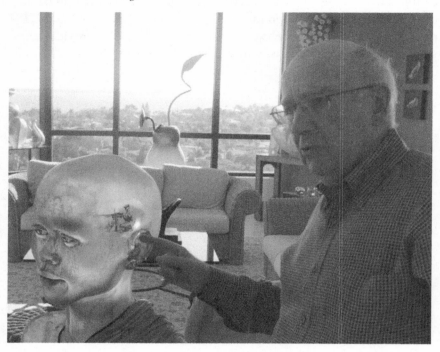

He was voted the first Leader in Marketing Thought by the American Marketing Association and named The Founder of Modern Marketing Management in the Handbook of Management Thinking. Professor Kotler holds major awards including the American Marketing Association's (AMA) Distinguished Marketing Educator Award and Distinguished Educator Award from The Academy of Marketing Science. The Sales and Marketing Executives International (SMEI) named him Marketer of the Year and the American Marketing Association described him as "the most influential marketer of all time." Kotler is in the Thinkers50 Hall of Fame[96], and is featured as a "guru" in the Economist[97]. He is the author Confronting Capitalism: Real

[95] www.pkotler.org
[96] *Thinkers50 Hall of Fame* http://thinkers50.com/hall-of-fame/
[97] "Guru Philip Kotler" *The Economist*
https://www.economist.com/news/2008/09/12/philip-kotler

Solutions for a Troubled Economic System,[98] 2015; and Democracy in Decline: Rebuilding its Future[99], 2016.

You have made a distinction between companies that care about their social obligations and companies that don't. Why is this important? Economists used to say that the only responsibility of business is to make a profit. Many companies still believe that. What do you say to that?

The idea of brand activism is not really a new one. In our book, *Corporate Social Responsibility*[100], we interviewed 45 companies. We asked each company: "Do you give money to charity? Have you adopted a favorite cause? Why did you choose that cause? Do you monitor whether the money has helped the cause? Do you know whether your company's reputation improved as a result?" Our book shows the findings. Consumers who are interested in buying from caring companies will have a better sense of whether the caring is real or just window-dressing.

But what is now critical is to understand is that the landscape has changed.

Millennials led the way, but now most customers have high expectations for brands. We live in a world filled with constant problems – air pollution, bad drinking water, crimes, income inequality. The brands that show real concern not just for profits but for the communities they serve, and the world we live in are the ones that are coming to the forefront. A caring company must make its activities visible to its customers. It needs to show its values and commitments early, and that it cares about its people, cities, communities, and the planet.

If you present the evidence, customers will reward you.

More and more customers are become aware of their voting power in the market place and that they favor buying from caring companies. And when you add social media to the mix, there is "instant activism."

---

[98] *Confronting Capitalism: Real Solutions for a Troubled Economic System* by Philip Kotler https://www.amazon.com/Confronting-Capitalism-Solutions-Troubled-Economic/dp/0814436455/
[99] *Democracy in Decline* by Philip Kotler https://www.amazon.com/Democracy-Decline-Rebuilding-its-Future/dp/147398050X/
[100] *Corporate Social Responsibility: Doing the Most Good for Your Company and Your Cause* by Philip Kotler https://www.amazon.com/Corporate-Social-Responsibility-Doing-Company-ebook/dp/B008N9IXLI

What do you think of the scuffle between Kraft Heinz and Unilever?

That is exactly the issue. We are fighting a battle, as Bill George[101] says, for the soul of Capitalism.

As George explains, you had Unilever's Paul Polman championing sustainable growth in earnings to raise long-term shareholder value. On the other side, you had KHC's Bernardo Vieira Hees and its Brazilian owner 3G Capital. They want to maximize short-term earnings to increase near-term valuation.

Of course, the outcry was loud, and 3G withdrew its offer just 50 hours after it was made.

I agree with George when he says that the *larger issue at stake here is not just the fate of a single company, but the fate of capitalism itself.*

Is it really that bleak? What can businesses do to understand their place in society?

We have a disconnect. Businesses that think they exist independent of society are not going to last. Perhaps it is the fault of our MBA education and perhaps it is the fault of our business culture that still emphasizes "maximizing shareholder value."

Even *Jack Welch* reversed his philosophy. In his now infamous interview[102] with the *Financial Times* he tells us – "On the face of it, shareholder value is the dumbest idea in the world. Shareholder value is a result, not a strategy… your main constituencies are your employees, your customers and your products. Managers and investors should not set share price increases as their overarching goal. … Short-term profits should be allied with an increase in the long-term value of a company."

Where did this idea of "maximizing shareholder value" come from?

I think it was Roger Martin who said that this mess begins with Michael Jensen and Dean William Meckling of the Simon School of Business at the University of Rochester. They published "Theory of the Firm: Managerial

---

[101] "CNBC: The Battle for the Soul of Capitalism Explained in One Hostile Takeover Bid" by Bill George https://www.billgeorge.org/articles/cnbc-the-battle-for-the-soul-of-capitalism-explained-in-one-hostile-takeover-bid/
[102] "Welch condemns share price focus" https://www.ft.com/content/294ff1f2-0f27-11de-ba10-0000779fd2ac

Behavior, Agency Costs and Ownership Structure" in the *Journal of Financial Economics*. That was in 1976.

The article was intellectually and philosophically incorrect. It basically said that shareholders are the owner of the business, while the executives are agents who are hired by the principals to work on their behalf. Jensen and Meckling argued that the goal of a company should be to maximize the return to shareholders.

And that was the biggest scam in business. Now anything goes under the mantra of "maximizing shareholder value."

What do you mean?

Well, let's reference Peter Drucker. He tells us that ***the only valid purpose of a firm is to create a customer*** I am convinced that the polarization in society, the stark rise in income inequality and the staggering rise in the levels of CEO pay are directly related.

I agree with Bill George when he says that unconstrained capitalism focusing on short-term gains can cause great harm to employees, communities and the greater needs of society.

And it is precisely because of this that we have the rise of populism around the world.

Our titans of industry are shooting themselves in the foot by not comprehending the existential threat populism holds for the future of their businesses.

But isn't this really about price? Don't customers deserve the best and lowest prices?

That is again a misapplication of the philosophy that low prices are the end-all.

Do we really want low-prices that are the result of exploitation, slave labor, or environmental degradation on the other side of the globe?

The true cost of low prices is that the cost is borne by society – to its detriment.

Globalization has brought many changes, and as we are learning now, not all of them were good.

The feelings of powerlessness and frustration in a world dominated by wealthy elites has led to the resurgence of nationalism, protectionism, and growing threats of war and violence.

Our business leaders forgot their history.

Let's discuss the concept of Demarketing. How does that play into all of this?

We have built this unsustainable world on the backs of consumer debt.

The question is how do we get people to use a scarce resource more carefully.

We started thinking about this in 1971 – the concept of demarketing[103]. If you recall, the 4Ps (product, price, place, promotion) provide solutions:

First, we design products that will use less water, such as by designing more efficient showerheads. Second, we raise the price of water to discourage consumption. Third, we make less water available in certain channels. Fourth, we use promotion to make people more ashamed of wasting water.

The demarketing idea is very generic. *We just reverse the direction of the 4 Ps.*

Make the product less necessary, more expensive, less available, and more shameful. Companies like Patagonia will sell you a jacket that lasts a lifetime. They'll even repair it for you. This is good sense. It should be a best practice for the future of product development.

Does the conflict also arise out of the power structure within organizations? How many CEOs were promoted from sales, where they are responsible for "maximizing revenue"?

If you look at a study done by *Harvard Business Review* on the *Best Performing CEOs*[104], we learn that there are so many reasons for leaders to focus on the short term: slow growth, shareholder activism, political turmoil—to name just a few. Yet the study highlights the CEOs that still manage to focus on the long term and deliver strong performance over many years.

---

[103] "Welcome to the Age of Demarketing" by Philip Kotlerhttp://www.marketingjournal.org/welcome-to-the-age-of-demarketing-an-excerpt-from-philip-kotlers-autobiography-philip-kotler/
[104] The Best-Performing CEOs in the World, *Harvard Business Review* https://hbr.org/2016/11/the-best-performing-ceos-in-the-world

Prior to 2015, the rankings were based *purely on financial returns*; by that measure Jeff Bezos of Amazon led the pack for three years running.

What's interesting is that when *HBR* started including ratings of companies' environmental, social, and governance (ESG) performance as a variable, there was a big shift in ranking.

There's a profound discussion led by Adi Ignatius on this – with Novo Nordisk CEO Lars Rebien Sørensen, WPP CEO Martin Sorrell, and Inditex CEO Pablo Isla – the three top ranked CEOs based on paying attention to their ESG performance.

So how should businesses change? How can they become more caring and still balance profit-making with the future?

Perhaps the best explanation of this comes from Ratan Tata[105] who tells us:

Profits are like happiness in that they are a byproduct of other things. Happiness, for example, can stem from having a strong sense of purpose, meaningful work and deep relationships. Those who focus obsessively on their own happiness are usually narcissists — and end up miserable. Similarly, companies need a purpose that transcends making money; they need sustainability strategies that recognize that you can make money by doing good things rather than the other way around.

Marketers need to lead the way, working with their CEOs to nurture the future. The $64,000 question is: How do we create and nurture markets, communities, and the future of society?

---

[105] "Why Making Money Is Not Enough" by Ratan Tata, Stuart L. Hart, Aarti Sharma and Christian Sarkar, *MIT Sloan Management Review*
https://sloanreview.mit.edu/article/why-making-money-is-not-enough/

11. LETTER TO BILL GATES (AND FRIENDS)

Dear **Bill Gates** (and friends),

You are giving back to society. But, as someone once famously said, **if you're giving back, you may have taken too much.** Nick Hanauer warns us that the "pitchforks are coming."

Nobody wants that, man.

You have shown through the work of your foundation that you are making a difference in the world. But this difference is being made because of your individual commitment.

What happens when you're gone? Wouldn't it be far better to create democratic institutions that are free of corruption – a government that solves the problems you say capitalism can't.

Your friends, the Koch brothers, and others of their ilk, think nothing of subverting our democracy in the name of freedom – buying their politicians and gaining unfair advantages through their lobbying efforts. How is this different from a banana-republic? Sure, their immense wealth allows them the luxury of ignoring public opinion if they wish. But their endless lobbying to further income inequality is simply evil. It means that everything you work for is subject to the whim of an autocrat.

Freedom means freedom for all, not just for the plutocrats.

Is there nothing you can do to act now to help restore a just political system in the USA? One that works for the public interest, the Common Good, and not just for corporate sponsors?

Surely that is a worthwhile challenge for your Foundation?

It's the one thing that will ensure your good work lives on.

Regards,

Christian Sarkar
Philip Kotler
January, 2020

12. JOIN US

If you have read this far, you qualify as someone who may be interested in joining us.

What is it you want me to join, you ask?

Two things:

One, work to transform your company into a force for good by becoming an impactful brand activist.

Two, work with others *outside* your company to make a difference. We are beginning work on the Wicked 7 – to find a path forward. Join us.

More information:
www.activistbrands.com and **www.wicked7.org**

ABOUT THE AUTHORS

Christian Sarkar is an author, entrepreneur, consultant, artist, and activist. He is the co-author, with Philip Kotler, of *Losing our Democracy* and with Michael Gordon, of *Inclusivity: Will America Find Its Soul Again?* He is also the co-founder (with Philip Kotler) and editor of *The Marketing Journal.* He is the founder of Double Loop Marketing LLC and Ecosystematic, an ecosystem mapping and strategy tool. He also leads the $300 House project. His latest project – co-founded with Philip Kotler – is The Wicked7 Project, a design project to "save humanity from itself" (see: www.wicked7.org).

Learn more: **www.christiansarkar.com**

Philip Kotler is known around the world as the "father of modern marketing." For over 50 years he has taught at the Kellogg School of Management at Northwestern University. Kotler's book *Marketing Management* is the most widely used textbook in marketing around the world. He has been honored as one of the world's leading marketing thinkers.

He received his M.A. degree in economics (1953) from the University of Chicago and his Ph.D. degree in economics (1956) from the Massachusetts Institute of Technology (M.I.T.), and has received honorary degrees from 22 universities including Stockholm University, the University of Zurich, Athens University of Economics and Business, Budapest School of Economics and Administrative Science, the Cracow School of Business and Economics, and DePaul University.

He is author of over one hundred and fifty articles and 60 books, including *Principles of Marketing, Marketing for Hospitality and Tourism, Strategic Marketing for Nonprofit Organizations, Social Marketing, Marketing Places, The Marketing of Nations, Confronting Capitalism,* and *Democracy in Decline.* His research covers strategic marketing, consumer marketing, business marketing, professional services marketing, and e-marketing.

He has been a consultant to IBM, General Electric, AT&T, Bank of America, Merck, Motorola, Ford, and others. He has lectured several times in Italy, Sweden, China, Japan, India, Indonesia, Australia, Mexico, Brazil, Chile, and many other countries.

Learn more: **www.pkotler.org**

Made in the USA
Las Vegas, NV
06 October 2021

31768372R00166